The Right to Education of Persons with Disabilities in Turkey

Selda Çağlar

The Right to Education of Persons with Disabilities in Turkey

Within the Context of the United Nations Convention on the Rights of Persons with Disabilities (CRPD). Gap Analysis

PETER LANG

Bibliographic Information published by the Deutsche Nationalbibliothek
The Deutsche Nationalbibliothek lists this publication in the Deutsche Nationalbibliografie; detailed bibliographic data is available online at http://dnb.d-nb.de.

Library of Congress Cataloging-in-Publication Data
A CIP catalog record for this book has been applied for at the Library of Congress.

Cover image: © Tupungato /

Fotolia.com

ISBN 978-3-631-76652-1 (Print)
E-ISBN 978-3-631-76898-3 (E-PDF)
E-ISBN 978-3-631-76899-0 (EPUB)
E-ISBN 978-3-631-76900-3 (MOBI)
DOI 10.3726/b14716

Peter Lang – Berlin · Bern · Bruxelles · New York · Oxford · Warszawa · Wien

This publication has been peer reviewed.

www.peterlang.com

Preface

This publication is a part of the project, conducted by UNDP and Ministry of Family and Social Policies (MoFSP), called "Support to the Implementation and Monitoring of the United Nations Convention on the Rights of Persons with Disabilities (CRPD) in Turkey" and which was completed in the end of 2014. In the scope of the project, an elaborated Turkish report was submitted to Ministry of Family and Social Policies (MoFSP). This report was shared with all related ministries of Turkey and the essential studies were started to resolve the examined gaps. This report has been regarded as a roadmap for legal and administrative regulations (including action plans) that should be made by Turkish government in the medium term. Another characteristic of this study, which makes it nationally significant and valuable is being the first and only study on this subject. It is the only resource for the academicians and researchers for those who will study in this field.

Our study is also significant for international disability law and the right to education. It is the only source of data, particularly for scientists and researchers who will conduct comparative studies, or for those who will conduct country studies.

On the other hand, the book has the characteristics of a shadow report for the relevant institutions of the UN, EU and Council of Europe. In case both the country reports given to the related institutions within the scope of the conventions which Turkey is a party to and the individual complaint mechanisms of the optional protocols of these conventions are operated, the related committees shall use this study as a shadow report. International non-governmental organisations will also be able to make evaluations, regarding this study in their reports about Turkey.

Our purpose of publishing the study in English and in the form of book is the reasons above mentioned. In other words, we would like to make the study accessible to international institutions and organisations and to scientists or unscientific people working on this field.

Contents

Introduction

With the aim to ensure that the Project implemented jointly by the United Nations Development Programme (UNDP) and the Ministry of Family and Social Policies (MoFSP) called “Support to the Implementation and Monitoring of the United Nations Convention on the Rights of Persons with Disabilities (CRPD) in Turkey” achieves its goal, it is necessary first and foremost to outline a normative framework for the provisions laying down CRPD’s purpose[1], general principles, rights and freedoms as well as the State’s obligations, and reveal the philosophy elaborated in the *Preamble* to the Convention. In other words, the Convention’s text must be addressed as a whole and analysed using scientific interpretation methods. As regards the interpretation of its provisions, an assessment of the word of the Convention will not suffice; historical, teleological and systematic interpretation methods will also be employed to determine the protection areas of the relevant norms. In that sense, to determine the norm-protected areas, General Comments issued by the Committee on the Rights of Persons with Disabilities[2] for the clarification of Convention’s provisions as well as its decisions for individual applications will be regarded as the basis. In addition, observations and recommendations on the reports of States Parties will also be referred.

The next step of this work to be taken within the scope of this Project is to reveal the compliance/non-compliance between the norms of the Convention and the positive law comprising of the legislation in force for the persons with disabilities in the national law and the judicial decisions. In other words, it is to identify the gaps between the positive law and the Convention’s provisions. However, since we are requested within the context of the Project only to determine the gaps regarding the right to education of the persons with disabilities, the Gap Analysis does not require us to evaluate all provisions of the Convention. However, as mentioned in the first paragraph, without conducting a classified analysis on the entire Convention, it is not possible to evaluate the Convention’s norms regulating the right to education of persons with disabilities with regard to meaning, extent and State Party’s obligations. It is because, granting protection and proper implementation of the right to education to persons with disabilities by States Parties to the Convention make it obligatory to observe other rights and freedoms related to the right to education as well as the general principles of the Convention.

In this framework, the Convention will first be evaluated on the basis of general principles, then the provision on the right to education and the extent of State’s obligations will be explained. Explanations and assessments on the Convention will

1 Hereafter the “Convention”. S.Ç.
2 Hereafter the “Committee”. S.Ç.

be accompanied by information on the legislation in Turkey which directly and/or indirectly regulates the right to education of the persons with disabilities and affects the right to education, and necessary assessments will be conducted in accordance with the comparative method.

Assc. Prof. Dr. Selda Çağlar*

* Faculty member at Trakya University, Faculty of Economic and Administrative Sciences, Department of Public Administration – Department of Law Sciences (scaglar@trakya.edu.tr).

PART I. Assessment Based on the General Principles of the Convention on the Rights of Persons with Disabilities

Under this subheading, the general principles listed in Article 3 of CRPD will be examined in terms of meaning and scope based on the respective content as accepted in the international human rights law and the explanations and assessments made by the Committee on the Rights of Persons with Disabilities, and then, an attempt will be made to determine the extent to which the Turkish law fulfils these principles.

A. Respect for an Individual's Independence, Autonomy Including His/Her Freedom to Make His/Her Own Decisions, And Dignity

The purpose of the Convention on the Rights of Persons with Disabilities is defined as "to promote, protect and ensure the full and equal enjoyment of all human rights and fundamental freedoms by all persons with disabilities, and to promote respect for their inherent dignity" (Art. 1).[3] Dignity and autonomy are regarded as important values on which the human rights law is built. Dignity[4] is an invaluable self-value owned by individuals as human beings, apart from the economic or other type of benefits they provide. Therefore, including those persons who have severe disabilities hindering them from participating in economic development, regardless of physical and intellectual abilities and skills of persons with disabilities, they are recognised as having the same value as any other person in the society.

Autonomy or self-determination is a principle that is based on the assumption that individuals possess the ability to stand in the centre of the decisions which have an effect on them and steer their behaviours and actions themselves.[5] During the preparatory stage of the Convention on the Rights of Persons with Disabilities, the term "self-determination" meaning "the ability to make relevant decisions on one's

---

3 UN General Assembly sixty-first session, A/61/611, 6 December 2006 Ad Hoc Committee on a Comprehensive and Integral International Convention on the Protection and Promotion of the Rights and Dignity of Persons with Disabilities, Eighth Session, New York, 14–25 August 2006.

4 For a treatment of the concepts of dignity and human rights in international law and comparative law, see: **Grant Evadné,** "Dignity and Equality", *Human Rights Law Review* 2007 7(2), pp. 301–309.

5 Human rights law is premised on four moral values: dignity, autonomy, equality and solidarity. See: Human Rights and Disability, http://www.unhchr.ch/disability/intro.htm, (11.02.2007)

own or determine one's own fate" was suggested instead of the term "individual autonomy".[6] It was stated that the term individual autonomy did not include individuals' right to make choices or decisions about themselves. The principle was expanded to include the term "self-determination" alongside the term "individual autonomy" as suggested by organisations including the European Union and was incorporated in the Convention's text. Therefore, a more comprehensive content was created as "individual autonomy including individuals' independence and freedom to make their own decisions".

The empowerment of persons with disabilities in terms of personal, economic, social, cultural and political matters and ensuring their individual autonomy and independence and therefore allowing them to enjoy all their rights as equals with others are expressed as the main purpose in the Preamble to the Convention (paragraph n) and many other articles. For instance, Article 19 "Living independently and being included in the community" of the Convention imposes certain obligations on States to ensure that persons with disabilities have the opportunity to make choices as equals with others as well as their full inclusion and participation in the society. Persons with disabilities must have the opportunity to choose the location, place and residence they want to live in, including whether to live with their families or on their own, have the opportunity to choose to live on an equal basis with others and must not be obliged to live in a particular living arrangement. Through the Convention which adopts the social model of disability, efforts are made to put an understanding in place to abandon the isolation and exclusion practices caused by the institutional care practice particularly for persons with intellectual disabilities, and shift to accommodation at places made more appropriate for persons with disabilities via reasonable accommodation or less restricting locations by providing necessary support. In other words, through the rights regulated by this general principle and other relevant provisions of the Convention, the Convention aims to prevent the practice of keeping persons with disabilities in institutions against their consent, and for compulsory situations, to ensure that the life at these institutions have *less restrictions and more independence* for persons with disabilities, to empower persons with disabilities in the physical, intellectual and societal sense and allow them to live in maximum independence.[7] In this framework, States Parties are under obligation to strengthen, supervise and extend the scope of habilitation and rehabilitation services and programmes used particularly in the areas of health, education, employment and social services and maintaining the integrity of family (Art. 26).

6 Selda Çağlar, Uluslararası Hukuk ve Türk Hukuk Sisteminde Engellilerin Eğitim Hakkı ve Devlet Yükümlülükleri [Right to Education of Persons with Disabilities and State's Obligations in International Law and Turkish Law], Beta, Istanbul, 2009, p.40.

7 UN Enable – Towards a Convention Comments on the Draft Text, Draft Article 15: Living independently and being included in the community, UN General Assembly, A/60/266, 17 August 2005.

B. Non-Discrimination

In the Convention, discrimination on the basis of disability is defined as, "...any distinction, exclusion or restriction on the basis of disability which has the purpose or effect of impairing or nullifying the recognition, enjoyment or exercise, on an equal basis with others, of all human rights and fundamental freedoms in the political, economic, social, cultural, civil or any other field. It includes all forms of discrimination, including denial of reasonable accommodation". (Art. 2). As is seen, the definition of "discrimination" in Article 2 of the Convention is clear. However, it is necessary to determine what the "prohibition of discrimination" includes or excludes. Therefore, in terms of the Convention which delivers the definition of reasonable accommodation and regards the lack of reasonable accommodation as discrimination, the expression which should be emphasised is the term "any discrimination". In order to determine which acts, situations or lack of actions are included in this expression which appears to be quite inclusive at first glance and therefore imposes obligations on States Parties in this scope, it would be appropriate to go through the discussions held during the preparatory works of the Convention. During the preparatory stage of the Convention draft, it was decided that all direct and indirect forms of discrimination would be included in the scope of the prohibition. Moreover, where any impartial provision, criterion or practice causes a certain disadvantage for a person with disability in comparison to others, it was prescribed that it would be regarded as indirect discrimination and its exception was also stated. Accordingly, if the relevant provision, criterion or practice makes the purpose of an appropriate and necessary regulation reasonable and justified in an objective manner or if it is not possible to take a measure to eliminate the disadvantage, it will not be regarded as indirect discrimination.[8]

There are no clues that will serve to draw the normative limits of "prohibition of discrimination" other than the discussions during the preparatory stage of the Convention and the written opinions submitted. Nor are there abstract evaluations prepared by the Committee on the Rights of Persons with Disabilities which is the supervisory body of the Convention. In fact, there is no general comment on the prohibition of discrimination principle and/or provision of the Convention by the Committee. However, for some of the applications lodged via the individual application mechanism, the Committee decided that the "non-discrimination and equality" provision regulated by Article 5 of the Convention was violated and made subjective evaluations on discrimination in these decisions. For instance, upon an application

8 UN Enable Contribution by Governments, European Union Proposed Modifications to Draft Article 7 – Equality and non-discrimination, p.2; For case legislation on prohibition of discrimination and equality and case precedents on indirect discrimination in the European Union law, see: **Timo Makkonen**, *Measuring Discrimination Data Collection and EU Equality Law*, European Commission, 2006, pp. 31–38, *Anti-Discrimination Law Review*, Issue No. 4, November 2006, European Commission, pp. 7–87.

lodged about a case where a person with a physical disability requested to build a hydrotherapy pool for rehabilitation on her own land and her request was denied by the Swedish administrative authorities on grounds of being contradictory to the urban development plan,[9] the Committee evaluated the meaning and scope of the prohibition of discrimination for the specific case as follows: "... *when the planning and building permit legislation in force is applied in a neutral manner without taking into consideration the particular circumstances of the individuals to whom it is applied, it may have a discriminatory effect. The rights granted under the Convention must be enjoyed without being subject to discrimination States Parties can only make it justifiable to treat differently the persons whose situations are significantly different by using objective and reasonable justification*". Moreover, according to the Committee, "... *the Planning and Building Act allows for departure from the development plan when necessary in a particular case. Nevertheless, when necessary in a particular case, an application for reasonable accommodation aimed at ensuring to persons with disabilities the enjoyment or exercise of all human rights on an equal basis with others and without any discrimination must be accepted*".[10] In this context, the Committee noted that the State Party, when rejecting the applicant's application for a building permit, did not address the specific circumstances of her case and her particular disability-related needs and therefore considered that the decisions of the domestic authorities to refuse a departure from the development plan in order to allow the building of the hydrotherapy pool were disproportionate and produced a discriminatory effect that adversely affected the applicant's access, as a person with disability, to the health care and rehabilitation required for her specific health condition; and concluded that the applicant's rights under Articles 5(1), 5(3), 25 and the State Party's obligations under Article 26 of the Convention, read alone and in conjunction with Articles 3 (b), (d), and (e), and 4(1) (d) of the Convention, were violated.[11]

In another application lodged against Germany where a person alleged that the inclusion of his/her son with disabilities into the labour market was not facilitated and the right to work of persons with disabilities was not promoted, the Committee concluded that the provisions 27/1-d, e and h of the Convention which regulated the right to work and employment as well as the general principles such as the prohibition of discrimination, equality of opportunity and full and effective participation in the society (Art. 3) and the provision 5/1 which regulated "non-discrimination and equality" were violated. In this decision, the Committee is of the view that the measures taken by the State Party's authorities to facilitate the inclusion of the applicant into the labour market do not meet the standards in the relevant articles

9 Committee on the Rights of Persons with Disabilities, CRPD/C/7/D/3/2011, Distr.: General 21 May 2012.

10 Committee on the Rights of Persons with Disabilities, CRPD/C/7/D/3/2011, Distr.: General 21 May 2012, para. 8.5–8.6.

11 Committee on the Rights of Persons with Disabilities, CRPD/C/7/D/3/2011, Distr.: General 21 May 2012, para. 8.8–8.9.

of the Convention and the existing model for the provision of integration subsidies does not effectively promote the employment of persons with disabilities. Another point emphasised in the decision is that the apparent difficulties faced by potential employers when trying to gain access to the integration subsidy that they are entitled to for the employment of a person with disabilities affect the effectiveness of the integration subsidies scheme. The Committee stated that the administrative complexities caused by the application which was alleged in the application file and not refuted by the State Party put the applicant in a disadvantageous position and resulted in indirect discrimination and hence ordered that the State Party Germany must take steps to prevent similar violations in the future, including by reviewing the content and functioning of the scheme for the provision of integration subsidies to individuals who are permanently disabled, to ensure its full compliance with the principles of the Convention, and by ensuring that potential employers can effectively benefit from the scheme whenever appropriate.[12]

As is seen, the prohibition of discrimination, in addition to being a very comprehensive general principle in the Convention's text, is also a fact that guarantees the enjoyment by persons with disabilities of their Convention-based rights and freedoms. This is the exact reason why the prohibition of discrimination is regarded as a *jus cogens*[13] principle in the international law. The decision examples provided from the applications lodged to the CRPD Committee demonstrate that, in accordance with the word and spirit of the Convention, the Committee puts the "prohibition of discrimination" beyond being a simple prohibition and prefers an interpretation that imposes strict obligations on the States Parties on the topic of meeting the requirements of this prohibition. When it is considered that the Convention does not have a nature of prohibiting absolute discrimination and is also not a list of freedoms but actually is a hybrid example which combines these two qualities, the emphasis placed on the prohibition of discrimination should be considered natural. Because, unless States take action to prevent and eliminate discrimination against disadvantaged groups of the society such as the persons with disabilities, it is not possible for these persons to enjoy their human rights as equals with everyone else. In this framework, as a State Party of the Convention, Turkey has a lot of work to do.[14]

---

12 Committee on the Rights of Persons with Disabilities, CRPD/C/11/D/2/2010, Distr.: General 4 April 2014, para. 6–7.

13 "Compelling law" in Latin. Peremptory norm from which no derogation is permitted in the international law.

14 The Convention on the Rights of Persons with Disabilities was signed by the Republic of Turkey on 30 March 2007; ratified by the Law No. 5825 enacted by the Turkish Grand National Assembly on 3 December 2008; and the ratification process was consummated by the Decree No. 2009/15137 of 27 May 2009 of the Council of Ministers. The Convention became binding upon Turkey on the thirtieth day from 28 September 2009 when the ratification instrument was deposited with the United Nations Secretariat.

The Constitution of 1982 is a guide for the place and function of CRPD in the Turkish law. According to Article 90 of the Constitution of the Republic of Turkey[15]; "International agreements duly put into effect have the force of law. No appeal to the Constitutional Court shall be made with regard to these agreements, on the grounds that they are unconstitutional. In the case of a conflict between international agreements, duly put into effect, concerning fundamental rights and freedoms and the laws due to differences in provisions on the same matter, the provisions of the international agreements shall prevail". Pursuant to the mentioned provision of the Constitution, *the Convention on the Rights of Persons with Disabilities* which is a duly approved international agreement, is on the same level as the Constitution text within the hierarchy of norms such as other human rights conventions. In this framework, the Convention provides a basis for all legal and administrative regulations made in Turkey, while also possessing the nature of being a norm to which the independent Turkish courts can make direct references.[16]

From the early 2000s, Turkey has put emphasis on legal fight against discrimination. With the amendment made in 2004, the Constitution of 1982 achieved a more protective nature in terms of "equality and prohibition of discrimination" and efforts were put into action for an assurance system embracing various segments of the society. However, there is no independent provision in the Constitution of 1982 on the "prohibition of discrimination". The prohibition of discrimination is included in the "equality before the law" provision regulated in Article 10 of the Constitution. Accordingly, "*Everyone is equal before the law without distinction as to language, race, colour, sex, political opinion, philosophical belief, religion and sect, or any such grounds*". (Cons. Art. 10/1) Although "disability" is not listed as a ground for prohibition of discrimination, an implication can be made that disability is included in the prohibition based on the "or any such ground" expression in the provision. However, in order to achieve full compliance with the Convention, the relevant provision of the Constitution should include "disability" as a ground for prohibition of discrimination.

With the amendment made in the Constitution in 2010, the provision *"Measures to be taken for children, the elderly, the impaired, widows and orphans of martyrs as well as for the disabled and veterans shall not be considered as violation of the principle of equality"* was added (Cons. Art. 10/3). It is confirmed that the positive measures to be taken for the social groups mentioned in the relevant provision will not violate equality and a constitutional assurance is provided, while the fact that there are no clear obligations imposed on the State makes it ambiguous who will actually carry out the equalisation of disadvantaged groups in terms of rights and freedoms

15 Hereafter the Constitution of 1982.

16 Engelli Hakları Sözleşmesi'ne ilişkin Türkiye Ulusal Rapor Taslağı [The draft Turkish National Report on the Convention on the Rights of Persons with Disabilities (designed as the inception report), p.1] http://engelli.oyhgm.gov.tr/sozlesme/dosyalar/sozlesme/national_rapor/, (29.06.2014)

and how it will be done. Although it is prescribed in the last provision of Article 10 that "State organs and administrative authorities are obliged to act in compliance with the principle of equality before the law in all their proceedings", unless the legislative body puts legal regulations in practice for ensuring actual equality of persons with disabilities and administrative and judiciary bodies interpret the Constitution and legal regulations based on the rights of persons with disabilities in their decisions and practices, it does not seem possible for the phenomenon of discrimination to be eliminated. Therefore, the Article should be recast by pointing out the rights of the persons listed in the relevant provision and State's obligation in this regard and it should be clearly emphasised that these persons and groups have the same rights as everyone else and the State is obliged to ensure this equality. In addition, the meaning and contents of equality in the Constitution should be clarified and a form should be assumed in compliance with the understanding accepted in the international law. Based on the experience demonstrating that the narrow interpretation of the understanding on the equality before the law is not adequate for protecting the rights, the provision on equality should be adjusted in a manner to involve all vulnerable and weak groups on the basis of equality of opportunity and actual equality.

This provision of the Constitution, which is limited to equality in the form, is used in the same manner in the Constitutional Court decisions as well and about the applications for annulment, the Constitutional Court, rather than determining whether the legal regulation subject to the annulment request is in conformity with equality, tries to determine with a strict positivist attitude whether it is against equality and rejects some requests on the ground that "the rule cannot be annulled with the aim to expand its field of application (or due to missing regulation)". While rejecting the inequality allegations made by persons or groups who are not able to enjoy a certain right or opportunity even though they are in the same situation and conditions as the subject matter of the legal regulation, it uses the argument "not being substantially contrary to the Constitution". In some of its decisions, it rejects the applications for annulment with evaluations such as "the field of application would expand because of the annulment of the provision subject to the appeal", "annulment requests cannot be lodged with the aim to expand the field of application of relevant articles and therefore ensure a more comprehensive application", "results caused by the missing regulation can be fixed with legislative acts".[17] However, in most of the legal regulations on fundamental rights and freedoms or public services, there are no special measures to be taken in favour of persons with disabilities and this situation causes inequality against persons with disabilities and also results in indirect discrimination. In order to eliminate such negative results, the "equality before the law" provision regulated in the Constitution should be rewritten in line

17 For early decisions, see: E.1963/172, K.1963/244, KT.21.10.1963, RG.1.2.1964/11622; E.1963/174, K.1963/115, KT.20.5.1963, RG.2.8.1963/11470; E.1963/205, K.1963/123, KT.22.5.1963, RG.14.8.1963/11480; E.1963/89, K.1964/36, KT.5.5.1964, RG.22.8.1964/11787.

with the suggestion above. The phenomenon of indirect discrimination will be addressed below.

Another measure to be taken with regard to harmonisation with the Convention is expressing the "prohibition of discrimination" in the Constitution with a content which is independent and/or involves all forms of discrimination along with equality, prohibiting direct and indirect discrimination and regarding the lack of reasonable accommodation as discrimination. By doing so, obligatory common standards can be achieved by taking into account the Convention on the Rights of Persons with Disabilities and other international conventions to which Turkey is a party, which would be mandatory for all State bodies, public entities and natural persons and institutions.

Regarding the extra-Constitutional legal measures on the prohibition of discrimination; first, the provisions of the Law No. 5378 on Persons with Disabilities (LPD) which is closely related to the fundamental rights and freedoms of persons with disabilities and the services to be provided should be reviewed. LPD has been through a gradual change since 2013 to eliminate all kinds of discrimination against persons with disabilities. While LPD was in force under the name *"Law on Amending the Law on Impaired Persons and Certain Laws and Decree-Laws"* before 25/4/2013, it was renewed with regard to language as well as in line with other legislation with an amendment enacted on this date. From this date forward, degrading expressions for persons with disabilities such as "impaired, being impaired, impairment, crippled, cripple" in the general or disability related legislation were abandoned, and the legislation was cleared of discriminatory and exclusive language. LPD went through a radical change on 6/2/2014 with an understanding that the phenomenon of discrimination is the most important barrier against the persons with disabilities enjoying their rights and freedoms on an equal basis as others and amendments were made in parallel with CRPD. Discrimination, which was prohibited in the Law via an abstract and short provision before the amendment, has gained a comprehensive meaning to involve all kinds of discrimination on the basis of disability including direct and indirect discrimination (Art. 4A/1), direct and indirect discrimination and reasonable accommodation were defined in the "definitions" article and the prohibition was materialised (Art. 3). However, unlike the Convention, the Law did not regard the lack of reasonable accommodation as discrimination and only sufficed to provide that necessary measures shall be taken for implementing reasonable accommodation for persons with disabilities in order to ensure equality and eliminate discrimination (Art. 4A/2). In the last paragraph of the Article on discrimination, it was laid down that "special measures to be taken for ensuring the full and equal enjoyment of rights and freedoms by persons with disabilities shall not be regarded as discrimination" (Art. 4A/3) and the function of other special measures as well as reasonable accommodation of preventing and eliminating discrimination and ensuring actual equality was reinforced. However, LPD was not able to meet exactly the prohibition of discrimination which was addressed as a general principle as the expression of an abstract prohibition in the Convention on the Rights of Persons with Disabilities and also enshrined with a material content in a separate provision. We can conclude the reasons why LPD was behind the Convention as follows:

i. LPD provides in its Article titled "discrimination" *that necessary measures shall be taken for implementing reasonable accommodation for persons with disabilities in order to ensure equality and eliminate discrimination"* and does not regard the lack of reasonable accommodation as discrimination. However, the approach of the Convention which considers the lack of reasonable accommodation in the scope of "discrimination on the basis of disability" and regards it as discrimination is more accurate and protective (Art. 2/4). Because, although the lack of reasonable accommodation in favour of persons with disabilities often causes indirect discrimination, sometimes it can cause discrimination on its own. For instance, unless there are reasonable accommodations implemented for the education of a child with dyslexia from educational materials to teaching techniques, it is not possible for this child to receive education on the same quality level as others. If the educational institution refuses to implement reasonable accommodation, legal remedies can be sought on the grounds that child's right to education is violated; however, it cannot be alleged that it is an act of indirect discrimination. Because, it cannot be expected from the educational institution to employ teachers who have knowledge in techniques and methods specific to children with dyslexia or other types of disabilities or procure appropriate materials before the concrete need manifests itself. As is seen in the specific example, regarding the lack of reasonable accommodation as discrimination is an important assurance for preventing discrimination. When it is not regarded as discrimination, or in other words, only considered as an obligation by the person involved, only a corrective solution can be suggested in terms of the occurred results and this corrective action is usually achieved via litigation. And this leads to a waste of time as well as high costs and also it does not guarantee the enjoyment of the relevant right and freedom until a conclusion is reached. Based on these explanations, it can be beneficial to amend LPD in a manner to resolve this deficiency.

ii. The Convention includes the prohibition of discrimination in the general principles while also explaining the scope of the prohibition and the State's obligations in a provision linked to equality. Accordingly, the States Parties are obliged to *recognise that all persons are equal before and under the law and are entitled without any discrimination to the equal protection and equal benefit of the law; prohibit all discrimination on the basis of disability and guarantee to persons with disabilities equal and effective legal protection against discrimination on all grounds; take all appropriate steps to ensure that reasonable accommodation is provided in order to promote equality and eliminate discrimination* (Art. 5). On the other hand, LPD prohibits discrimination on the basis of disability with the "general principles" provision, but the fight against discrimination is left to the fields of policies for persons with disabilities (Art. 4). The Law also contains a separate Article titled "Discrimination", but this Article only prohibits all kinds of direct and indirect discrimination and states that necessary measures shall be taken for reasonable accommodation for persons with disabilities in order to ensure equality and eliminate discrimination. The State's obligations and the responsibilities of private persons and entities are not mentioned (Art. 4A). Yet, it is the duty of the State also in the national law as well as the international law to prevent and eliminate discrimination and to plan and implement all kinds of fight against legal and actual inequality caused by discrimination.

While it is not an obligation for the States Parties to directly transpose all types of obligations imposed by the Convention into their national laws, this way is an important assurance for protecting persons with disabilities against discrimination. Although it is prescribed in Article 90 of the Constitution of 1982 that in the case of a conflict between international human rights agreements and the national law, the agreements shall prevail; the State's obligations are programmatic provisions which should be materialised via national law norms and cannot be considered within the context of norm conflicts. Therefore, preventing and fight against all kinds of legal and actual discrimination against persons with disabilities should be included in the field of all policies including the law and all State bodies should be obliged to perform this duty.

In addition to general provisions on the prohibition of discrimination, LPD also prohibits discrimination related to certain rights and freedoms and lists necessary measures to be taken in order to eliminate them. The Article titled *Employment* (Art. 14) and the Article regulating *Education and training* (Art. 15) in the Law were amended on 6.02.2014 and provided more assurance for persons with disabilities in terms of discrimination regarding these rights. In Article 14 of the Law, it was prescribed that discriminatory practices on the basis of disability shall not be implemented in any matter related to employment including application and recruitment for work, recommended working periods and conditions as well as the continuance of employment, career advancement, healthy and safe working conditions and employees with disabilities shall not be treated differently than other persons based on their disability in a manner to cause disadvantage to them and persons with disabilities were protected against discrimination in the employment process and throughout their working period. In addition, the obligation to take measures in the employment processes for eliminating barriers and challenges which persons with disabilities who work or apply for jobs may encounter and to implement reasonable accommodations in workplaces where persons with disabilities work are imposed on organisations and entities which have the duties, powers and responsibilities in this regard as well as the employers. Labour laws and civil servant legislation besides LPD also contain mandatory quotas regarding the employment of persons with disabilities. The legislation appears to be in harmony with the Convention with regard to preventing and eliminating discrimination regarding the right of persons with disabilities to work. However, there are problems in terms of practice.

Regarding the prevention of discrimination against the right to education of persons with disabilities provision 15/1 of LPD, it is regulated as the fundamental rule of education that, *the right to education of persons with disabilities shall not be hindered under any justification and persons with disabilities shall enjoy life long education while their special conditions and differences are taken into account, in areas integrated to the environment they live in, on the basis of equality and without being subject to any discrimination.* In the subsequent paragraphs of the Article, special measures to be taken for ensuring that persons with disabilities enjoy this right at all levels of education and throughout their lives are mentioned. However, LPD does not provide a detailed regulation on how the discrimination will be prevented and eliminated, which is the most important barrier in front of full and effective enjoyment of the right to education by persons with disabilities. For instance, it does not mention the necessity of implementing reasonable accommodation in educational settings and/or method and does not regulate through which concrete measures the integration in education at all levels of education should be achieved. However, as mentioned in the General Comment No. 5 of 1994 of the Committee on Economic, Social and Cultural Rights on persons with disabilities (E/1995/22), results of discrimination on the basis of disability are felt severely particularly in areas of education, employment, housing, transportation, cultural life and access to public places and services. Therefore, as in the case of Article 14 of LPD which regulates the employment of persons with disabilities, we believe that it would be beneficial to implement necessary measures for preventing discrimination in a manner to involve all educational processes in a detailed manner. Such an amendment would be effective in resolving the lack of harmony between LPD and the Convention on the Rights of Persons with Disabilities which provides a powerful protection against discrimination for persons with disabilities. Because, in the right to education provision of the Convention, States Parties are put under the obligation to ensure that persons with disabilities access general higher education, vocational training, adult education and lifelong education without being subject to discrimination and on equal conditions with other individuals and for this purpose, to provide reasonable accommodation according to the needs of persons with disabilities (Art. 24/5).

If we continue to evaluate the legislation in terms of the relationship between the right to education and prohibition of discrimination, it becomes important to what extent the prohibition of discrimination in education is expressed in the context of the Basic Law No. 1739 on National Education (BLNE) which regulates the education in Turkey on the national level. Because, this Law covers all the formal/adult education processes of all individuals with or without disabilities. Law No. 1739, in its section *Fundamental Principles of Turkish National Education* under the title *Generality and Equality,* prescribes that educational institutions are open for every individual without any discrimination on the basis of their language, race, sex or religion and no privilege shall be granted in education for any person, family, group or class (Art. 4). Besides this provision in BLNE which implicitly regulates the prohibition of discrimination, there is no comprehensive provision which explicitly prohibits discrimination in education in all forms within the context of contemporary human rights. Through the additions to be made in the fundamental principles section and relevant provisions of the Law, which was adopted in 1973 and has not been through a comprehensive amendment, it would be a positive step to ensure that the prohibition of discrimination is also implemented in the area of education and training.

In some of the legal regulations in force in Turkey, it is observed that there are provisions which may cause direct discrimination against certain groups with disabilities. For instance, in the Regulation on Special Education Services (RSES), it is stated that "every individual who is in need for special education has the right to get education in the same institution as their peers" and integrative education is accepted as the fundamental principle. However, in the provision of the Regulation which regulates the criteria for receiving education via integration, most of the children with disabilities who are at the compulsory education age were excluded from this education. The primary ones of these groups are individuals with medium or severe level of intellectual deficiency as well as persons with autism. A distinction was made for these children with disabilities within this group on the ground of whether they can or cannot follow the programmes implemented in elementary schools, and for the ones who cannot follow, it was stated that they would receive education in special education application centres in two tiers each consisting of four years. In this case, the children with severe intellectual disabilities and the ones with medium level intellectual disability who cannot pursue the purpose of elementary school programmes as well as children with autism were excluded as a group who will not benefit from integrative education, and automatically left for a separated education in special schools and institutions designated for these groups (Art. 40/3-b). As it is known; the negative impact of discrimination caused by separated education on children with disabilities lasts for a life time. Because, children who start their education in such a way and do not benefit from integrative education in any step of their education encounter a lower level of education with lower quality compared to their peers who do not have any deficiency and usually lose their chance of transition into regular educational processes in the next steps. Also, the graduation certificates they receive are not equivalent to the diplomas given by the institutions which give provide regular education.

RSES also had a similar regulation regarding the persons who continue their education via inclusion (integration).[18] Until the amendment made in the Regulation on 21.07.2012, all students who were receiving education in special education classes within the schools which provided regular education were subject to the same legislative provisions as special education schools and institutions which were designated for the individuals with the same deficiency. Therefore, they were receiving different education programmes and different diplomas. With the amendment made in the regulation, this categorical discrimination was partially eliminated. According to the new regulation, special education classes could be opened for individuals who are at the compulsory education age and are able to follow elementary school or middle school programmes, but the education to be given in these classes

---

18 The text of RSES failed to deliver a unity of terminology on this matter. It refers, at some places, to "kaynaştırma" (which means "fusion, melting/welding together" in Turkish), some others to "bütünleştirme". (which means "making whole" or "integration"). "Our recommendation is to screen the entire legislation, abandon the term "kaynaştırma", adopt "integration" or preferably "kapsayıcı" (inclusive) to be more aligned with international law. S.Ç.

would be the same as the education programme of the school or institution. Also, the graduation certificates they receive would be the same as the ones which their peers without any deficiency would receive after completing the same education (Art. 26, Art. 27). While this legislation amendment is positive with regard to preventing discrimination, there are still provisions in the Regulation which bear the risk for discrimination among persons with disabilities. Namely, while it is ensured that students who are visually or hearing impaired and receive education in the special education class receive education in the same class as their peers starting from the 5th grade (Art. 26/1-c), the same opportunity is not provided for students with intellectual deficiency or autism (Art. 26/1-ç).

The actual source of the distinction of being suitable or unsuitable for integration is LPD. In the provision "persons with disabilities shall enjoy life long education while their special conditions and differences are taken into account, in areas integrated to the environment they live in, on the basis of equality and without being subject to any discrimination" of the Law, the expression "while their special conditions and differences are taken into account" is interpreted in a wrong way. Although LPD aims the implementation of appropriate integration models according to special conditions and differences of persons with disabilities via this expression, in the Regulation on Special Education Services and some legal regulations, "special conditions and differences" were perceived as "differences that will hinder some persons with disabilities from benefiting from integrative education". Yet, taking into account the special conditions and differences indicates a measure. As it is known, discrimination occurs on the basis of certain grounds and reasons through certain acts such as distinction, exclusion, restriction and preference. Excluding certain persons or groups in the society, showing distinct treatments towards them, restricting their rights solely based on this ground or preferring others solely based on this ground is discrimination. Discrimination is usually defined as "situations/results against equality". However not all situations contradictory to equality poses discrimination. While it is obligatory to create/establish different situations when implementing the rules, if the different situation is not established correctly, if what is not supposed to be included in that situation is included or if someone or something is not included in the situation he/she/it is supposed to be in, then there is contradiction to equality; in this context, equality and discrimination are synonymous.[19]

Another provision which could be regarded as direct discrimination in education used to be in the Regulation on Pre-School Educational Institutions. In the regulation which stated that the children at the pre-school age except for the ones who

19 **Selda Çağlar,** "Engelli Hakları Sözleşmesi'nde Ayrımcılık Yasağı ve Türkiye'nin Uyum Sorunu" ["Non-discrimination in the Convention on the Rights of Persons with Disabilities and Turkey's Problem of Harmonisation"], *Türkiye Barolar Birliği Dergisi [Journal of Turkish Union of Bar Associations*], Eylül-Ekim 2011 [September-October 2011], Yıl:24 [Year: 24], Sayı:96 [Issue: 96], pp. 162–163.

has severe or very severe intellectual disabilities as well as the ones with multiple disabilities would be registered in regular pre-school educational institutions within a quota, again the children with severe or multiple disabilities were excluded from the inclusion education (Art. 10-c).[20] On 26.07.2014 the new Ministry of National Education Regulation on Pre-School and Elementary School which regulates pre-school educational institutions as well as elementary schools went into force and produced a solution which solved this problem to a certain extent. The new Regulation which regulated the pre-school education of full-time inclusive education students in the same direction as the old Regulation provision, resolved that children who have severe deficiency that hinders them from continuing their education in the full-time inclusion method as well as the children with multiple disabilities can be registered in special classes to be opened in the institution as long as the physical environment is suitable and special education teachers are employed (Art. 11/5-d). However, the fact that the opportunity of children with severe deficiency or multiple deficiencies to have education together with their peers is linked to the suitability of the physical environment and employment of special education teachers creates the risk that children in this group may continue to be excluded in practice. Educational institutions can avoid registering these children on the ground that they do not have suitable physical structure or educational staff. A regulation should be made for an effective solution that will end the discrimination in education against persons with disabilities in certain groups, to be implemented as a rule without being subject to such conditions for ensuring that all children receive education in the same institutions. To this end, pilot applications should be initiated, and necessary needs and problems should be determined, and appropriate solutions should be created. Of course, there will be children with disabilities who will not be able to benefit from such applications. However, this should only remain at the level of exceptions.

When the legislation on special education is examined as a whole, it is observed that children with severe intellectual disabilities and multiple disabilities are not able to participate in the integration throughout the compulsory education period and after (including adult education). The legislation which excludes certain disability groups from integrative education or remains neutral in this regard should be recast with explicit and clear expressions in a manner to ensure that all persons with disabilities receive education in compliance with the inclusive education principle. Moreover, functions, principles and purposes of special education institutions should be amended in a way to achieve harmony with international law norms and this amendment should be included in LPD as well as the legislation on special

20 Okul Öncesi Eğitim Kurumları Yönetmeliği, Resmi Gazete (RG): 08.06.2004/25486, Tebliğler Dergisi: Temmuz 2004/2562, m.10/c (Değişik: 21.07.2012/28360 RG) [Regulation on Pre-school Educational Institutions, Official Gazette: 08.06.2004/25486, Journal of Communiques: July 2004/2562, Art. 10/c (Amended: 21.07.20012/28360 OG)]

education institutions.[21] The State's obligation to avoid discrimination on the basis of disability also includes preventing discriminatory acts to be performed by other persons, organisations or private enterprises besides the public entities. The Convention on the Rights of Persons with Disabilities regulates in the provision which generally regulates the obligations of States Parties that States shall take necessary measures in this regard (Art. 4/e). In other words, the obligation to respect the right to education of persons with disabilities includes the State avoiding discrimination on the basis of disability as well as necessary measures to be taken in order to prevent third parties from performing discriminatory acts. Discrimination caused by persons and institutions outside the government more commonly occurs in practice in connection with private sector educational institutions. It is obligatory for the State to ensure that private sector educational institutions comply with the principles and standards it imposes regarding the right to education of persons with disabilities and take necessary measures to prevent and discourage the development of discrimination against persons with disabilities in the relevant sector by conducting necessary inspection and supervision activities.

Another regulation to be evaluated regarding the fight against discrimination on the basis of disability in the Turkish legislation is the Turkish Criminal Code (TCC) No. 5237 which went into force in 2004 and criminalised discrimination. Article 122 of TCC prescribed that any person who made discrimination between individuals on the basis of language, race, colour, sex, impairment, political opinion, philosophical belief, religion, sect and similar reasons and thereby prevented them from performing the acts, benefiting from the services or carrying out the services listed in the Article or refused to render public services be sentenced to imprisonment or imposed judicial fine. The Article which generally prohibits direct discrimination, in other words, does not include the discrimination which may result from an equal

21 Special education institutions should no longer be places that give education in the form of a school; they should be places that give education sessions to meet special educational needs. In addition, special education institutions should cooperate with schools that provide inclusive education or inclusive education for all and become resource institutions for expertise, knowledge and experience on special education. Therefore, the following legislative pieces need to be amended which govern the structure, functions and operations of special education institutions: Özel Eğitim Hakkında Kanun Hükmünde Kararname, Kararname Tarihi: 30.05.1997, No:573, Yetki Kanununun Tarihi: 03.12.1996, No: 4216, RG: 06.06.1997/ 23011(Mükerrer), Madde. 18–20 [Decree-Law on Special Education, Decree date: 30.05.1997, No: 573, Date of the Authorising Law: 03.12.1996, No: 4216, Official Gazette: 06.06.1997/ 23011(bis)], Art. 18–20; Özel Eğitim Hizmetleri Yönetmeliği, RG: Tarih. 31.05.2006, Sayı. 26184, Madde. 37–46 [Regulation on Special Education Services, O.G.: Date 31.05.2006, Issue 26184], Art. 37–46; Milli Eğitim Bakanlığı Özel Eğitim Okulları Çerçeve Yönetmeliği, RG: 22.7.2205/25883, Tebliğler Dergisi: Ağustos 2003/2551, Madde. 6–7 [Framework Regulation on Special Education Schools of the Ministry of National Education, Official Gazette: 22.7.2205/25883, Journal of Communiques: August 2003/2551], Art. 6–7.

treatment to persons in the same or similar positions into the scope of protection was subject to various criticism back in the day. It was alleged that the narrow scope of the Article which is only limited to certain acts would be inadequate in terms of the fight against the prohibition of discrimination which is a phenomenon encountered in all areas of social life and it was pointed out that, instead of limiting the scope of the Article to some acts, it would be more coherent to make a general regulation or remove the prohibition of discrimination from the subjects of the criminal code. In addition, there were problems in the application of the Article. The first was the difficulty to prove. In addition to the general difficulty in proving regulations on discrimination, the fact that the crime in the Article was a crime which could be committed with special intent along with its other aspects made it almost impossible to prove this crime except for the acts explicitly contrary to the law. Since the Article was a provision of criminal code, it was also unimaginable to reverse the burden of proof against the defendant.[22]

Attitudes and decisions of public prosecutors regarding the criminal complaints lodged by persons with disabilities or their families based on Article 122 of TCC also demonstrates the problems in the implementation of the relevant article and shows that such criminalisation could not achieve the purposes of preventing and deterring discrimination against persons with disabilities or other disadvantaged groups. Indeed, in the case of a 6-year-old child with autism who went through an educational assessment and received a report from the relevant public authority that he could attend inclusion (integration) education but was rejected on his request to be registered to a private school in his neighbourhood by the school, when the child's family lodged a criminal complaint based on Article 122 of TCC, the public prosecutor's office decided that there was no need for litigation based on this Article. The family lodged an appeal according to the rules of Code of Criminal Procedure against the decision of non-prosecution, however since they could not achieve a result, they applied personally to the European Court of Human Rights (ECtHR). The application was considered to be acceptable by the ECtHR but has not yet been concluded.[23]

Another example is the case where Hakan Özgül, who has an orthopaedic disability and is wheelchair-bound has lodged an application for filing a public case against the Municipality on the ground that the Municipality Service Building built in the district he lives in years after the Law No. 5378 went into force and its pavements were not constructed to appropriate standards and therefore he could not have the accessibility opportunity which persons without disabilities had and this condition hindered him from receiving services on an equal basis. The reason why

22 **Ulaş Karan,** "Türk Hukukunda Ayrımcılık Yasağı ve Türk Ceza Kanunu'nun 122. Maddesinin Uygulanabilirliği" [Non-discrimination in Turkish Law and Applicability of Article 122 of the Turkish Criminal Code, *Türkiye Barolar Birliği Dergisi [Journal of Turkish Union of Bar Associations*], Sayı 73 [Issue 73], 2007, p.168.

23 The only information we have is the application number to ECtHR: 77023/12.

this application had a negative conclusion was, since in the Turkish law there is an obligation for getting a permit from the civil administrator in cases of trials of civil servants, and the permit for trial was not granted for the involved Municipality civil servants by the Beylikdüzü District Governorship on the ground that the allegations in the application submitted by the Public Prosecutor's Office lacked legal basis. The appeal lodged by the plaintiff to Istanbul Regional Administrative Court was rejected by decisions E.2009/798 and K.2010/160[24] on the basis that adequate information and documentation was not included in the file. The allegations on discrimination were ignored both by the Authority of District Governorship and Istanbul Regional Administrative Court.[25] A similar attempt was the case when Olgun Yılmaz, who was visually impaired, lodged a criminal complaint against the requirement by the bank of him to bring two witnesses when he wanted to have banking transactions at the teller's desk and against such a practice. The Public Prosecutor's Office submitted the file to Ankara 7th Criminal Court of Peace with the request for a public case, the public case was opened under the number E.2009/457, however after the trial, it was decided by the court that the act performed by the employees of the bank did not have the intent and the employees of the bank were acquitted.[26]

Due to the criticism made by some criminal lawyers regarding Article 122 of TCC as well as the material decisions on the implementation of the Article, the relevant article was amended on 2.03.2014.[27] The title of the Article was amended as *Hate and Discrimination* and the grounds for discrimination were listed which included disability and the acts similar to the acts listed in the old article committed in these situations with the motive of hate were accepted as crime. In its new form, Article 122 of TCC is neither a hate nor a discrimination crime. While it is not possible for

---

24 See Annex-6: Istanbul Regional Administrative Court's Decision No. E.2009/798 and K.2010/160.

25 Türkiye'de Engellilik Temelinde Ayrımcılığın İzlenmesi Raporu Raporu 1 Ocak – 30 Haziran 2010, Hazırlayanlar: Arzu Şenyurt Akdağ ve diğerleri, İstanbul Bilgi Üniversitesi İnsan Hakları Uygulama ve Araştırma Merkezi, Şubat 2011, İstanbul [Report on Monitoring Discrimination on the Basis of Disability in Turkey 1 January – 30 June 2010, By Arzu Şenyurt Akdağ et al, Istanbul Bilgi University, Human Rights Application and Research Centre, February 2011, Istanbul], p. 47.

26 Türkiye'de Engellilik Temelinde Ayrımcılığın İzlenmesi Raporu Raporu 1 Ocak – 30 Haziran 2010, Hazırlayanlar :Arzu Şenyurt Akdağ ve diğerleri, İstanbul Bilgi Üniversitesi İnsan Hakları Uygulama ve Araştırma Merkezi, Şubat 2011, İstanbul [Report on Monitoring Discrimination on the Basis of Disability in Turkey 1 January – 30 June 2010, By Arzu Şenyurt Akdağ et al, Istanbul Bilgi University, Human Rights Application and Research Centre, February 2011, Istanbul], p. 47; for a similar decision, see: ibid p.46.

27 6529 Sayılı Temel Hak ve Hürriyetlerin Geliştirilmesi Amacıyla Çeşitli Kanunlarda Değişiklik Yapılmasına Dair Kanun, Kabul Tarihi: 2/3/2014, RG Tarihi:13 Mart 2014, Sayı:28940, Madde.15 [Law No. 6529 on Amending Various Laws to Improve Fundamental Rights and Freedoms, Date of Enactment: 2/3/2014, Official Gazette Date: 13 March 2014, Issue: 28940], Art. 15.

us to evaluate criminal code as a Constitutional lawyer, we can say that the new article will have a very limited discouraging effect in preventing discrimination since it penalises discrimination with a certain motive.

C. Social Belonging, Full and Effective Participation

Inclusion in the community means active participation in the community together with everyone else as well as in all areas of social life (economic, social, political, cultural and public). Only living in the society does not necessarily mean inclusion in the community. Because, although persons with intellectual disabilities can physically take part in the social area, they cannot participate in the social life on the equal basis as others due to acts of distinction and exclusion occurring in socio-cultural and economic areas.[28] However, the enjoyment of personal, political, economic, social and cultural rights by persons with disabilities depends on granting them the same opportunities and chances as other individuals and their existence in the society as active and effective individuals. The Convention on the Rights of Persons with Disabilities also adopts this philosophy which can be summarised as the social model of disability.

Pursuant to the social model approach which dominates the entire Convention, the barriers against the participation of persons with disabilities in the social life and activities are addressed under the 'environmental factors' framework under three titles as; physical, institutional and attitudinal factors. Physical factors refer to the obstacles in the physical environment either created by humans or existing naturally. As long as the roads, buildings, houses and means of transportation constructed for persons without disabilities and not allowing persons with disabilities to participate in the social life are not accommodated in a manner to allow persons with disabilities to access and benefit from or are not restructured, it is suggested that persons with disabilities cannot be an active part of this system. According to theoreticians and activists of the model, persons with disabilities are also excluded from the institutional system. As a result of negligent or systematic exclusion performed by social, educational, legal, religious or political institutions, persons with disabilities face troubles in accessing these institutions as well as being subject to various acts of discrimination. In addition to all of this, due to the rooted personal or social prejudices and stereotypes about the human environment, they are not perceived as a part of the social order. Because, dominant attitudes and values of the cultural,[29] economic and social life are established by people who are healthy, educated, working and producing and in that sense, regarded as "normal".[30]

---

28 Ad Hoc Committee A/58/118 & Corr.1, 3 July 2003.

29 For impact of cultural imperialism on persons with disabilities, see: **Colin Barnes/ Geof Mercer,** *Disability,* Polity Press, 2002, London, pp. 21–22.

30 For social model theory, see: **Alison Harris/ Sue Enfield**, *Disability, Equality and Human Rights A Training Manual for Development and Humanitarian Organisations,*

In the Article 19 of the Convention, "being included in the community" is addressed together with "living independently" and regulated in accordance with the social model approach. According to the article, persons with disabilities should have access to a range of in-home, residential and other community support services, including personal assistance necessary to support living and inclusion in the community, and to prevent isolation or segregation from the community (Art. 19/b). Community services and facilities for the general population should be available on an equal basis to persons with disabilities and should be responsive to their needs (Art. 19/c). It is the responsibility of States Parties to ensure that persons with disabilities are involved in the decisions concerning them in order to ensure their inclusion in the community and full participation in all areas of the life and create opportunities for them to take part in the political and public life (Art. 29)[31]; as well as the social and cultural areas by ensuring their participation in the cultural, artistic, intellectual, recreational and sports activities (Art. 30).[32]

As is seen, one of the obligatory elements of "full and effective participation" is that persons with disabilities have access to rights and services. The principle of "being included in the community, full and effective participation in the society" is in an inter-relationship with the general principle of "accessibility" as well as the "prohibition of discrimination". Because, there is a mandatory connection between the "prohibition of discrimination" and "accessibility". The Convention was written with the belief that in order for persons with disabilities to achieve the goal of an independent life, they need to be fully included in the society and provided with the possibility to benefit from all areas of life on an equal basis with others and in that sense, the general principle of equality of opportunity lays the function of being a protective shield on the prohibition of discrimination and accessibility over other general principles. This subject will be addressed in the explanations below on accessibility.

Oxfam GB, 2003, ISBN 9780855984854, pp. 17–18, https://policy-practice.oxfam.org.uk/publications/disability-equality-and-human-rights-a-training-manual-for-development-and-huma-115363(20.03.2018); **MJ Oliver,** "The Disability Movement and the Professions", *International Journal of Therapy and Rehabilitation,* Vol.6, Issue.8, 1 August 1999, pp. 377–379; **Jenny Morris**, "Impairment and Disability: Constructing an Ethics of Care that Promotes Human Rights", *Hypatia,* Vol.16, No. 4, 2001, pp. 1–5; **Michael Oliver& Bob Sapey,** *Social Work with Disabled People, Practical Social Work,* Series Editor: Jo Campling, BASW, Second Edition, 1998, pp. 21–25.

31 UN Enable Daily Summary related to Draft Article 18 – Participation in political and public life, Volume 3, # 5, January 9, 2004.

32 UN Enable Daily Summary related to Draft Article 24 – Participation in cultural life, recreation and leisure, Volume 3, #7, January 13, 2004.

D. Showing Respect for Differences and Accepting Disabilities as a Part of Human Diversity and Humanity

As mentioned above, according to the defenders of the social model[33], regarding the full participation of persons with disabilities and their right to have a say in their lives, they are excluded and ignored. In that sense, the real obstacle for persons with disabilities is caused by environmental factors. As a negative result of the understanding fed by the fact that the dominant attitudes and values of the cultural,[34] economic and social life consist of the social segment comprising of persons who are healthy, educated, working and producing and in that sense, regarded as "normal"[35] as well as the medical model which accepts disability as a medical and personal problem, social prejudices and stereotyping have continued against persons with disabilities and these persons were excluded from social living areas. In the preamble of the Convention, which adopts the social model developed with the aim to break the judgments which regard persons with disabilities as objects of help who are approached with feelings of pity, fear and worry instead of subjects of rights, disability is recognised as an evolving concept and it is accepted that disability results from the interaction between persons with impairments and attitudinal and environmental barriers that hinders their full and effective participation in society on an equal basis with others (Preamble-e).

Another one of the obstacles regarding the full and effective participation of persons with disabilities in the society is the existing public and social reluctance to accept and respect the difference of persons with disabilities. The inter-relationship between the "full and effective participation in the society" and "accepting and respecting the distinctness of persons with disabilities" is quite obvious. When the society regards the distinctness of persons with disabilities as a usual matter and takes responsibility in providing necessary and appropriate opportunities, it will make it easier for persons with disabilities to live as individuals included in the society. As a result of the inclusion of persons with disabilities in the social life through the measures taken and channels provided by the State, the society will

---

33 **Tom Shakespeare & Nicholas Watson**, "Defending the Social Model", Chapter 18, in *Disability Studies: Past Present and Future,* edited by Len Barton and Mike Oliver, Leeds: The Disability Press, 1997, pp. 263–273.

34 For impact of cultural imperialism on persons with disabilities, see: **Colin Barnes/ Geof Mercer** *Disability,* Polity Press, 2003, pp. 21–22.

35 For social model theory, see: **Alison Harris/ Sue Enfield**, *Disability, Equality and Human Rights A Training Manual for Development and Humanitarian Organisations,* Oxfam GB, 2003, pp. 17–18; **MJ Oliver,** "The Disability Movement and the Professions", *International Journal of Therapy and Rehabilitation,* Vol.6, Iss.8, 1 August 1999, pp. 377–379; **Jenny Morris**, "Impairment and Disability: Constructing an Ethics of Care that Promotes Human Rights", *Hypatia,* Vol.16, No. 4, 2001, pp. 1–5; **Michael Oliver& Bob Sapey,** *Social Work with Disabled People, Practical Social Work,* Series Editor: Jo Campling, BASW, Second Edition, pp. 21–25.

accept persons with disabilities in time and begin trusting them and respecting their distinctness. This connection is expressed in the Preamble of the Convention as, "*recognising the valued existing and potential contributions made by persons with disabilities to the overall well-being and diversity of their communities, and that the promotion of the full enjoyment by persons with disabilities of their human rights and fundamental freedoms and of full participation by persons with disabilities will result in their enhanced sense of belonging and in significant advances in the human, social and economic development of society and the eradication of poverty*" (Preamble-m).

It is of course important that the State puts into practice the necessary legal and administrative regulations in order to ensure continuous protection of the rights of persons with disabilities and to allow persons with disabilities to enjoy their rights and supervises the practices accordingly. However, it is more important to transform the perception of the society about disability to the positive through informing and educating the society, instead of creating pressure and forced acceptance on the society via laws and practices. Article 8 of the Convention titled *Awareness-raising* imposes the obligation on States Parties to adopt immediate, effective and appropriate measures in order to achieve their goals in this direction. In the provision which lists in detail the measures to be taken in order to raise awareness throughout society, including at the family level, regarding persons with disabilities, and to foster respect for the rights and dignity of persons with disabilities; to combat stereotypes, prejudices and harmful practices relating to persons with disabilities, including those based on sex and age, in all areas of life; and to promote awareness of the capabilities and contributions of persons with disabilities, emphasis is put particularly on breaking judgments and raising awareness among the society via education and mass media.

E. Equality of Opportunity

Equality of opportunity is the type of equality which states that certain persons or groups may be different than others from the beginning due to their special conditions and these persons cannot be equal to the rest of the society unless their access to opportunities is ensured and they are provided with legal assurance. In that sense, the equality of opportunity advocates for "equality at the beginning". In other words, it is important to possess the same chance as others, but the result of the enjoyment of this chance may not be equal for everyone.

The common view of international human rights regulations is that prohibition of discrimination is not sufficient for persons and groups who are excluded from the social life to enjoy human rights on an equal basis with others. In addition to the prohibition of discrimination, it is required that persons with disabilities are provided with access to the opportunities to enjoy their rights and become equal to other members of the society regarding the enjoyment of rights. Instead of the general concepts such as positive action and positive discrimination[36] used in the international conventions to equalise the opportunities of persons with disabilities, the Convention on the Rights of Persons with Disabilities has brought the concepts 'universal design' and 'reasonable accommodation' into the normative law order but also has not abandoned the established expression 'special measures'.[37] Universal design means creating environments usable by all people, while reasonable accommodation means obligations which ensure that where universal design is not applied, persons with disabilities actively exist in the society and all areas of life. In the Convention, States Parties undertake the obligation to take all appropriate steps to ensure that reasonable accommodation is provided with the aim to ensure equality and eliminate discrimination (Art. 5/3). Also, it is stated that specific measures which are necessary to accelerate or achieve de facto equality of persons with disabilities shall not be considered discrimination under the terms of the Convention (Art. 5/4).

In the Preamble of the Convention, the aim of contributing in making a significant contribution to redressing the profound social disadvantage of persons with disabilities and promote their participation in the civil, political, economic, social and cultural spheres with equal opportunities (paragraph y). In that sense, efforts were made to ensure that equality of opportunity gains content with new concepts added to human rights positive law and by pointing out the State's obligation for positive actions on making sure that persons with disabilities can enjoy their rights. In some provisions of the Convention, this situation is expressed as "opportunity of persons with disabilities to enjoy rights and freedoms on an equal basis with others" (Art. 29 – Participation in political and public life); in the provision which regulates the right to work and employment, "equality of opportunity" is emphasised as an element which serves to ensuring fair and appropriate working conditions as well as an obligation of States Parties (Art. 27).

F. Accessibility

Accessibility refers to possessing the opportunities to access primarily both human-made and natural physical environment as well as economic, social and cultural environment, benefit from the services provided in these environments and contribute to them. Similar to the mutual and holistic relationship between human rights and freedoms, the enjoyment of all rights in all generations depends on provision of access. Having opportunities for access is one of the mandatory elements of full and effective participation in all areas of life. In that sense, it is obligatory that physical, institutional and attitudinal barriers within the social life are eliminated and access is provided for persons with disabilities.

36 Ad Hoc Committee, Report of the third session, A/AC/265/2004/5, 9 June 2004, p.62.
37 For discussions on which of "special" or "positive" to precede "measures", see: Ad Hoc Committee, A/AC/265/2005/2, 23 February 2005.

The one and only convention that conceptualises accessibility on its broader extent and regulates it with a single provision is the Convention on the Rights of Persons with Disabilities. In the special provision of the Convention on accessibility, the measures to be taken by States in order to ensure that persons with disabilities benefit from all services provided in the public sphere were listed and the matter of ensuring that persons with disabilities can easily access buildings and institutions as well as information was regulated in detail (Art. 9). According to the article, in order to enable persons with disabilities to live independently and participate fully in all aspects of life, States Parties shall take appropriate measures to ensure to persons with disabilities access, on an equal basis with others, to the physical environment, to transportation, to information and communications, including information and communications technologies and systems, and to other facilities and services open or provided to the public, both in urban and in rural areas. How and via which means these measures will be taken, which also includes determination and election of all obstacles to access, were listed by means of examples.

"Accessibility" which is used as a key concept in the social model of disability, is also included in the "general principles" of the Convention on the Rights of Persons with Disabilities and emphasised as the main element in the Preamble (paragraph c) and most of the provisions. It is the responsibility of States to ensure the protection and participation of persons with disabilities in the justice system under the article titled "Access to justice"; and ensure that all communication channels are opened for persons with disabilities to enjoy their freedom of thought and expression under the article titled "freedom of expression and opinion, and access to information" (respectively Art. 3-f, Art. 9, Art. 13, Art. 21). Besides, in the Convention, equal access to quality and free primary education and secondary education is expressed as an element of the right to education; right to benefit from the highest attainable standard of health as an element of right to health; accessibility to assistive devices and technologies as an element of habilitation and rehabilitation; equal access to labour markets, general technical and vocational guidance programmes, placement services and vocational and continuing training as an element of the right to work; and the access to housing, retirement opportunities and programmes as well as clean water, appropriate and affordable services, devices, means and services suitable to their needs and the access of poor persons with disabilities and their families to the State aid regarding their expenses on education, consultancy, financial aid and care as an element of the right to adequate standard of living and social protection (Art. 24-b, Art. 25, Art. 26/3, Art. 27/1 and 27/1-d, Art. 28).

Obligations and responsibilities imposed by the Convention regarding the accessibility of persons with disabilities are not limited to the structure and services of the public sector, it was allowed that persons with disabilities can benefit from all services open to public and therefore enjoy their rights and freedoms as everyone else and assurance was provided. Pursuant to the Convention, States Parties are obliged to encourage private sector entities which provide services to the public and ensure that they apply universal design, reasonable accommodation and take special measures which can be realised in a certain time period as well as supervising the phenomenon of accessibility. As a result of their obligation to protect rights, States must also prevent violations to be committed by third persons against persons with disabilities. In cases where public services are privatised and free market policies are becoming widespread, non-State actors (private sector employers, private sector service providers) have the obligation to care for and respect the equality of persons with disabilities.[38]

In its personal application decision made in 2013, the Committee on the Rights of Persons with Disabilities investigated the allegations of persons with visual disabilities who asserted that they were not able to benefit from the banking ATM services provided by a private finance company on the equal basis as others in terms of the Article 9 of the Convention and concluded that the State of Hungary violated the relevant provision. Because, the State Party had not established minimum standards on how the banking services provided by private finance companies would be executed together with persons with disabilities regarding other persons without disabilities and had not fulfilled its obligation to make and implement the legal regulations which enable accessibility to services for everyone via information and communication means and impose sanctions for contradictions to these measures. The Committee also stated that the State must oblige the banking companies to make ATM services suitable for the access of persons with disabilities via reasonable accommodation or build new ATMs in this quality in order to ensure that persons with disabilities can fully benefit from ATM services.[39]

In the inception reports submitted by States Parties, due to the popularity of problems on the accessibility of persons with disabilities to rights and freedoms, the Committee highlighted the importance of this issue by the reference it made to this application in its General Comment Decision on the Article 9 of the Convention (General Comment No. 2-Article 9: Accessibility).

The Committee on the Rights of Persons with Disabilities made a decision regarding "accessibility" in its General Comment Decision No. 2 made public in 2014[40] and recognised that this phenomenon, which is regulated under Article 9 of the Convention, is the prerequisite for persons with disabilities to live independent lives, participate in the society fully and on the equal basis as others, and enjoy all human rights and freedoms on the equal basis without being subject to any limitations. Moreover, according to the Committee the phenomenon of accessibility should be regarded as *a right* and addressed with a special perspective for persons with disabilities. Because, the concept of equality has evolved from a form-based equality to material equality in today's world and this transformation creates a substantial impact on the obligation of States. This new duty, which can be called the obligation

38 Committee on Economic, Social and Cultural Rights, General Comment No. 5, Persons with disabilities, Eleventh session, 1994(Contained in Document E/1995/22).

39 Committee on the Rights of Persons with Disabilities, CRPD/C/9/D/1/2010, Distr.: General 21 June 2013, para. 9–10.

40 Committee on the Rights of Persons with Disabilities, General comment No. 2 - Article 9: Accessibility, Distr.: General 11 April 2014 Advance Unedited Version Original: English.

to provide accessibility, is an essential and mandatory element of the obligation of States to respect and protect rights and perform them fully on the basis of equality. From this point of view, the right to accessibility of persons with disabilities should be exercised by assuring that the accessibility standards are implemented meticulously. The recommendation of the Committee on this issue is reviewing the barriers regarding existing buildings, facilities and devices and products, services open or dedicated to the public until the goal of accessibility is fully achieved, eliminating them via reasonable accommodation in a systematic and more importantly continuous (perpetual) and gradual manner and structuring new assets, products, instruments and devices as well as regulation and technologies and services exactly according to the universal design principle.[41]

The Committee also explains in detail in the mentioned General Comment the inter-relationship between the right to accessibility and other rights and freedoms regulated in the Convention. This connection will be addressed later in the explanations on the right to education of persons with disabilities and the State's obligations.

G. Equality of Women and Men

Article 4 of the Covenant on Civil and Political Rights (CCPR), under the "gender equality" title, resolves that States Parties to the CCPR made commitments to ensure "equal rights" in enjoyment of personal and political rights.[42] The Covenant on Economic, Social and Cultural Rights (CESCR), in its Article 3 which makes the same right more clear, states that States Parties made commitments to ensure equal rights to women and men in the enjoyment of the rights in CESCR.[43] Also, in the international human rights documents in the field of women's rights and on the elimination of discrimination against women,[44] no special rights were requested for

41 Committee on the Rights of Persons with Disabilities, General comment No. 2 - Article 9: Accessibility, Distr.: General 11 April 2014 Advance Unedited Version Original: English, para 13–26.

42 **Leyla Uyar (Derleyen),** *Birleşmiş Milletler'de İnsan Hakları Yorumları İnsan Hakları Komitesi ve Ekonomik, Sosyal ve Kültürel Haklar Komitesi 1981–2006,* İstanbul Bilgi Üniversitesi Yayınları, 1. Baskı, Eylül 2006, s.349 [**(compiled by)** *Human Rights Comments in the United Nations, Human Rights Committee and Committee on Economic, Social and Cultural Rights 1981–2006,* Istanbul Bilgi University Publications, First Edition, September 2006], p.349.

43 **Leyla Uyar (Derleyen),** *Birleşmiş Milletler'de İnsan Hakları Yorumları İnsan Hakları Komitesi ve Ekonomik, Sosyal ve Kültürel Haklar Komitesi 1981–2006,* İstanbul Bilgi Üniversitesi Yayınları, 1. Baskı, Eylül 2006, s.380 [**(compiled by)** *Human Rights Comments in the United Nations, Human Rights Committee and Committee on Economic, Social and Cultural Rights 1981–2006,* Istanbul Bilgi University Publications, First Edition, September 2006], p.380.

44 See: **Mehmet Semih Gemalmaz**, *Ulusal Üstü İnsan Hakları Hukukunun Genel Teorisine Giriş,* Güncelleştirilmiş ve Geliştirilmiş 5. Baskı, Legal Yayınevi İstanbul, 2005,

women. What is demanded and expected is, putting an end to the discrimination developed against women particularly in political and public areas and equalisation of their rights and freedoms to the ones of the rest of the society.

However, the juxtaposition of the status as women with race, colour, language, religion, political or other views, national or social origin, property, birth or other statuses which may aggravate their disadvantaged position in terms of age, ethnicity, disability, marital status, refugee and migrant status has caused the emergence of different types of discrimination against women[45] and resulted in multiple victimisations.[46] Therefore, only protecting women against gender based inequality and discriminatory acts have not been sufficient on its own. Depending on different situations, there are also segments among women who experience discrimination on a deeper lever. Disability is one of these situations. This situation is emphasised explicitly in the Preamble of the Convention on the Rights of Persons with Disabilities, concerns were expressed on the difficult conditions faced by persons with disabilities who are subject to aggravated forms of discrimination and it was underlined that women and girls with disabilities are often at greater risk, both within and outside the home of violence, injury or abuse, neglect or negligent treatment, maltreatment or exploitation (Preamble-p, q). Especially, if girls and women who are in a disadvantaged position regarding the rights on education and working also have disabilities, their exclusion from these areas can become more systematic.

Due to the discriminatory acts and de facto inequalities based on disability and gender, women with disabilities need special protection and additional measures should be taken for them to enjoy their rights.[47] To this end, there is an independent article added to the Convention on the Rights of Persons with Disabilities about women with disabilities. In the Article 6 of the Convention, it is recognised once again that women and girls with disabilities are subject to multiple discrimination and the obligation was imposed on States to take measures to ensure the full and equal enjoyment by this group of all human rights and fundamental freedoms. Again, States Parties are obliged to take all appropriate measures to ensure the full development, advancement and empowerment of women, for the purpose of guaranteeing them the exercise and enjoyment of the human rights and fundamental freedoms set out in

ss.466–488 [*Introduction to the General Theory of Supranational Human Rights Law*], Legal Publication, Updated and enlarged Fifth Edition, Istanbul, 2005], pp. 466–488.

45 For State's obligations on this matter, see: Committee on Economic, Social and Cultural Rights, General Comment No. 16 (2005), 11/08/2005. E/C:12/2005/4. (General Comments); Committee on Human Rights, General Comment No. 28: Equality of rights between men and women (Article 3) 29/03/2000, CCPR/C/21/Rev.1/Add. 10, General Comment No. 28. (General Comments)

46 The Convention on the Rights of Persons with Disabilities explicitly refers to this on the provision on women with disabilities (Art. 6).

47 Committee on Human Rights, General Comment No. 28: Equality of rights between men and women (Article 3). 29/03/2000, CCPR/C/21/Rev.1/Add. 10, General Comment No. 28. (General Comments)

the present Convention. In addition to the provision on general protection of women, there is also a provision in the Convention which prescribes prioritised protection for women and girls with disabilities. Accordingly, under the "adequate standard of living and social protection", States are obliged to ensure access by persons with disabilities, in particular women and girls with disabilities and older persons with disabilities, to social protection programmes and poverty reduction programmes (Art. 28).

In the Article 16 of the Convention titled "Freedom from Exploitation, Violence and Abuse", women and girls are protected implicitly. Pursuant to Article 16, States Parties are obliged to take all appropriate legislative, administrative, social, educational and other measures to protect persons with disabilities, both within and outside the home, from all forms of exploitation, violence and abuse, including their gender-based aspects. While there is no specific emphasis on women and girls in the mentioned provision, as it is stated in the Preamble of the Convention, women and girls are at higher risk for being subject to such acts and therefore need to be specially protected. Also, in the Reporting Guide which is prepared by the Committee on the Rights of Persons with Disabilities and contains the principles that States Parties to the Convention must comply with in the reports they are going to submit, it is also specified that this article makes sure that persons with disabilities are not subject to exploitation both within and outside the home and are not exposed to violence and abuse and also takes into consideration particularly the children and women with disabilities.[48] In the Reporting Guide it is stated that information is requested from States on special measures and assurances provided for women and girls with disabilities regarding the Article 6 and Article 27 titled "Work and Employment" of the Convention. In relevance with Article 6, the request was stated that all articles of the Convention should be interpreted in a gender responsive manner, however pursuant to this specific article, the reports to be submitted by States Parties should contain steps taken for full development, advancement and empowerment of women in order to ensure that they enjoy the human rights and freedoms prescribed in the Convention and benefit from them and States Parties were requested to report on these issues:

- Whether the gender inequality against girls and women with disabilities is recognised on the legislative and political level as well as in programme development,
- Whether girls and women with disabilities enjoy all human rights and fundamental freedoms on the equal basis as boys and men with disabilities,
- Whether girls and women with disabilities enjoy all human rights and fundamental freedoms on the equal basis as other girls and women with disabilities.[49]

---

48 Committee on the Rights of Persons with Disabilities, "Guidelines on treaty-specific document to be submitted by States Parties under Article 35, para. 1, of the Convention on the Rights of Persons with Disabilities", CRPD/2/3. 18 November 2009, p. 10.

49 Committee on the Rights of Persons with Disabilities, "Guidelines on treaty-specific document to be submitted by States Parties under Article 35, para. 1, of the Convention on the Rights of Persons with Disabilities", CRPD/2/3. 18 November 2009, p.18.

Regarding the Article 27 which comprises of the State's obligations regarding protection and enjoyment of the right to "work and employment" of persons with disabilities, it is specified that, information is requested from States Parties on the significant differences between the employment of men and women with disabilities and whether there are policies and legislation for eliminating these differences in order to ensure advancement of women with disabilities.

H. Respecting the Development Capacity of Children with Disabilities and Their Right to Protect Their Identities

Protection of identity, in the broader sense, is the person protecting his/her own self. And that is about "dignity" to a great extent. It is important that the identities of persons regarding their ethnicity, religion, language, gender or disability status are protected and their existing identities are recognised. Regarding persons and children with disabilities, social acceptance together with their disabilities is important for them to continue a healthy development. Because, the world of a child comprises of different needs compared to the adulthood and the perceptions and understanding of the childhood era is also different. This process can become even more sensitive for children with disabilities. Especially the use of labels and stereotypes pointing out the disabilities of children can be more hurtful and humiliating during the childhood period. In this process, in order to ensure that children can experience their development in parallel to their peers without their "disabilities" being highlighted, it becomes important to prevent the encounter of children with negative attitudes resulting from their differences and to build and also reinforce their self-confidence.

Committee on the Rights of the Child recognises the childhood development as a holistic concept which embraces the entire Convention on the Rights of the Child (CRC).[50] The right to development is addressed not only in regard to physical and intellectual development, but also within a concept which includes, along with the inalienable rights of all individuals, participation and contribution in political, social, economic and cultural development as well as enjoying these rights and freedoms.[51] Therefore, many rights related regulations of CRC on health, education, association, protection against violence and abuse, social security and adequate standard of living serve for the aim of exercising the right to development.[52] The principle on

---

50 **Susan Marks/ Andrew Clapham**, *International Human Rights Lexicon*, Oxford University Press, 2005, ISBN: 9780198764137, p.25.

51 **Dominic McGoldrick**, "The United Nations Convention on the Rights of the Child", in *Children's Rights*, Volume II, Edited by Michael D.A. Freeman, Ashgate/Dartmouth, 2004, ISBN: 075462336X (alk. paper) 9780754623366 (alk. Paper), p.139.

52 For detailed information, see: **Javaid Rehman**, *International Human Rights Law: A Practical Approach,* London, Longman, 2003, pp. 384–386; Rehman discusses inconsistencies in terms of cultural relativism between Article 5 of the convention governing the respect for the parents' rights and responsibilities on the development of abilities of the child and the right to development in this provision.

"respect for the right of children with disabilities to development" is a principle applicable in the society by the inclusion of children with disabilities into the society. Children with disabilities who take part in the all practices of social and cultural life together with their peers will be more prepared for the adulthood life. Meeting their special needs by respecting their dignity and identity and also with measures and applications for taking their capacities to the highest level possible will help children with disabilities to become independent individuals.

In case of the children with disabilities, the concept of "best interest of the child" becomes even more important. As explained above in the general principle on equality of women and men, children are also in a weaker and more disadvantageous position like women regarding rights and freedoms. Therefore, international human rights documents have developed new rights and protection provisions specific for children. Where the child has a disability, the violations of rights and freedoms increase even more. Throughout the history, children with disabilities have been subject to violations and victimisation regarding the access to education and training, family life, proper health care, playing games and leisure activities and right to participate in regular childhood activities. Children with disabilities constitute the group who is most frequently exposed to the acts of social exclusion as a denial of fundamental rights within the whole population of children.[53] Moreover, they suffer multiple discriminations due to the addition of other factors and their victimisation escalates. For instance, combinations such as being a girl and having a disability or being refugee and having a disability or being a member of a minority and having a disability create differences regarding the type and severity of victimisation among children with disabilities. Committee on the Rights of the Child, in the General Comment Decision No. 9 it adopted in 2006 on children with disabilities, in order to eliminate the discrimination against children with disabilities and ensure that they enjoy all human rights on the equal basis as other children, it emphasises that the "best interest of the child" should always be considered within the scope of the special conditions of children with disabilities.[54]

Also, in the Convention on the Rights of Persons with Disabilities, an obligation is imposed on States Parties to implement special measures for children with disabilities. Article 7 of the Convention regulates the obligation to ensure the full enjoyment by children with disabilities of all human rights and fundamental freedoms on an equal basis with other children and that in all actions concerning children with disabilities, the best interests of the child shall be a primary consideration (Art. 7/1,2) and complementary information is requested in the State reports to be submitted regarding this article indicating the steps taken to ensure the full

---

53 United Nations Committee on the Rights of the Child, Day of General Discussion, CRC/C/66, Annex V, 16th Session, 6 October 1997 http://www.ohchr.org/EN/HRBodies/CRC/Documents/Recommandations/disabled.pdf (20.03.2018)

54 Committee on the Rights of the Child, General Comment No. 9 (2006) The rights of children with disabilities, CRC/C/GC/9, 27 February 2007.

enjoyment of children with disabilities of fundamental human rights and freedoms that these steps assure that the best interest of children with disabilities are considered. In the Reporting Guide which clarifies what complementary information involves, it is stated that explanatory information is requested from States Parties on which fundamental principles the decision making processes for girls and boys with disabilities are based, whether children with disabilities have the right to freely express their opinions on all matters affecting them and whether a support is provided suitable to their disabilities and age for the granting of this right to them, differences of the girls and boys with disabilities regarding their conditions and whether children with disabilities are regarded as right owners under the same conditions as other children.[55]

In the State reports, information is requested on the measures taken regarding the children with disabilities about the articles of the Convention which regulate the liberty of movement and nationality and the rights to education, health and participation in cultural life, recreation, leisure and sport. One of the noteworthy pieces of information among these is the steps taken for all children born with disabilities to be registered in the civil registry immediately after birth and receive a name and citizenship. Registry is extremely important for ensuring that the children with disabilities which can be detected during birth can receive early rights and services such as education, health and rehabilitation etc. as soon as possible.[56] As a matter of fact, it is known that the information requested pursuant to the article of the Convention, which regulates the right to education, about the steps taken for ensuring that children with disabilities attain early childhood education, compulsory primary, secondary and higher education as well as the number of girls and boys at the early childhood education period and the information on health services aiming to prevent the occurrence of new conditions of disability and minimising them as well as early diagnosis and prevention programmes depend on the detection of the existence of children as citizens registered in the civil registry.

---

55 Committee on the Rights of Persons with Disabilities, "Guidelines on treaty-specific document to be submitted by States Parties under Article 35, para. 1, of the Convention on the Rights of Persons with Disabilities", CRPD/2/3. 18 November 2009, p.18.

56 Committee on the Rights of Persons with Disabilities, "Guidelines on treaty-specific document to be submitted by States Parties under Article 35, para. 1, of the Convention on the Rights of Persons with Disabilities", CRPD/2/3. 18 November 2009, p.11, 13, 14.

PART II. Assessment of the Turkısh Legıslatıon and the Convention on the Rights of Persons wıth Disabilities in Terms of the Right to educatıon and state's obligations

In the first part of this section, explanations will be provided on the development of the right to education in terms of normative content and the State's obligations, based on the recognition of the right to education as a human right and in the second part, the conceptual, meaning, quality and elements related transformation the right to education went through regarding persons with disabilities will be addressed based on the Convention on the Rights of Persons with Disabilities along with other related conventions. Legal regulations and judgments in force within the Turkish law system will be evaluated in terms of the extent to which they comply with this transformation.

A. Right to Education in the International Law in General

Education is both a human right in and of itself and an inalienable instrument for the realisation of all other human rights. As an empowering right, education is the basic instrument for adults and children who are excluded from the society in economic, social and other areas to find the way to save themselves from poverty and participate fully in the society in which they live. Education has a vital role in empowerment of women as well as persons with disabilities, protecting children from exploitation and dangerous labour and sexual abuse, development and emplacement of human rights, democracy and the notion of active citizenship and protection of the environment.

In the international law, since the time it was recognised as a "right", education has been regarded as a dynamic right which continuously develops in parallel to human life and development of societies in terms of content, scope and objectives. It is an inevitable obligation to interpret the right to education in the day the Universal Declaration was adopted and the education which has to adapt to the needs of the competitive and global world of today, differently in terms of scope, elements and content. Therefore, UN canalises the efforts of international independent organisations and institutions to expand the scope of the right to education and to ensure that education is a usable right for everyone without distinction. First product of this effort is the Convention against Discrimination in Education adopted in 1960.[57]

---

57 Convention against Discrimination in Education Paris, 14 December 1960; for text of the Convention http://portal.unesco.org/en/ev.php-URL_ID=12949&URL_DO=DO_TOPIC&URL_SECTION=201.html (24.06.2014); Hereafter the "Convention". S.Ç.

In the first article of the Convention, discrimination in education is defined as any distinction, exclusion, limitation or preference, based on certain reasons which has the purpose or effect of nullifying or impairing "equality of treatment in education"; and particularly which acts will be regarded as discrimination in education were explained. In that sense, *"depriving any person or group of persons of access to education of any type or at any level", "limiting any person or group of persons to education of an inferior standard", Subject to the provisions of Article 2 of this Convention, establishing or maintaining separate educational systems or institutions for persons or groups of persons"* or *"inflicting on any person or group of persons discrimination, exclusion, limitation or preference which are in-compatible with the dignity of man"* will be regarded as discrimination. However, it is necessary to point out that the Convention not only aims at preventing and eliminating discrimination in education, but also imposes the obligation on States Parties to adopt positive measures in order to ensure the equality of opportunity and treatment in the field of education.[58]

In the Convention on the Rights of the Child adopted in 1989[59], education for children is recognised as a right to be achieved progressively and on the basis of equal opportunity and States are obliged to make primary education compulsory and available free to all (Article 28). Convention does not only regard the right of the child to education as a matter of access but also states that it is a matter of content (Article 29). Therefore, after the Article 28 which regulates the right-related dimension of education and focuses on the obligations of States Parties in establishment of education systems and ensuring access to these systems, the right to personal and subjective access to a certain quality education with certain purposes is regulated. This article, which is consistent with the emphasis in the Convention on the importance of acting by considering the best interest of the child, gives the message of child-centred education: Accordingly, the main goal of education is developing the personality, skills and competences of the child as an individual; meanwhile it must be recognised that every child has unique properties, interests, skills and education needs. Therefore, the curriculum must be directly related to the social, cultural, environmental and economic conditions of the child as well as his/her existing and future needs; while completely considering the developing skills of the child.

Teaching methods should also be shaped according to the different needs of children in different positions. Education should also aim at ensuring that every child learns basic life skills and no child leaves school without acquiring the background to deal with situations he/she may encounter in life. Basic skills not only refer to literacy and numeracy, but also to life skills which go beyond these. These skills

---

58 For brief information on the Convention, Hector Gros Espiell, Significance of the Convention against Discrimination in Education (1960), UNESCO 2005.

59 For the full text of the Convention, see: http://www.shcek.gov.tr/Cocuk_Haklari, (04.10.2007); For the original text in English, http://www.ohchr.org/english/law/crc.htm, (04.10.2007)

include the skills of balanced decision making and resolving conflicts without resorting to violence, as well as healthy life styles which enable children to choose their paths in their lives according to their own decisions, positive social relationships and sense of responsibility, critical thinking, creative skills and others.[60]

The right to education has begun to refer to the understanding that education should be delivered in a manner to include the rights in education, involve everyone in terms of purpose and content without discriminating anyone, consider personal differences, put forward the personal and special educational needs and approaches the development of the child/individual in a holistic way. The "inclusive education" concept used to explain the education which involves everyone without distinction was used in the decisions of UN Commission on Human Rights[61], also the Committee on the Rights of the Child and Committee on Economic, Social and Cultural Rights issued decisions interpreting the provisions on the right to education in terms of the related Conventions and recognised inclusive education as a compulsory element of the right to education in these decisions.[62]

General Comment No. 13 of the Committee on Economic, Social and Cultural Rights adopted in 1999 which explains the objectives and principles in the Article 13 of CESCR regulating the right to education[63] is of particular importance as it presents the qualities regarding the normative content and scope of the right to education. In its General Comment on the right to education, the Committee refers to the 4A rule (available, accessible, acceptable and adaptable) developed by the UN Right to Education Special Rapporteur Katarina Tomasevski in determining the scope of the State's obligations on the right to education, as applicable to all elements in the provision 13/2 of the Convention[64] and explains the nature of the right to education as follows:

---

60 General Comment No. 1: **The Aims of Education** (Article 29/1), CRC/GC/2001/1, April 2001.

61 The Right to Education, Commission on Human Rights Resolution 2002/23, 49th meeting, 22 April 2002 [Adopted without vote. E/2002/23-E/CN.4/2002/200, see chap.X.], The right to Education, Commission on Human Rights Resolution 2005/21, 51st meeting, 15 April 2005 [Adopted without vote. E/CN.4/2005/L.10/Add.10, see chap.X.]

62 General Comment No. 1: **The Aims of Education** (Article 29/1), CRC/GC/2001/1, April 2001; The right to education (Art. 13): 08/12/99. E/C.12/1999/10. (General Comments), CESCR Committee on Economic, Social and Cultural Rights, Twenty-first session 15 November – 3 December 1999.

63 The right to education (Art. 13): 08/12/99. E/C.12/1999/10. (General Comments), CESCR Committee on Economic, Social and Cultural Rights, Twenty-first session 15 November – 3 December 1999.

64 **Katarina Tomasevski,** "Human rights obligation: making education available, accessible, acceptable and adaptable", *Right to Education Primers No. 3,* International Development Cooperation Agency, Sida, 2001.

Available: Refers to States Parties having functioning educational institutions and programmes available in sufficient quantity, meeting the needs for buildings, providing education in healthy and hygienic facilities with safe drinking water and the needs for relatively trained teachers who work for appropriate salaries, teaching materials and similar needs. In the implementation of institutions and programmes requiring more advanced needs, this quality should be taken into account.

Accessible: Refers to ensuring that educational institutions and programmes are accessible in law and fact to everyone, within the jurisdiction of the State. Committee addressed accessibility on three dimensions:

1. Non-discrimination – It means that all types of discrimination on any of the prohibited grounds particularly regarding the groups under risk about obtaining the right will violate the right to education.
2. Physical accessibility – It is about the locations education is delivered as well as the educational setting and opportunities. Education has to be within safe physical, proper and appropriate geographical locations or delivered by using technological advancements (for instance remote access).
3. Economic accessibility – Provided that it is in compliance with the rules of Article 13/2 of the Convention, education has to be affordable to all.

Acceptable: The form and substance of the education have to be acceptable to all students and, in appropriate cases, parents while meeting the minimum educational standards as well as educational goals in the Convention.

Adaptable: Refers to the flexibility of education. With this quality, the Committee highlights an education system which can meet both the needs of changing and developing communities and the needs of students in different social and cultural settings. This element is also closely related to the content, adaptability and comprehensiveness of education.[65]

CESCR points out that these qualities should be addressed as a whole and "the best interest of the student should be considered" above all.

In the "Education for All Summits"[66] the term "basic education" which makes reference to elementary school with "early childhood care and education" was enriched in terms of scope and quality and basic education was recognised as a type of education referring to providing to everyone the education they need throughout their lives within the formal and adult education system. In international conventions on human rights, education is regulated or interpreted with a content based

65 The right to education (Art. 13): 08/12/99. E/C.12/1999/10. (General Comments), CESCR Committee on Economic, Social and Cultural Rights, Twenty-first session 15 November – 3 December 1999.

66 For the content of "basic education" discussed at Jomtien and Dakar summits, see: The challenge of universal primary education, Strategies for achieving the international development targets, Department for International Development (DFID), January 2001, p.8.

on an individual oriented and rights-based approach rather than a service mentality which puts forward the interests of the State and aims at raising good citizens.

As is seen in the brief explanations, education, as recognised in the international law order, has to be physically and economically accessible to all in law and fact in compliance with the prohibition of discrimination, particularly for persons with disabilities and vulnerable groups. "Accessible education/accessibility of education" which refers to not making anyone subject to discrimination regarding the enjoyment of the right to education; ensuring the physical access of everyone to educational institutions; not excluding anyone from education due to economic deprivation or other reasons; and ensuring via necessary special measures full enjoyment of the education provided in educational institutions by everyone is accepted as an inseparable element of the right to education. The form and substance of education, including the curriculum and teaching methods, should be acceptable to all students and, in appropriate cases, parents, by considering the principle of "best interest of the child", adaptable to the needs of changing societies and communities and flexible enough to meet the educational needs of students who come from different social and cultural settings and possess different properties.

B. Right to Education of Persons with Disabilities and State's Obligations

Although it is one of the most frequently researched subjects in the international law order and also a right on which a serious emphasis is laid due to its developmental impact on other human rights, the right to education has not been a right which is fulfilled and protected on the same level for everyone and a universal success has not been achieved for certain social segments. The right to education, which is developed and protected under conventions on human rights and extra-Conventional decisions and documents, is at the position of being a right which is not fulfilled completely or properly for certain social segments including persons with disabilities. At the World Conference on Education for All held in 1990 in Jomtien, it was claimed that there were 600 million persons with disabilities in the world. According to the estimates of UN, only 2% of the 150 million children under the age of 15 included in this figure were able to receive education.[67] According to the recently conducted research, there is an increase in the number of children with disabilities who are able to access education. According to the results obtained from countries which are more successful in collecting data and developing statistics, 40 million of 115 million children with disabilities do not go to school. In that case, it is possible to say that approximately 1/3 of children with disabilities have never been enrolled to school or have dropped out of school. This ratio is twice as higher

67 "Inclusive Schools & Community Support Programmes", *Report 1996 – First Phase 1997*, UNESCO, p.10.

compared to the one of regular children.[68] According to the data from 2007; one third of 77 million children between ages 6 to 11 who are not able to receive education have a disability. In order to change this tragic picture, equalise the education level and ratio of children with disabilities to their peers or at least create a balance, it has become inevitable to develop the interpretation of the right to education in terms of persons with disabilities.

When the provision on the right to education and other articles of the Convention on the Rights of the Child are evaluated together, it is observed that education is a right which carries certain properties for every child without discrimination and imposes active obligations on States. However, there is no special emphasis on the education of persons with disabilities in the Convention. While there are no provisions specific to children with disabilities in the Convention, in the specific provision, care and protection of children with disabilities are the topics addressed more prominently and the goal of their integration with education and society within these limits is mentioned. It is stated that, financial assistance will be provided to the parents or others caring for the children with disabilities if necessary and this assistance will be designed to ensure that the child has effective access to education, vocational training and other services listed (Art. 23/3). The aim of this provision is not to determine the scope and content of the right to education in terms of children with disabilities, but to impose an obligation on the State for the protection of children with disabilities.

"Tallinn Guidelines for Action on Human Resource Development in the Field of Disability" adopted by UN in 1989[69] took the right to education regarding persons with disabilities one step further compared to the Convention on the Rights of the Child and imposed rules to guide governments and politicians on the education and employment of persons with disabilities. While the Tallinn Guidelines addressed the education as a means for employment and recruitment with a holistic approach, some of the fundamental principles involve a contemporary interpretation of the right to education specific to persons with disabilities. For instance, Rule 23 regulates that vocational training programmes as well as primary, secondary and higher levels of education should be available to persons with disabilities at the regular schools and institutions within the general (regular) educational system. In the States where education is delivered in a double system as general-private education, it should be considered as an evolution that education is delivered for persons with disabilities within the general educational system as much as possible together with

68 "The Right to Education for Persons with Disabilities: Towards Inclusion, An EFA Flagship", *Conceptual Paper December 2004*, p.7; it is indicated that most of the children included in this figure do not have disabilities visible to the eye or easily diagnosable. This means that children with emotional or intellectual disabilities are more frequently excluded from education that their counterparts with physical disabilities. (S.Ç.)

69 "Tallinn Guidelines for Action on Human Resource Development in the Field of Disability", UN General Assembly, A/RES/44/70, 8 December 1989.

their peers in the same classrooms, in order words, adoption of inclusive education. Although the Tallinn Guidelines do not use the term inclusive education, it is possible to say that it is the first international document with a content which has the same meaning and purpose.

Another extra-Conventional document adopted after the Tallinn Guidelines is the "Standard Rules on the Equalization of Opportunities for Persons with Disabilities".[70] The aim of Standard Rules is to eliminate the obstacles against the equal participation in the society and access to education and other services. It is stated that this goal can be accomplished if children, teenagers and adults with disabilities are provided with the opportunity to receive education with others in regular educational institutions at all levels of education and training and by keeping the education delivered in separate private educational institutions as exceptional. Accordingly, private education should only be used within the general educational system as a system which should be resorted when special needs of persons with disabilities cannot be met (Rules 3 and 6).

The term "special education" used in the Standard Rules was clarified by the Salamanca Statement and Framework for Action published as a result of the World Conference on Special Needs Education: Access and Quality[71] organised by UNESCO in 1994. The term "inclusive education" added to the human rights terminology by the Salamanca Statement on Special Needs Education[72] has been used widely in the studies and regulations conducted on the rights to education after this date. Essence of inclusive education is based on the recognition that every child is different and thus has different needs. Every child is unique regarding his/her interests, skills, needs for education and properties. Educational systems should include educational programmes and regulations taking into account properties and needs differing for every child. Needs of the children who need special education should be met via child-centred educational methods and scientific approaches in regular schools. It is mandatory to provide opportunities to every child to ensure learning on an acceptable level. The principle of inclusive education aims to ensure support for "education for all" by eliminating the access-related obstacles against the education of children who cannot receive education, persons with disabilities and disadvantaged groups as well as women and girls.

The newest document which presents a synthesis of all studies on the right to education of persons with disabilities in the field of international human rights is the

---

70 "Standard Rules on the Equalization of Opportunities for Persons with Disabilities", UN General Assembly resolution 48/96 of 20 December 1993, A/RES/48/96, 4 March 1994, hereafter "Standard Rules".

71 "World Conference on Special Needs Education: Access and Quality, Salamanca, Spain", 7–10 June 1994, UNESCO & Ministry of Education and Science Spain.

72 "The Salamanca Statement and Framework for Action on Special Needs Education", Adopted by the World Conference on Special Needs Education: Access and Quality, Salamanca, Spain, 7–10 June 1994, UNESCO & Ministry of Education and Science Spain.

Convention on the Rights of Persons with Disabilities.[73] The Convention regulates the right to education in a similar manner to the content of the Salamanca Statement. However, it has taken a step further compared to the Salamanca Statement, as a legally binding document which takes into account the developments in the perception of disability since the 1960s, changing needs due to social, scientific and technological advancements and problems encountered by persons with disabilities and finds solutions to these problems. In addition, the Optional protocol was added to the Convention in order to activate the mechanism for monitoring and supervising the rights and an effort was made to provide assurance for the rights of persons with disabilities on the international level.

The right to education of persons with disabilities is regulated in the Convention in a detailed and comprehensive manner. The first paragraph of Article 24 where the right to education is regulated lays down the fundamental principles to be considered in the education of persons with disabilities and the aims of this education (24/1). The measures and methods by which the right to education can be performed by the States are regulated in the second paragraph (24/2), while it is regulated in the last paragraph what the obligation to enable persons with disabilities to learn life and social development skills to facilitate their full and equal participation in education includes (24/3).

The most innovative aspect of the Convention is that it addresses the right to education as a right effective in different periods of life instead of limiting it to certain age periods. It is recognised that many uneducated or low educated adults with disabilities who did not have education during their childhood or have such an opportunity also have educational needs and regulations were incorporated regarding the right to education of this group. The Convention, which resolves that "lifelong learning" can provide employment opportunities to teenagers and adults with disabilities and that education of persons with disabilities should be supported by vocational and tertiary education programmes in order to develop their work competences (Art. 24/5), gives the priority again to children with disabilities and imposes the obligation to ensure their participation in all stages of education (Art. 24/2, a). It is a fundamental necessity that this obligation is performed by acting according to the best interest of the child (Art. 24/2, b).

There are many evidences that inclusive education is recognised in the Convention on the Rights of Persons with Disabilities. One of them is the provision stating that education should be delivered by taking effective individualised support measures dedicated to persons with disabilities, in environments that maximise academic and social development skills (Art. 24/2, e). In addition, in order to ensure their effective enjoyment of the general educational system, the goals of meeting their needs within this system, providing reasonable accommodation and thus ensuring the continuation of their regular education should be regarded in this direction

73 "Convention on the Rights of Persons with Disabilities", UN General Assembly A/61/611, 6 December 2006.

(Art. 24/2, c, d). UNESCO defines "inclusive education" as a process referring to determining and meeting the different needs of all students in order to determine the factors hindering the enjoyment of the right to education; reduce the exclusions in education and increase participation in learning.[74] The subject of inclusive education is to remove the barriers to participation regarding the education of children who cannot receive education, persons with disabilities and disadvantaged groups as well as girls and women and to support "education for all".[75]

The subjects of inclusive education are children or persons who have disabilities or are geniuses, foreigners or nomads, working, living on the street or are members of minorities or other groups with disadvantages or ones excluded in a socio-economic sense. According to the framework shaping the inclusive education principle; schools should be made appropriate for all children and teenagers regardless of their physical, intellectual, social, emotional, lingual or other conditions. In this educational system, unlike the integrated education, children with disabilities are not accommodated to the regular setting, but the schools are changed to become appropriate for children with disabilities. Since no organisational changes are made in the regular school settings according to the "integration in education" model, children with special educational needs are not able to benefit enough from the education provided. Most of them have no choice but to take alternative courses on academic topics or take education in a separate classroom. The basic philosophy of the Convention on the right to education is that inclusive education is the only and effective way of ensuring that the right to education becomes enjoyable by persons with disabilities. The fact that no private education schools and institutions are mentioned and measures and practices to be implemented by States for the realisation of inclusive education are regulated in detail confirms this argument (Art. 24/3,4).[76]

In order to make an assessment regarding the legislation and judgments which determine the fundamental principles of the right to education of persons with disabilities in the Turkish law, draw the lines on the normative meaning and scope of the right with its nature and elements and regulate the obligations of the State and the responsibilities and duties of persons and communities, it is obvious that Article 24 of the Convention should be taken as the basis. Article 24 of the Convention, which regulates the education of persons with disabilities, regulates the

---

74 UNESCO Paris and UNESCO Bangkok join hands to build consensus on Inclusive Education, http://www.unescobkk.org/index.php?id=3123&tx, (30.07.2008), UNESCO worked intensively in subsequent years to expand the scope of inclusive education. For works, see: http://www.unescobkk.org/index.php?id, (30.07.2008)

75 **Olof Sandkull**, "Strengthening Inclusive Education by Applying a Rights-based Approach to Education Programming", *ISEC 2005 Paper*, August 2005, UNESCO, Bangkok, p.1.

76 For more information, see: "Disabilities from Exclusion to Equality Realising the Rights of Persons with Disabilities", *Handbook for Parliamentarians on the Convention on the Rights of Persons with Disabilities and its Optional Protocol*, UN, UN OHCHR, Inter-Parliamentary Union, No. 14, 2007, pp. 81–85.

right-related dimension of education based on certain fundamental principles as well as the field of responsibility of the State with its purpose and nature, based on concrete indicators and elements. In the first paragraph of the provision which consists of 5 paragraphs, the right to education is built on 4 fundamental principles; equality of opportunity, prohibition of discrimination, inclusive and lifelong education (Art. 24/1). In the same provision, both individual and social goals of education are listed based on these principles; ensuring respect for human dignity, rights and fundamental freedoms and differences; ensuring development of persons with disabilities in every aspect to their fullest potential and their effective participation in the society (Art. 24/1-a, b, c).

When conducting research in the Turkish legislation in this regard, a comparative method should be used, in other words, an examination should be conducted in order starting from the first paragraph of the article of the Convention which regulates the right to education. However, in order to provide an analytical point of view, it would be appropriate to first study the constitutional and general educational legislation on the right to education of persons with disabilities and then evaluate the regulations on the private education legislation.

C. Right to Education of Persons with Disabilities in the Convention on the Rights of Persons with Disabilities vs. Right to Education of Persons with Disabilities in the Turkish Education Legislation: Differences – Gaps – Adaptations

I. Regarding CRPD Art. 24/1

1. *Right to Education of Persons with Disabilities in the General Legislation*

In this regard, first, it should be considered whether right to education is a constitutional right in Turkey. In the Constitution, which is recognised as the most superior instrument of law, education is regulated together with training on the dimensions as a right, freedom and also duty. Accordingly; *No one shall be deprived of the right to education* (Art. 42/1). This regulation emphasises that the right to education belongs to everyone without exceptions and prohibits discrimination and exclusion. However, in the provision, there are no regulations highlighting the fact that in compliance with the prohibition of discrimination, education must be accessible for all in law and fact, especially for persons with disabilities and vulnerable groups physically and economically. We mentioned before that in the provision where the Constitution prohibits discrimination in general and regulates equality before the law, one paragraph lays down a regulation on the measures for ensuring the equality of persons with disabilities. In addition to the criticism we made above against this provision which we addressed under the "prohibition of discrimination" context, we can say that; in the specific provision of the Constitution on the right to education (Art. 42), emphasis should be laid on the matter that everyone has physical access to educational institutions without being subject to discrimination, no one is excluded from education due to economic deprivation or other grounds and an accessible educational system is required for ensuring the full enjoyment of all of the education provided in educational institutions.

While in the Article 42 of the Constitution it is laid down that, "*the State shall provide scholarships and other means of assistance to enable students of merit lacking financial means to continue their education and take necessary measures to rehabilitate those in need of special education so as to render such people useful to society*", it is against the universal regulations on the right to education as well as CRPD that the access to right to education is bound to certain conditions. Stipulating that scholarships and other means of assistance and aid are subject to merit and restricting the measures to be taken for persons in need of special education with the objective of "rendering useful to society" are not among the leading appropriate measures ensuring the full actualisation of the right to education for persons with disabilities. The priority objective of special education is not rendering the child useful to society but ensuring his/her individual and social development with all aspects and to the highest level as well as empowering and liberalising him/her to the extent that he/she fully participates in independent life. Such an expression should be incorporated in the Constitution and it should be clearly stated that it is an obligation of the State to meet the needs of persons with disabilities within the general education system in order to ensure that they effectively benefit from this system, to perform reasonable accommodation and thus ensure that they continue their regular education.

It may also be considered as a deficiency that the general and individual objectives of education are not mentioned in the Constitution. In the Article 42/ 3 of the Constitution, the restriction that "*education shall be conducted along the lines of the principles and reforms of Ataturk, based on contemporary scientific and educational principles, under the supervision and control of the State and educational institutions contravening these principles shall not be established*" is about the contents and nature of the education rather than its objectives and it is addressed to private entrepreneurs. There is also a provision in the Constitution which prescribes that the freedom of education and training does not relieve the individual from loyalty to the Constitution and it also emphasises the limitations of the freedom to enjoy the right (Art. 42/4). However, addition of a provision which incorporates the social and individual objectives of education to the Constitution could be beneficial in terms of shedding light on the ways and methods to be followed regarding the right to education in general as well as the education of persons with disabilities. In this scope, individual objectives of education should put the child and the individual to the centre, adopt the method of meeting different needs on the basis of differences, be suitable to ensure the individual and social development on the highest level and based on the principle of the best interest and participation of the child.

A provision of the Constitution, which is written with a content appropriate to the Convention on the Rights of the Child, Covenant on Economic, Social and Cultural Rights and the Convention on the Rights of Persons with Disabilities to which Turkey is a party, which prescribes that education shall aim *to empower the child by developing his/her competences, learning and other competences, human dignity, self-respect and confidence and ensure his/her full and active participation in all areas of life* would also have a positive function for protecting the right to education of persons with disabilities.

Fundamental Principles of Turkish National Education are provided in the Basic Law No. 1739 on National Education which is recognised as the general law for the Turkish education system. The provision on the principle of "Generality and Equality" in this section of the Law was amended in 2014 and the word *disability* was added after the expression language, race, gender and it was specified that educational institutions are open for anyone without discrimination on the basis of any of these grounds (Art. 4). As mentioned before, "equality of opportunity and means" was also accepted as one of the fundamental principles in the same section. According to this provision, it was stated in general that everyone shall be provided with the equality of opportunity and facility without discrimination by gender and it was mentioned that necessary assistive and special measures shall be taken in cases of deprivation of financial sources and the need for special education and protection. Therefore, the idea was supported that disadvantages of this nature should be eliminated on the basis of equality of opportunity and facility (Art. 8).

It is a positive regulation that in the Law No. 1739, equality of facility is also mentioned among the fundamental principles of education in addition to the equality of opportunity. Because, equality of opportunity is a type of equality which advocates that certain persons or groups are different than the others from the beginning due to their special conditions and that they cannot be equals with the rest of the society unless their access to opportunities are provided and enshrined by law. In that sense, equality of opportunity advocates for "equality at the beginning". Which means, it is important to have the same chance as everyone else, but the outcome of the enjoyment of this right may not be equal for everyone. In other words, equality of opportunity makes reference to the first steps to be taken for ensuring actual equality. Equality of facility, on the other hand, goes beyond the equality of opportunity and reflects the need for positive measures and actions which will ensure the enjoyment of these opportunities. The relevant provision of the Law No. 1739 should be interpreted according to this point of view, personal needs of persons with disabilities should be considered in the education to be provided within the general education system, legislative and institutional regulations should be aimed to ensure the protection and actualisation of the right to education of persons with disabilities.

The Basic Law on National Education, as given in its name, is a Law which lays down the fundamental principles and procedures regarding education and training. Moreover, education and training are regulated separately based on processes which include children of certain age groups. We will also examine the legislation in terms of education systems by taking into account these processes.

a. Pre-School Education Period

There is no special law for the period of pre-school education. This period is carried out based on a regulation in the nature of a by-law. Principles and procedures regarding the establishment, administration, education, duties and operations of public and private and pre-school educational institutions affiliated with the Ministry of National Education were regulated according to the Regulation on Pre-School Educational Institutions and the implementation had been carried out based on this Regulation for years. As explained in the part on the prohibition of discrimination, this Regulation was superseded on 26.07.2014 by a new regulation which regulates pre-school educational institutions together with primary schools. In the Regulation which entered into force under the name Regulation on Pre-School and Primary School Institutions of the Ministry of National Education. Unlike the old Regulation on Pre-School Educational Institutions, the new Regulation incorporates the measures required to be taken for children in the pre-school age and in need of special education with a more rights-based perspective. For instance, children in need of special education who were referred by a counselling and research centre report can be enrolled in any school regardless of their address in the national address database, provided that they document their condition (Art. 11/4).

The actual important development is that, while in the old Regulation children with severe deficiencies and those with multiple deficiencies used to be excluded from inclusive education as a category in pre-school education, in this new Regulation, while being dependent on certain conditions, they can be enrolled in special education classes. In accordance with the report from the special education assessment board, children with severe deficiency who cannot pursue their education in a full-time inclusive method and those who have multiple deficiencies can be enrolled to special education classes which will be opened on the condition that the physical space is suitable and special education teachers are employed in these institutions (Art. 11/5-d). We previously mentioned the risk that these conditions may hinder the children in this group from participating in a part-time inclusive education. Nonetheless, it is still a significant step that children with severe or multiple disabilities are not excluded from ordinary pre-school education system as a category.

As we are going to see later in concrete examples, regulations and practices for classifying persons with disabilities based on ratios or some degrees and making the enjoyment or exclusion of certain rights conditional on these criteria is quite prevalent in the Turkish law. The General Director of Services for Persons with Disabilities and the Elderly, Aylin Çiftçi, whose opinion was asked for the Review Report on the Rights of Persons with Disabilities prepared by the Committee on Human Rights Inquiry of the Turkish Grand National Assembly (4.07.2013) criticises the fact that the diagnosis for disabilities is made based on a ratio of loss of medical functionality, in other words only persons with a loss of medical functionality higher than a certain ratio are recognised as persons with disabilities and that the enjoyment of certain rights and services is determined based on these ratios and highlights that the medical approach on disabilities will be changed with the new legal regulations.[77] Another example of abandoning the medical approach and adopting an approach for persons with disabilities in need of special education suitable to the requirements of the social model is expanding the practice of support education rooms in a manner to include the pre-school period (Art. 84/1). The old Regulation did not provide for opening support education rooms for inclusive education students in the pre-school education period. However, meeting the special educational needs of children within the same institution who pursue their pre-school education with peers without any deficiencies is a method which is a practical way for both the child and the family which also increases the effectiveness of inclusion. Therefore, a mistake was avoided in the new Regulation and it was made possible that support education rooms could be opened albeit within the limits of on physical means.

b. Primary Education Period

Law No. 222 on Primary Education which regulates the education and training period of the children of the age of 6–13 in Turkey, due to being an older law than the Basic Law on National Education and being subject to only a few amendments since the day it went into force in 1961, it does not incorporate fundamental contemporary principles of the right to education such as the prohibition of discrimination, equality of opportunity, respect for differences and integrative education. In the first articles of the Law, it is laid down that the children of this age group are subject to compulsory education regardless of their gender and the education of persons with disabilities is mentioned in an article which is written with a language which is no longer in use. The article of the Law, which states *"Special education and training shall be provided to children who are impaired mentally, physically, intellectually and socially in spite of being in the age of compulsory education"* (Art. 12) has not been amended to date. Although the whole legislation was screened in 2012 an all "impaired" terms were replaced with "persons with disabilities", it is open to criticism that in such a fundamental law, the term "impaired" which is regarded as derogatory and discriminatory by persons with disabilities and their families is still being used. We think that, Law No. 222 which is obsolete in terms of language, far from the contemporary interpretation of the right to education and does not include any measures specific to persons with disabilities and other disadvantaged children groups should be repealed and a new law should be prepared which addresses education in this significant period of education with a rights dimension.

The issues and deficiencies we criticised in the Law No. 222 were tried to be eliminated with the Regulation on Primary Educational institutions of the Ministry

77 Turkish Grand National Assembly Commission on Human Rights Inquiry Rights of Persons with Disabilities Inquiry Report, 24th Assembly 3. Legislative Year 2013, pp. 5–11.

of National Education. In the Regulation, a non-discriminatory language was used which respects differences and primary education was regulated as a process in compliance with the contemporary view of the right to education in terms of both goals and fundamental principles. It was stated with a regulation parallel to the provisions of the Basic Law No. 1739 on National Education that, primary educational institutions are open for anyone without discrimination (Art. 6/d), everyone will be provided with the equality of opportunity and facility and special measures will be taken for the cases of economic inefficacy and for raising children in need of special education and protection (Art. 6/f). The distinction of the Regulation which puts it a step further compared to other educational regulations is that there are provisions which prescribe that students will be accepted and valued as they are in the primary education (Art. 6/k) and it is essential that individuals in need of special education pursue their education together with their peers via inclusive practices (Art. 6/n). It is possible to say that the phrase "accepting students as they are" which is listed as one of the "general principles" in the Regulation is parallel to the "principle of respect for differences". However, as mentioned above, the Regulation on Primary Educational institutions has been repealed. In the new Regulation which regulates the primary educational institutions together with pre-school educational institutions, such provisions are not included. It is possible to say that the new Regulation, which does not incorporate any of the fundamental principles of the Convention on the Rights of Persons with Disabilities on the right to education, is not in compliance with the Convention in this regard. To explain from the opposite side, in this regard, the old Regulation on the Primary Educational institutions was a more compatible regulation with the Convention.

In the Turkish law, open education opportunities are provided to adults who could not complete their primary education and exceed the age limit for compulsory primary education to complete their primary education and these processes are regulated by regulations. Regulation on Open Primary Schools which is one of these regulations was renamed as Regulation on Open Secondary Schools with an amendment published in the Official Gazette of 21 July 2012. In this Regulation, it was resolved that age records will not be sought for persons who document that they have physical disabilities and those prove with a document to be obtained from the Special Education Services Board that they need special education and it was accepted that persons with disabilities can also pursue their education by benefiting from this opportunity. However, under the enrolment conditions for such education, a condition was included that persons have to document that they completed the fourth grade of primary school. It will not be possible for persons with disabilities who did not complete up to this level of primary school to benefit from this system.

c. Secondary Education Period

The secondary education period is regulated in the Turkish law with a regulation, not a law. Since the compulsory education period was increased to 12 years in 2012, secondary education refers to the education period of 4 years which is compulsory to attend after the primary education period which consists of two tiers consisting of four years each. To this end, the Regulation on Secondary Education was renewed in 2013 in a manner to include the new education system. According to the Regulation, a secondary educational institution is defined as an institution which refers to any of the public or private formal education schools or institutions providing four years of education and training after middle school or imam and preacher middle school. The Regulation, which bears similar provisions to the Regulation on Primary Education in terms of the goals and principles of educational institutions, unlike this regulation, recognises the "ensuring that individuals adopt lifelong learning" as one of the goals of secondary education (Art. 7/1-h). While the main goal of secondary education is preparing students to higher education and training, it is also of uttermost importance that "lifelong learning" principles are placed within the secondary education in order to ensure that particularly the persons who are not able to pursue higher education after compulsory education due to their deficiencies keep preparing for the life with different methods.

Another aspect of the Regulation which distinguishes it from the Regulation regulating primary education that it defines "inclusive education". Accordingly, inclusive education refers to special education practices which are based on the principle that persons in need of special education pursue their education together with their peers while being provided with support education services as well (Art. 4/1-i). In addition to other provisions of the Regulation, when it is considered together with the provision which regulates education and training activities; "*Students in need of special education shall avail of programmes opened in secondary educational institution with their development aspects based on individual competences being considered in order to improve their skills and meet their needs for learning* (Art. 8/3). We can say that the inclusive education corresponds to the inclusive education view in the Convention.

Since the vocational and technical education process is also usually included in the scope of secondary education and training, this legislation should be reviewed. This area is regulated by the Law on Vocational Education. "Vocational and Technical Education Schools and Institutions" are defined in the Law as, secondary educational institutions which lead to a degree in vocational and technical education as well as formal and adult education and training institutions of all types and levels where qualification and certification programmes are applied. The Law is a regulation which regulates the principles of the training of apprentices, journeymen and masters as well as the vocational training to be provided in schools and businesses, which covers the education and training in organisations, entities and workplace in the public and private sectors in the occupations to be determined by the Vocational Education Board as well as in the vocational and technical education schools. This Law does not involve any provisions for the students with disabilities who pursue their education in vocational and technical education schools. It is ambiguous how these students will do their internships and who will take preventive and supportive measures. The Law only resolves in its Article 39 that, special vocational courses will be organised by the Ministry for persons in need of special education for preparation to duties valid in the work life; that interests, needs and competences or these persons will be considered while organising and implementing these courses and that as long as they continue to the course, the participants of the course will benefit from the same rights the Law grants to apprentices and students. In terms of this Law, it can be concluded that persons in need of special education will be given vocational and technical education in separated settings and the status of these institutions will not be schools but courses providing certificates or documents.

In the first text of the Regulation on Vocational and Technical Education which was issued based on this Law, it was laid down that students/trainees with disabilities who pursue their education in vocational and technical schools and institutions who are in need of special education will be availed of the programmes to be opened in institutions, placement will be done with a balanced distribution by considering the disabilities of persons with disabilities, the number of people in the classes to which persons with disabilities attend will be decreased, physical arrangements will be carried out, visually-impaired and hearing impaired persons and those with orthopaedic disabilities will be included in suitable occupations/fields or programmes. With the amendment made in 2008, inclusive education was defined in the Regulation (Art. 4) and measures were incorporated on the enrolment of persons in need of special education in institutions as well as regarding the classes in which they will be placed and their education (Art. 41/c-e). Accordingly, measures will be taken for a balanced distribution of persons in need of special education among the institutions suitable for their deficiencies, in cooperation with the special education services board in accordance with the special education assessment board report pursuant to the provisions of the Regulation on Special Education Services, visually-impaired and hearing-impaired persons as well as persons with orthopaedic disabilities will be taken to suitable occupational fields/branches or programmes and whether persons with intellectual deficiency will be included in the inclusive education in vocational and technical education programmes and the programmes to which those who will be included can pursue will be decided in cooperation with institutions and counselling and research centres. However, the Regulation on Vocational and Technical Education was repealed by the Regulation on Secondary Education of the Ministry of National Education which was published in the Official Gazette of 7 September 2013 and it was resolved that until a new regulation is issued, provisions of this regulation on the operation of vocational training centres, maturation institutes and tourism education centres as well as adult education practices will continue to be in force. As we know, a new regulation has not yet been issued.

The open education high school system, which was established with the aim to provide the opportunity to persons who completed primary education but did not continue to secondary education as well as those who left or graduated from secondary education and those who left or graduated from higher education, to pursue their education in different fields and thus providing the opportunity for education and training is also regulated by a regulation. Although the Regulation includes "contributing in equality of opportunity and facility on the secondary education level" in its goals (Art. 5), it is regulated explicitly that persons with intellectual disabilities cannot be enrolled and the registration of those who are already enrolled will be erased upon discovery and therefore this group is excluded from distance education as a category without even having the need to grade persons by intellectual disabilities (Art. 15/d). However, it is possible for persons with mild or medium level intellectual disabilities to complete the primary education. It should be remembered that such categorical exclusions are an example of direct discrimination and the Regulation should recast according to the principles and rules of the Convention on the Rights of Persons with Disabilities.

The fact that there are no special measures for the education of persons with disabilities who will benefit from the education to be provided under this Regulation is another deficiency of the Regulation.

d. Higher Education Period

The basic law which regulated the higher education period is the Law No. 2547 on Higher Education (LHE). In the Law, higher education is defined as, all education and training at all levels comprising of a minimum of four semesters, based on secondary education, within the national education system (Art. 3/a). Types of education and training within the higher education are formal, open, external and adult education. (1) Formal Education: Refers to the type of education-training in which students are obliged to attend courses and exercise throughout the education-training period. (2) Open Education: Refers to the type of education-training provided to students via radio, television and educational materials. (3) External Education: Refers to the type of education-training conducted in certain branches of higher education, without an attendance obligation besides the obligation to participate in mid-term examinations and final examinations. Students who pursue this type of education take the common compulsory courses and certain other ones deemed necessary, at the courses to be organised at relevant educational institutions whenever deemed suitable after working hours. (4) Adults education: Refers to the type of education-training aims to provide knowledge and skills to all segments of the society in different fields (Art. 3/u).

In terms of the goals of higher education, the Law contains a list of goals suitable to the official ideology of the period when it went into force (6.11.1981) and it is observed that it was written with a State-oriented perspective rather that personal and social goals of education (Art. 4). The only provision in compliance with the Convention on the Rights of Persons with Disabilities in terms of fundamental principles is the provision which regulates that measures shall be taken for ensuring the equality of opportunity and facility in higher education (Art. 5/e). The provision of the Law on entrance and placement in higher education was amended in 2012 and it was prescribed that the entry and placement processes in higher educational institutions shall be carried out according to the principles and procedures determined by the Council of Higher Education, provided that measures for ensuring the equality of opportunity and facility are taken, (Art. 45 – (Amended: 30/3/2012 – Art. 6287/14). The LHE which is practically the basic law governing the higher education period simply ignores persons with disabilities. Measures specific to persons with disabilities should have been included in LHE in terms of selection, enrolment and education-training processes regarding higher educational institutions in line with the Law No. 5378 on Persons with Disabilities which entered into force in 2005.

Preparations for a law superseding the LHE currently in force and restructuring the higher education are in process. In fact, a draft bill has been prepared in this regard and submitted to the opinions of the public. The new draft bill which aims to fulfil the need for a structural change in higher education seems to have been written in a manner appropriate to the contemporary human rights view in terms of both fundamental principles and freedom of education and training. In the "fundamental principles" provision of the draft, it is prescribed that higher education shall be planned, regulated and carried out based on the principles of equality, prohibition of discrimination, academic and scientific freedom, institutional autonomy, diversity, transparency, accountability, participation, cooperation, scientific competition and quality (Art. 3). In the provision titled "Freedom of education and training", it is emphasised that education and training is a right and a freedom and that all students shall be able to enjoy this right and freedom on an equal basis without discrimination based on political views, language, religion, sect, belief, race, colour, gender, choice of clothing and other grounds (Art. 4).[78] In the draft, duties of higher educational institutions were regulated based on a human rights view; higher educational institutions are assigned with the duty to equip individuals with knowledge, skills and competences to ensure that individual and social projects are put into practice in a more successful manner pursuant to equality of opportunity and principle of lifelong learning and to ensure that students are provided with education-training services according to universal standards which will turn them into individuals who are not afraid of taking initiative and assuming responsibility, who have critical thinking abilities and are loyal to human rights and democracy, respectful to cultural values and active (Art. 26). It is possible to interpret the draft provision which prescribes that entry and placement processes in higher educational institutions shall be carried out according to the principles and procedures determined by the Turkish Council of Higher Education, provided that measures for ensuring the equality of opportunity and facility are taken (Art. 35/1-a), in favour of students with disabilities and assume that support and regulations specific to persons with disabilities will be provided in such processes.

However, when the draft bill is examined as a whole, although it distinguishes itself from the LHE in force as a text which reflects the view of human rights in general and right and freedom to education specifically, the intended new law should have prescribed that persons with disabilities can participate in higher education; taken these persons into account; and designed the restructuring process based on principles of general equality-prohibition of discrimination by determining the

78 Draft text available at http://yeniyasa.yok.gov.tr/?page=yazi&c=90&i=120. (10.07.2014)

special needs of persons with disabilities regarding higher education as well as the institutional and structural system by endeavouring to make these needs visible and respond to them.

We previously mentioned that LHE in force, which assumes that all persons who attend or will attend higher education fit the healthy and dynamic human model, ignores the persons with different needs and deficiencies. This deficiency in the LHE was only notices in 2006, the Regulation on Counselling and Coordination of Impaired Persons in Higher Educational institutions was issued based on the Article 15 of Law No. 5378 on Persons with Disabilities.[79] This Regulation was repealed in 2012 and replaced with the regulation on Counselling and Coordination of Persons with Disabilities in Higher Educational institutions.[80] Pursuant to the purpose provision of this Regulation which was amended in 2014, the purpose of the Regulation is to provide the necessary academic setting for facilitating the educational life of persons with disabilities who attend higher education and to regulate the principles and procedures of Council of Higher Education Commission for Students with Disabilities, Counselling and Coordination Unit for Students with Disabilities, OSYM (Assessment, Selection and Placement Centre) Counselling and Coordination Unit for Persons with Disabilities and units for students with disabilities to be established within higher educational institutions, in order to take necessary measures and make regulations for ensuring their full participation in education and training processes (Art. 1 – Amended: OG-14/2/2014-28913).

While the regulation has a purpose arrangement suitable for ensuring the actualisation of the right to education of students with disabilities, it represents a retrogression with its definition of "student with disability". In fact, a student with disability is defined as *"a higher education student who has problem in adapting to social life and meet his/her own daily needs due to loss of physical, intellectual, mental, emotional or social competences on various degrees for any reason congenitally or afterwards, who is in need of protection, care, rehabilitation, counselling and support services"* (Art. 4/c-Amended: OG-14/2/2014–28913). Moreover, this article is a regulation made after the date the definition of persons with disabilities was amended in the Law No. 5378 on Persons with Disabilities and harmonised with the Convention and it is based on the definition of persons with disabilities of the Law No. 5378 before the amendment of 6.2.2014. It is an inevitable obligation to amend this definition which reflects the medical view on disability and make a regulation parallel to Law No. 5378.

Unlike the old regulation, the new Regulation has made the Commissions and Units on Students with Disabilities more efficacious in terms of both quality and quantity. As a new unit, a counselling and coordination unit for students with disabilities was established under the Assessment, Selection and Placement Centre (Art. 9). By doing so, it was ensured that for the students with disabilities who are

79 Official Gazette Date: 20/6/2006, Official Gazette issue: 26204.

80 Official Gazette Date: 14.08.2010, Official Gazette issue: 27672.

reached the step of higher education, the central examination places where they will take the examinations as well as the support they need during the examination were determined before and also other counselling services were put into practice (Art. 10/1). With the amendment made regarding the Council of Higher Education Counselling and Coordination Unit for Students with Disabilities included in the previous Regulation, temporary members of the Unit were replaced with permanent members and thus the ground was laid for carrying out the difficult duty of guiding, supporting, ensuring coordination and oversight for higher educational institutions in terms of measures to be taken for students with disabilities in an uninterrupted and more functional manner (Art. 7).

The Council of Higher Education Commission for Students with Disabilities is a commission which consists of members selected for a certain time period with the aim to determine the needs of students with disabilities who reached the level of higher education under the Council of Higher Education or who are pursuing higher education; plan the administrative regulations to be carried out according to the determined needs; and ensure coordination among relevant higher educational institutions by establishing required infrastructure standards (Art. 5). In the Commission, there is also a student with disability who represents students with disabilities. In addition to this central structure under the Council of Higher Education, pursuant to the Regulation, all higher educational institutions are obliged to establish a unit for students with disabilities within their own structures (Art. 11). Units for students with disabilities are assigned with the duty to take all measures for ensuring that students with disabilities enrolled in the programmes within their institutions receive appropriate and high-quality education on the equal basis with other students. In addition to this important duty, they also have the duty to create solutions for determination and elimination of shelter, transportation, social, cultural etc. needs of students with disabilities; ensure that these duties are carried out in coordination; develop programmes and projects for increasing the level of awareness and sensitivity regarding disabilities via monitoring and oversight; and organise events such as seminars, conferences and similar activities (Art. 12).

Although the measures taken at the level of the Regulation seem to be appropriate and adequate, in practice, it is observed that the same level of success have not been achieved in all higher educational institutions, while some universities take these measures as a whole and achieve the goals of "campus without handicap", "education without handicap" by fulfilling accessibility conditions for persons with disabilities, units for students with disabilities seem to be non-functional or inadequate units which only exist on the paper in most of the higher educational institutions. This situation indicates that the practices are not audited by authorised central bodies, monitoring activities are not carried out and coordination is not ensured. Therefore, it would be beneficial to restructure central units in a more functional manner and support higher educational institutions with reward and incentive methods.

e. Adult Education – Life Long Learning Period

Adult education has been regulated in the Turkish law as a whole by the Regulation on Educational Institutions. In the Regulation which entered into force in 2010, adult education refers to, *"all lifelong education, training, production, counselling and exercise activities provided in various periods and levels for the economic, social and cultural development of persons who has never entered the formal education system or who is at any level of formal education or have left or completed this level in line with their interests desires and competences"* (Art. 3/1-p). The Regulation which includes the view of "lifelong learning" in both its definition and goals as a requirement of the fundamental philosophy of adult education, explains the purpose of this view as, *to ensure scientific, entrepreneurial, technological, economic, social and cultural development of persons and get them to adopt the habit of utilising and using their free time the best way possible and provide opportunities to develop their competences* (Art. 4/1-g). However other purposes of adult education such as the fundamental principles of "right to develop", "equality of opportunity in education" and "prohibition of discrimination" and human rights were not incorporated.

Education, which is recognised as a right dependent on certain principles in the Convention on the Rights of Persons with Disabilities, should aim to develop the personality, abilities and creativity as well as intellectual and physical competences or persons with disabilities to their fullest potential (Art. 24/1-b). The steps to be taken by States to achieve this goal are also provided. In the same article, an obligation is imposed on States Parties to ensure that persons with disabilities are able to access vocational training, adult education and lifelong learning without discrimination and on an equal basis with others and to this end, ensure that reasonable accommodation is provided to persons with disabilities (Art. 24/5). The adult education and lifelong learning mentioned in the Convention correspond to the process in Turkey called as adult education. However, the Regulation on Adult Education only points out limited measures for persons with disabilities in this process and lists the goals of adult education as; *teach how to read and write to individuals in need of special education and help them increase their knowledge and competences according to their development aspects and in line with their individual competences* (Art. 4/1-ğ).

The Regulation regulates that persons in need of special education shall participate in adult education in separate special classes and/or via other courses within inclusive education. These courses aim to increase the knowledge and competences of persons in need of special education in vocational and technical as well as social and cultural areas, reintegrate them in life and turn them into productive individuals. Collaborations will be established with relevant entities and institutions in organising the courses, education and training services will be carried out according to the provisions of the Regulation on Special Education Services (Art. 29). In practice, courses are organised for persons with disabilities mostly by preparing separate classes and those who are able to participate in courses together with other persons via inclusive education only represent a small group. Because, usually persons with physical disabilities which are not severe, hearing impaired persons, persons with mild intellectual disabilities and persons with disabilities who do not have any social adaptation problems are included in this group. Such provisions which may cause separating, excluding persons with disabilities also in adult education should be amended. To this end, amendments should be made in the Regulation which will be based on methods and means to ensure the development of persons with disabilities to the highest level and which recognise that they will receive adult education in a manner to help them get prepared for an independent life based on the equality of opportunity and prohibition of discrimination for their full and effective participation in the society.

2. *Right to Education of Persons with Disabilities within the Legislation on Special Education*

In Turkey, principles, purposes, methods and institutional structure regarding the education of persons with disabilities are to a great extent subject to special legal regulations. As explained above, the subject of the education of persons with disabilities / persons in need of special education is almost non-existent in the general educational legislation.

The basic law on the right to education of persons with disabilities is the Decree-Law of 1997 on Special Education (DLSE).[81] However, since in LPD No. 5378 the right to education is regulated specifically, assessment should begin with the provisions of this Law. Since the relevant provisions of the Law were explained before in the assessments conducted in terms of the general principles, we are going to make the assessment of the provisions on the right to education without repeating these parts. In this scope, Article 15 of the Law should be interpreted in terms of the fundamental principles of the Convention. According to the Article 15 of the Law, *the right to education of persons with disabilities shall not be hindered by any reason. Persons with disabilities shall be provided with the opportunity of lifelong learning on the basis of equality in the environment they live in, within integrated settings with their special conditions and differences being taken into account* (Art. 15/first paragraph). *Integrative planning shall be incorporated in the general education system to ensure that persons with disabilities participate in all levels of education* (Art. 15/second paragraph). This part of Article 15 is in compliance with the Convention in term of the general principles of the right to education. We also previously mentioned that efforts have been made to eliminate the incompliance in the first text of the Law by the amendments made in 2014.

In the Decree-Law on Special Education, principles for ensuring that persons in need of special education enjoy their right to general and vocational education in line with the general purposes and fundamental principles of Turkish National education as well as the regulations on the education services to be provided directly or indirectly to persons in need of special education and the schools, institutions

81 Hereafter the "Decree".

and programmes which will provide these services are prescribed (Art. 1, Art. 2). In the Decree-Law, "person in need of special education" is defined and an insight is provided on the educational settings and methods via the subjects of the right to education and definitions of "special education" and "inclusive education". "Person in need of special education" refers to the individual who, for various reasons, shows significant difference compared to the level expected of his/her peers in terms of individual properties and educational competences; "special education", refers to the education pursued in settings suitable for the disability condition and properties of persons in need of special education in order to meet their educational needs by the personnel trained specially for this purpose, via developed education programmes and methods; "inclusive education" refers to the educational settings developed for ensuring that persons in need of special education are included in mutual interaction with other persons and to actualise their educational goals on the highest level (Art. 3-a, b, c).

Fundamental principles of special education are referred as "fundamental principles on special education in line with the general principles governing the Turkish National Education". In this context, without readdressing the general principles listed above within the general education legislation, we are only going to address the principles specific to special education in connection with principles of Convention. Prohibition of discrimination, equality of opportunity, inclusiveness and full and effective participation in the society or any other phrases in the same meaning as these principles are not listed in the relevant provision of the Decree-Law. Although it is possible to interpret this situation as due to the reference made to the National educational legislation it has not been deemed necessary to repeat, it would be appropriate for the Decree-Law which is the basic regulation in terms of the right to education of persons with disabilities not to avoid such a repetition, to incorporate all general principles of the Convention and therefore to reinforce in terms of legislation by expressing clearly the foundation on which the special education will be based. It is not possible to say that the principle "special education services shall be planned in a manner to include the process of interaction and mutual adaptation of persons in need of special education with the society" (Art. 4/i) completely corresponds to the "inclusiveness" and "full and effective participation in society" principles of the Convention. Similarly, the principle "all persons in need of special education will be provided with special education services in accordance with and to the extent of their interests, desires, competences and abilities" (Art. 4/a) is far from expressing the prohibition of discrimination. Although the phrase *all persons* prevents the discrimination among persons with disabilities as a guarantee for the enjoyment of special education in a certain direction and to a certain extent, it will not serve for ensuring equality with others in terms of education.

Another aspect which causes inconsistent between the Decree-Law and the Convention is that "special education" is regulated with a service mentality instead of being a right. When persons with disabilities are concerned, special education is a fundamental human right. As is known, the concept "special education" is not included in the Convention and it only regulates the education with an emphasis on the right to education of persons with disabilities. Special education in Turkish law mostly refers to the system regulated with reference to persons with disabilities. Therefore, it should be clearly declared in the legislation either that education is a right for persons with disabilities as well or special education should be regulated not only as a service but also as a right. The difference between them is that, while a *service* can be carried out via policies even without laws, a *right* is necessarily the object of regulations in the nature of laws and is enshrined by law. Although special education services are regulated with many of their aspects in the Decree-Law and enshrined by law, the criterion of a *right* is much stronger than the criterion of a *service* in terms of judicial protection, including constitutional jurisdiction.

Regulation on Special Education Services is the repetition of the Decree-Law on Special Education in terms of the principles to be regarded as the basis for special education services (Art. 6). Unlike the Decree-Law, in the Regulation, purposes of special education are addressed in a separate article by making a reference to general purposes and fundamental principles of Turkish National Education. Only one of the purposes listed corresponds to one of the fundamental principles of the Convention on the Rights of Persons with Disabilities; provision 5/1-b which states the purpose of *development of fundamental life skills of persons in need of special education in order to ensure that they live independently within the society and become self-sufficient.* However, the Regulation is newer than the Decree-Law and it has been amended a couple of times in the context of harmonisation with the Convention. But in none of these amendments the provisions regulating the fundamental principles and purpose of special education were addressed and the prohibition of discrimination and equality of opportunity has not been incorporated. Purpose and scope articles of legal regulations are the provisions reflecting the philosophy of the regulation which enables an assessment on the whole regulation. Therefore, the relevant articles in the Regulation which as an arrangement parallel to the Decree-Law should be rewritten in a manner to include the fundamental principles and purposes of the Convention.

Regulation on Special Education Services recognises the inclusive method as the main method in some of the provisions regarding the planning and implementation of the special education process and thus incorporates yet another one of the principles of the Convention on the right to education. The provisions of the Regulation which resolve that; when placing persons in need of special education in suitable educational settings, a placement in a way to enable them to pursue their education starting from the least classified settings then moving to the mostly classified settings shall be considered such as starting with the classes where their peers without deficiencies pursue their education, then moving to special education classes, day special education schools/institutions and boarding special education schools/institutions (Art. 12/2-a); that at all levels of education, decisions shall be made for placing the individual in a new suitable school or institution according to his/her development and educational performance (Art. 12/2-f) seem to be in compliance with the Convention in this regard.

It is not possible to interpret provision 23/1 of the practice of "inclusive education" mentioned in the Decree-Law on Special Education to a narrow extent, which looks like a fundamental system covering all educational processes of persons in need of special education in terms of the Regulation in the same sense. In the provision, inclusive education is defined as, special education applications which are based on the practice of persons in need of special education pursuing their education together with their peers without deficiencies while being provided with support education services in public and private; pre-school, primary education, secondary education and adult educational institutions. The phrase based on used in the definition, in our opinion, does not mean that inclusive education is the main and priority educational model in all public and private institutions providing pre-school, primary education, secondary education and adult education (Art. 23/1–2), but it indicates the foundation on which the inclusive education is based. Although it seems at first glance that the Regulation restricts the practice of "inclusive education", in the following articles it becomes clear that it prescribes a practice which includes all segments in need of special education. In the first article of the Practices of Inclusive Education section, it is specified that this practice shall be carried out as "full-time education in the same class" and "part-time education in special education classes" and part-time inclusive education practices shall be carried out as students participating in some courses in the same classes or extra-curricular activities with their peers without disabilities (Art. 23/2-b). However in the following part of the same article, it is prescribed that measures shall be taken for the participation of students who attend special education schools and institutions in some courses and social activities in the context of inclusive education in schools and institutions where their peers without deficiencies pursue their education and a guarantee is provided that none of the students in need of special education shall be subject to completely separated education (Art. 23/2-ı).

Another point which needs to be pointed out regarding the Regulation is that inclusive education is not regarded as a one-way association but as a practice which enables opposite inclusion, which allows students without deficiencies to enrol in classes to be opened in special education schools near them, upon request (Art. 23/2-k).

Although the Regulation is based on meeting the special educational needs via inclusive education, when it is examined as a whole, it can be seen that there is a preference of pursuing education in special education classes and separate special education institutions. While the Regulation regulates inclusive education, which is accepted as the primary method, in two articles (Art. 23, 24), education in special education classes is regulated in three articles (Art. 25, 26, 27) and education in special education schools and institutions is regulated in eight articles (Art. 35, 37, 38, 39, 40, 44, 45, 46). Number of articles allocated for special education types and practices is a form related issue and of course not the sole determinant. Scope and content of the sub-regulations of articles is also important. In this regard, it can be observed that all mentioned articles have several paragraphs and are quite long texts. But this common feature is applicable to all articles and does not affect content.

Moreover, in the section of the Regulation titled Special Education Services in Types and Levels of Education which was amended comprehensively in 2012, it should also be added that provisions separately regulating special education in preschool and primary and secondary education periods have a mixed nature, in other words, they also regulate the special education to be provided in separate schools/institutions/classes in addition to inclusive education practices and that phrases which seem to offer the opportunity to choose between two systems were used in these provisions. In the sentence used in almost all practices regarding educational processes; "Persons in need of special education can pursue their education at the level of..., primarily together with their peers via inclusive education practices or in schools/institutions opened for persons in need of special education". The phrase can pursue (Art. 30,31) is a less precise expression compared to it is essential that they pursue. This phrase is not even incorporated in the provision on special education services in adult education, it is mentioned that persons in need of special education under inclusive education will be ensured to participate in adult education programmes under the collaboration to be made with other public and private entities and institutions (Art. 32/1-d) and special education classes may be opened (Art. 32/1-f).

The provision of the Regulation on Special Education Services based on providing at-home educational services for the persons in the age of compulsory education and in need of special education, but not able to directly attend education and training institutions (Art. 34/1) is a deficient regulation due to not including fundamental principles on the right to education of persons with disabilities and moreover it gives a broad discretion to administration and endangers the full actualisation of the right to education of persons in this group. The Regulation, which gives the power to determine the *"persons who are not able to directly attend education and training institutions"* and plan their education to the board on special education services (34/1-a, b) has preferred to shape the practice as a Directive, instead of regulating such a sensitive matter in terms of the right to education and training in the most explicit way possible. However, it is a well-known legal principle that fundamental rights cannot be restricted by a Directive which is a piece of legal arrangement below the Regulation in the hierarchy of norms and usually does not concern third parties and more commonly directs the practices of government entities; that the normative protection area of the right, from the determination of principles of fundamental rights up to limits of discretion power given to the administration, must necessarily be done by law. However, there are no regulations in the Decree-Law on Special Education on the education to be provided at home or hospitals.

Article 14 of the Decree-Law titled "support for special education" only prescribes that *educational programmes shall be implemented for persons of compulsory education age in need of special education who are in no condition to pursue any educational institution in order to meet their needs for developing basic life skills and learning regardless of the level of which they are affected by deficiencies.* As obvious in the provision, it is stated that special educational needs of persons of compulsory education age should be met in settings outside educational institutions as well, however fundamental principles such as "best interest of child", "equality of opportunity" and "prohibition of discrimination" and the principles and standards for the selection of the persons to be in this group and the nature of the education to be provided are not included in this kind of education. Therefore, we think that the Decree-Law on Special Education, which we already find quite old and insufficient in most of its aspects, should be repealed, a new law should be made which will include all settings of special education with a rights-based approach, regulate the right to education of persons with disabilities in every way by binding it to principles and standards and also include monitoring, oversight and remedy mechanisms for full protection and actualisation of the right. This is the only way which can provide a legal basis for the Regulation on Special Education Services and other regulations of the same nature. It would not change this situation that the Directive on Education Services at Home and Hospitals of the Ministry of National Education which was renewed in 2010 is completely of the nature of a regulation in terms of form and content. In fact, the practice of home schooling, which directly affects a fundamental right such as the right to education is not an issue to be left completely to a regulation. Because, such an education is in fact a separation. The most important reason for providing education on an institutional basis is to enable children to learn the necessities of collective living and contribute in their personal and social development. Home schooling should be a type of education which should not be preferred unless it is obligatory. Thus, in determination of obligatory and necessary conditions, a medical and objective assessment to be given by medical institutions, consent of the family and if available the child, as well as a decision from educational investigation and assessment boards consisting of several steps should be sought and the best interest of the child and equality of opportunity should necessarily be taken into account.

The new draft text presented to the public under the name Regulation on Special Education and Counselling Services which superseded the Regulation on Special Education Services, despite having aspects to be criticised, relatively complies with the Convention due to incorporating some of the principles of the Convention on the Rights of Persons with Disabilities on the right to education and also due to regulating the decision, oversight and monitoring mechanisms as well as the education planning which will be effective on the process of special education at home and hospitals, with a rights-based approach. However, even if the draft Regulation is adopted in its current form, we believe that it would be beneficial to repeal the Decree-Law on Special Education and make a new law in the nature we recommended.

II. In terms of CRPD Art. 24/2

Second paragraph of the Article 24 of the Convention on the Rights of Persons with Disabilities, according to the principles prescribed in the first paragraph, regulates how the right to education, content of which was specified, will be actualised by

States Parties, in other words, the areas of obligation of States regarding the right to education of persons with disabilities. In our opinion, this provision of the Convention determines the essence of the right to education for persons with disabilities and the minimum area of obligation for States. The measures and actions pointed out in this provision about not excluding persons with disabilities from the general education system and free and compulsory primary education or secondary education opportunities on the basis of disability; providing them the access to inclusive, quality primary and secondary education on an equal basis with others; providing reasonable accommodation in this regard; providing them effective, suitable and individualised support within the general education system, in environments that maximise academic and social development are obligatory minimum conditions for persons with disabilities to participate in quality and suitable education on the equal basis with their peers. While in Turkey, which is one of the States Parties to the Convention, persons with disabilities are not excluded from free and compulsory education, it is observed that there are some problems in their inclusion in this process and special legal measures particularly regarding starting pre-school special education, continued attendance to schools/institutions and preventing drop-outs are not sufficient. A bigger problem is encountered in the access of persons with disabilities to quality and suitable education and their participation in integrative education by implementing reasonable accommodation. In the following section, the degree to which these elements are incorporated in legal regulations will be examined and evaluated, again starting from the Constitution and moving towards the lowest level legislation.

1. *Free and Compulsory Education*

Ensuring the enjoyment of the right to free and compulsory education by persons with disabilities depends on several conditions. Most important one is that this right is enshrined by the Constitution and other legal regulations. Other condition for persons with disabilities to enjoy this right is determining the population who will benefit from this right and ensure their enrolment and continued attendance to schools. In the Turkish legislation, education is free and compulsory within a certain time period. Pursuant to the Article 42/5 of the Constitution which prescribes that "primary education is compulsory for all citizens of both sexes and is free of charge in State schools", Turkish citizens are obliged to complete their education.[82]

Primary education in State schools is also free of charge in basic laws on education currently in force.[83] Although there is no provision in the Basic Law on National Education which emphasises that education is free, it is possible to interpret the

82 Pursuant to the amendment made to the education system in 2012, while the compulsory and free education process was expanded to include secondary education, the relevant provision of the Constitution was left unchanged. This amendment must be made. Otherwise the laws on education will continue to contradict the Constitution.

83 Basic Law on National Education Art. 22, Art. 38; Law on Primary Education Art. 2.

provision which regulates that primary education is a right and obligation for all citizens, as this process is free of charge. Since economic accessibility to education is an issue related to the equality of opportunity, it is stipulated in the Law that educational costs of students of merit lacking financial means shall be covered by various types of aid until they complete the highest level of education in order to ensure equality of opportunity in education and it is resolved that special measures shall be taken for those in need of special education and protection (Art. 8). In 2012, the year when the education system was restructured, Article 22 of the Law was amended, and it was prescribed that the compulsory primary education period would cover the children of 6–13 age group. In the regulation regarding the secondary education period, it is pointed in the provision which explains the scope of this period that it is "compulsory" (Art. 26). However, there is no phrase stating that education in these compulsory processes is free of charge. The only provision of the Law which establishes the linkage between education-training and money is that Article 38 which specifies clearly that higher education is not free of charge. It can be regarded as a deficiency that there is no emphasis on the education in the period before higher education being free of charge.

Also, in the Regulation on Primary Educational institutions of the Ministry of National Education, in line with the Law, it is highlighted that primary education is a right for every Turkish citizen within the compulsory primary education age. Ensuring the equality of opportunity and facility is listed among the general principles of primary education and it is prescribed that students lacking financial means shall be provided with opportunities during the primary education period such as public boarding schools and scholarships and necessary special measures shall be taken for those in need of special education.[84] For the students who are in no condition to cover their educational costs, there is also the opportunity to pursue education in public boarding primary and secondary schools affiliated with the Ministry of National Education. Pursuant to the Law No. 2684 on Enabling Primary and Secondary Education Students to Pursue Education in Public Boarding Schools or Under Scholarships and the Social Aids to be Provided to Them,[85] students at public boarding schools are also provided with educational materials and equipment as well as food, clothing, pocket money and health aid within the education period (Art. 10). These facilities are also provided to the boarder students

84 Ministry of National Education Regulation on Primary Education Institutions, Official Gazette: 27.08.2003/25212, Journal of Communiques: September 2003/2552 Correction November 2003/2554, Art. 6/f **(Amended: 2.05.2006/26156 OG.)**

85 Official Gazette: 19.06.1992/17729; for the relevant Regulation, see: Regulation on Scholarships, Free Boarding and Social Aid in Primary and Secondary Education Institutions of the Ministry of National Education, Decree of the Council of Ministers: 05.10.1983-83/7166, Official Gazette: 8.12.1983/18245.

in Apprentice Training Centres affiliated with the Ministry of National Education under the scope of adult education.[86]

Free education, which is one of the universalised rules of international law and emphasised in the Convention on the Rights of Persons with Disabilities as a mandatory element of the right to education is a facility which serves for the purpose of ensuring economic accessibility to education. Participation of everyone in a certain part of the education period regardless of their economic power depends on the condition that education is free of charge in every way. When persons with disabilities are concerned, free education has another different function. Because special education is an expensive type of education and some persons with disabilities need to receive special education throughout their lives. Special education is a unique type of education with its trainers, materials, instruments and equipment, techniques and settings used and besides being a means serving to ensure the accessibility of persons with disabilities to quality and suitable education and participation in education on the equal basis with others, it is also a right. Therefore, it is resolved in the Constitution that education, which is among the fundamental rights and freedoms, shall be free of charge in primary education period, students lacking financial means shall be provided with support by the State and necessary measures shall be taken for those in need of special education. Same regulations have been incorporated in the Basic Law on National Education and inclusion of persons with disabilities in compulsory and free education is stipulated in a restricted manner connected to the need for special education. In the Law on Primary Education, after defining the primary education period, it is clearly stated that this period is compulsory and free in State schools (Art. 2) and that children with disabilities shall also benefit from the right to primary education which is compulsory and free in State schools, despite using a slightly derogatory language (Art. 12).[87]

Free education is a right for persons with disabilities as well and the actualisation of this right depends on the provisions in the general education legislation. Moreover, opportunities for economic accessibility to education are also included in the legislation on persons with disabilities and special to a certain extent. Within the legislation on persons with disabilities, a provision was added to the basic law which is LPD No 5378 on financial aid and contribution to the special education

86 Regulation on Providing Free Boarding Education at Apprentice Training Centres and Social Aid, and Administration of Boarding Houses, Official Gazette: 30.04.1995/22273, Journal of Communiques: 22.05.1995/2431.

87 While the expression in the relevant article of the Law that "special education shall be provided to children with intellectual, physical, mental and social impairments in compulsory primary education age" does not exclude children with disabilities from the right to free and compulsory education, it is nevertheless a discriminatory language. With the recent recognition of the expression "impaired" as discriminatory and degrading, all the legislation was screened and replaced by such less derogatory expressions as "with disability", "person with deficiency", "developing differently than peers", this provision of the Law was not amended.

of persons with disabilities without being limited to their compulsory education period as well as an article to the Law on the Organisation and Duties of the Ministry of National Education (Art. 35). Pursuant to the article added to the Law on the Organisation and Duties of the Ministry of National Education, persons with visual, hearing impairments, language/speech impediments, spastic, intellectual, orthopaedic or mental impairments who are proven to have a minimum of 20% impairment via a medical board report by a healthcare institution or entity authorised to issue medical board reports for impairment and those who are deemed suitable to attend in support education provided in special education schools and special education and rehabilitation centres opened under the Law No. 5580 of 8/2/2007 on Special education institutions after their educational assessment and diagnosis is conducted by special education assessment boards, a certain amount of their educational expenses to be determined by the Ministry of Finance shall be paid from the allowance included in the budget of the Ministry of National Education for this purpose. Impairment groups, degrees and scope and duration of educational programmes depending on the nature of their impairments of these persons with impairments shall be determined by a regulation to be prepared by the Ministry by consulting the Administration for the Disabled People[88] and enter into force within the 6 months following the publication of this Law (Supplementary Article 3 – Supplement: 1/7/2005-5378/35 Art.; Amended: 24/7/2008-5793/25 Art.).

As is seen, measures were included in LPD for ensuring that persons with disabilities receive supportive education from special education schools and centres opened by private persons and entities in addition to public entities and efforts were made to lighten the burden on families regarding the economic aspect of accessibility to the right to special education. This bona fide measure is not in compliance with the provision of the Convention on the Rights of Persons with Disabilities which regulates that *persons with disabilities shall receive the support required, within the general education system, to facilitate their effective education.* The goal should be to restructure and arrange all public schools and institutions where persons with disabilities receive education within the compulsory education period in a manner to meet all special education related needs of persons with disabilities together with supportive education. States Parties to the Convention are obliged to conduct required reasonable accommodation, take or cause to take other supportive measures within the general education system for the education of persons with disabilities, regardless of the fact that whether institutions where persons with disabilities pursue integrative education or separated institutions offering special education are public or private. It is not a favoured method for the need

88 The Administration for Disabled People was abolished upon the establishment of the Ministry of Family and Social Policies. Its functions and powers are discharged by the General Directorate of Services for Persons with Disabilities and the Elderly within the Ministry. Therefore, for prospective regulations, the opinion of the Ministry and General Directorate will be consulted.

for support education to be met in different environments, by different institutions and also in very limited time periods. In the laws and regulations regulating the relevant provision of LPD, this duration is limited to 8 hours a month for personal education and 4 hours a month for group education. This duration is far from corresponding to the continuity and intensity of the support provided. Especially, the more intense and suitable is the education provided to persons with disabilities in earlier periods, the more their deficiencies recede and their chance to win their independence increases. The obligation mentioned in the Convention pointing out for meeting the special educational needs in the same educational settings should also be interpreted in this direction.

However, the Convention has toned down this obligation by stipulating that personalised effective supportive measures for persons with disabilities should be provided in accordance with the objective of the full participation of persons with disabilities in settings which improve academic and social development. But it is clear that this measure can only be implemented by putting certain conditions in practice. For instance, it is of course possible and important that support education is provided externally via State aid by expert institutions to a person with speech impediment who could not receive adequate speech therapy in terms of duration and quality in his/her own institution. However, despite some exceptional institutions, the ones providing such supportive education in Turkey are usually not competent. Many of the special education and rehabilitation centres lack proper trainers and therapists and have physical deficiencies regarding the education environment. It is not possible to say that personalised supportive measures are always effective in such institutions and that they improve the academic and social development of persons with disabilities. Therefore, the relevant legislation should approach special education as a right and recast in a manner to reflect this point of view. The practice of support education being provided in private sector institutions should only be referred when the adaptations are specific to obligatory conditions and needs which cross the limit of reasonability and an effective oversight system should be developed for such institutions.

Another regulation which incorporates a measure which partially aims to ensure economic accessibility of persons with disabilities to education is the Decree-Law on Special Education. According to the relevant provision of the Decree-Law, as long as the persons in need of special education pursue their education and training in public schools, all kinds of materials and equipment for ensuring their effective enjoyment of these services will be provided by the Ministry (Art. 27). There is also another provision in the Regulation on Special Education Services in this regard (Art. 87). In addition, in the Decree-Law on Special Education and the Regulation on Special Education Services, there are provisions prescribing that "special education students shall be transported to their schools for free regardless of their economic status" and efforts are made for facilitating physical and economic accessibility of persons with disabilities to education. Moreover, it is also regulated in the Regulation on Special Education Services that children in this group shall be provided with free lunch. Pursuant to these regulations, measures shall be taken by the Ministry of National Education for providing free transportation to day students in special education schools and institutions as well as special education classes and students studying in boarding or day special education schools and institutions and possessing the requirements for public boarding schools shall be provided free lunch from the allowance granted from the general budget (Art. 90, Art. 91).

In the legislation screening to be conducted in terms of the element of obligation which is the key characteristic of the right to education, the important part is through which measures this process is carried out for children with disabilities rather than the duration of compulsory education. In this regard, compulsory education regulations should be evaluated based on 3 parameters; acceptance/enrolment to educational institutions, continued attendance and graduation. States in the Convention on the Rights of the Child are obliged to promote regular attendance to education and preventing absence (Art. 28/1-e). In the General Comment issued by the Committee on Economic, Social and Cultural Rights, compulsion refers to "parents, guardians or the State not having the chance to choose whether the child will begin education or not".[89] The obligation of families and the State in this regard is not only limited to not preventing their children from starting school, but also they are actively under obligation to ensure that their children begin and continue school. In this regard, for fulfilling all requirements of compulsory education, States are obliged to turn compulsory education into a right to children and an obligation for families via other measures as well as legal regulations and impose sanctions for acts contrary to the compulsion. In addition, administrative and judiciary institutions of States are obliged to facilitate the actualisation of the right to education by monitoring and auditing whether the legal compulsion is put into practice.

Ministry of National Education is responsible for carrying out education and training services in Turkey in compliance with laws and for conducting oversight and supervision.[90] Pursuant to the Law No. 222 on Primary Education, *"every child shall be enrolled and accepted to a primary school at the end of the school year in which he/she enters the compulsory primary education age. Every parent, guardian or head of the family is obliged to enrol their children at a primary school on time"* (Art. 46).[91] Children identified by the school administration to be in the compulsory education age shall be automatically enrolled in the school by the school administration. Enrolment and placement processes are regulated in the Regulation on Pre-School and Primary Educational institutions of the Ministry of National Education in several provisions based on the age factor in primary education period, and for persons with

89 CESCR, Plans of action for primary education (Art. 14). 10/05/99. E/C.12/1999/4. (General Comments), para.6.

90 Basic Law No. 1739 on National Education, Date of Enactment: 14.06.1973, Official Gazette: 24.06.1973/14574, Art. 56; Law No. 3797 on Organisation and Functions of the Ministry of National Education, Date of Enactment: 30.04.1992, Official Gazette: 12.05.1992/21226, Edition 5 Volume 31, Art. 2.

91 Law No. 222 on Primary Education, Date of Enactment: 05/01/1961, Official Gazette: 12.01.1961/10705, Publication Series: Edition 4, Volume 1, Page. 1460.

disabilities, a provision is incorporated prescribing that new enrolments of children in need of special education who are referred via a report from a counselling and research centre can be made in any school they want regardless of their address in the national address database, provided that they document their condition (Art. 11/4). In the old Regulation there used to be a provision stipulating that those who are in the compulsory education age but not diagnosed for special education and did not receive a decision for placement were also going to be enrolled in primary schools. In the new Regulation, it is only laid down that children who are in the compulsory education age and have not been enrolled in any school for any reason and do not know how to read and write will be enrolled in first grade and special education and placement was not mentioned. However, provision 11/4 of the Regulation covers this deficiency to a certain extent.

During the census conducted after the legal regulation made in 2006 on the address-based registration system, questions were also asked for determining children and persons with disabilities within residences. Although this census of 2007 had the quality to determine the phenomenon of disability more accurately compared to the 2002 Research on the Impaired, it did not correspond to international standards completely and no updates were made for disabilities of children born after 2007 or the ones occurring afterwards. Unless persons go to a healthcare institution regarding their medical condition or apply to a public entity for any reason, it is left for the initiative of families to determine the need for special education particularly during the pre-school period and initiate the compulsory education period. Therefore, the compulsory education period usually starts for children with disabilities with their enrolment in primary schools. Compulsion of pre-school education only exists in laws, but it cannot go beyond being a measure that cannot be put into practice effectively. Therefore, we care a lot about mobile health screenings and recommend that regular screenings should be conducted, and healthy data should be collected in Turkey in order to facilitate early detection of disabilities, ensure that required healthcare, rehabilitation and education support is provided and therefore the chance of children with disabilities to live independently is increased.

There is no clear provision in the special education legislation on the education being compulsory for persons with disabilities and there is a deficiency in the Decree-Law on Special Education which is regarded as the basic law. Efforts were made for covering this deficiency with the Regulation on Special Education Services, Compulsory education was defined for persons in need of special education with the provision added to the Regulation on 21.07.2012. According to the definition, compulsory education is the education and training period which begins with the pre-school education period and covers the secondary education period (Art. 4/1-aa). Other than this explicit phrase, compulsion is included in various provisions of the Regulation as an element of education and training of children in need of special education (Art. 26/1, Art. 27/1). It is resolved all persons whose need for special education in pre-school and compulsory primary education period was determined or whose diagnosis or placement decision was not made will be enrolled in schools and institutions irrespective of the period specified in the annual work programme

(Art. 75)[92], and the institutions for enrolment were stated. Accordingly, persons who turned 37 months old will be enrolled in pre-school educational institutions, those who turned 66 months old will be enrolled in primary schools or special education schools and institutions which provide 1st tier education services to persons in the compulsory education age (Art. 76). While the obligation of families to enrol their children is not mentioned in the Regulation or other special education regulations, there is also no reference made to the relevant laws (general education legislation). Because of the deficiency in this regard, general provisions need to be referred and it needs to be stated that relevant provisions of the Basic Law of National Education and the Law on Primary Education will apply. It is possible to deduce this conclusion from the Article 77 titled "Acceptance of enrolment". Because, pursuant to this article, a requirement for having a placement decision is not sought for persons in need of special education for enrolment in schools and institutions and it is stated that school/institution administration can initiate formal processes for a placement decision for these persons, if the school or institution in which the student is enrolled is in compliance with the placement decision, student can pursue his/her education in that school or institution, and if there is a different placement decision, processes shall be initiated for transferring the student to a school in accordance with the placement decision.

Regarding the issue of ensuring continued attendance, Law No. 222 includes several measures on this regard. Law No. 222 on Primary Education imposes the obligation of "ensuring" the continued attendance of the child to the families and the obligation of "helping and taking necessary measures" for families and schools administrations to the civil administrators, primary education inspectors and the municipal police organisation (Art. 52). School administrations and primary education inspectors are obliged to research the causes for absence and try to eliminate the causes hindering attendance and notify civilian authorities in cases when they cannot resolve the problem (Art. 53). The school administration is obliged to notify the neighbourhood master in villages and civilian authorities in other places about the parents, guardians or heads of families who do not let their children go to school for reasons other than the force majeure prescribed in the Law, who exceed the leave period, get outside the school district and disappear without a trace and do not notify the school administration about the absence of their children without any excuses. In the notification made by these units to the families it will also be announced that those who do not do what is necessary will be imposed an administrative fine (Art. 55).[93] In the Regulation on Primary Education attendance

92 Regulation on Special Education Services, Official Gazette: 31.05.2006/26184.

93 Parents may be imposed by the local civil administrator 100 TL per day of non-attendance of the child. For parents who do not send their child to school following the fining, the directorate of national education will make a criminal report to the prosecution office and the court of criminal peace may impose a light prison sentence of 20 days to two months. See: *Eurybase The Information Database on Education*

of students in primary educational institutions is obligatory and with a reference made to the Law No. 222, it is explained that this obligation is imposed on families and other relevant public authorities. Moreover, the situations which will be regarded as absence and notification to be made to parents is stated and it is prescribed that absence of students who get outside the residential unit in which the school is located, whose address cannot be found or who go to a place without schools will be entered in the absence section of e-school by the school administration and their absence will continuously be followed by school administrations on the e-school system. For the students who go abroad, it is resolved that, their overseas address will be added to the e-school system by the school administration and measures will be taken by the Ministry to ensure their continued attendance to schools abroad and these records will not be erased until the students pass the age of compulsory education.

The basic law which regulates compulsory education for persons with disabilities is the Decree-Law on Special Education.[94] With the Decree-Law, the compulsory education period starts at the pre-school period for persons in need of special education who are diagnosed (Art. 7). This process is explained in detail in the Regulation on Special Education Services and the obligation is repeated. Pursuant to the provision of the Regulation which was amended in 2012, "Pre-school education is obligatory for persons of the age of 37–66 months who are in need of special education. However, pre-school education for these persons can be extended up to 78 months based on the end of September according to the Special Education Assessment Board Report and the signed consent of the parent (Art. 29/1).[95] While there is no obligation clearly stated in the Decree-Law on Special Education regarding the next educational processes, there is a provision which implies that after the pre-school education of the children in need of special education their primary education is also included in the scope of compulsory education. Accordingly, *Preparatory classes can be opened for children in need of special education who completed pre-school education or in the age of compulsory education* (Art. 8). However, since there has been no amendment made in the Decree-Law in accordance with the compulsory education period extended to 12 years in 2012 there is no compulsion prescribed for the secondary education period. An amendment must be made in the Decree-Law in this regard.

There is no special regulation for the continued attendance of persons with disabilities who pursue their education within the compulsory education period. In this regard, regulations in the general education legislation shall apply. Regulation

---

Systems in Europe 2007–2008 Türk Eğitim Örgütlenmesi, Eurybase – Turkey (2007–2008), pp. 30–31 http://eacea.ec.europa.eu/ressources/eurydice/eurybase, (16.12.2008)

94 Decree-Law on Special Education, Decree date: 30.05.1997, No:573, Date of the Authorising Law: 03.12.1996, No: 4216, Official Gazette: 06.06.1997/ 23011(bis)

95 Regulation on Special Education Services, Official Gazette: 31.05.2006/26184, (Amended 21.7.2012/28360 R.G.) Art. 29.

on Special Education Services only has a special provision for the continued attendance of students who attend special education application centres (schools), special education work practice centres (schools) and special education vocational training centres (schools); students who pursue these institutions will repeat the grade due to absence if they are absent for 60 work days without any excuse in spite of at least two written warnings issued by the school administration.

Although the obligation imposed by law for ensuring that persons with disabilities start their education during the pre-school (37–72 months) period is quite important, regulations with special measures are required for detecting the children within this age period and their enrolment in schools/institutions, ensuring their continued attendance in all steps of compulsory education along with this period and for having and completing a continuous and intense educational period. Measures in the general legislation regulations are not sufficient for protecting the right to education of children with disabilities in all aspects. The issue of education of persons with disabilities is a more sensitive issue compared to children without disabilities and has vital importance for certain disability groups. Especially for those with severe disabilities and physical disabilities, beginning special education and rehabilitation in an early period, pursuing education and rehabilitation without interruption, in which each hour is valuable, is quite meaningful for ensuring that these children connect with life. While a 10-day break would not cause a regression in the development of a child whose development is normal, it may cause serious loss for many children with disabilities. Therefore, after children with disabilities are enrolled in schools, it should be recognised as an obligation by Turkey stemming from the Convention on the Rights of the Child and the Convention on the Rights of Persons with Disabilities to make good use of this opportunity as a requirement of the best interest of the child and to take all legal measures.

Persons with disabilities, who constitute 12.29% of the total population of Turkey, have difficulties in accessing a quality education which is their right. Lack of birth and population records, which is a prevalent problem in Turkey, makes early diagnosis and intervention ineffective,[96] and as a result, pre-school education which is made compulsory for 37–66-month age group cannot be put into practice. In the booklet Statistical Data on Persons with Disabilities published in 2014 by the Ministry of Family and Social Policies General Directorate of Services for Persons with Disabilities and the Elderly, the number of children with disabilities in the 0–4 age group was 37 207 and those in the 5–9 age group was 109 837.[97] Although there

---

96 A Multi-Indicator Cluster Study in 1995 indicated that 26% of the children in the age group 0–4 had no birth and population records. For information, see: Türkiye'de Çocukların Durumu Ön Rapor [Preliminary Report on the State of Children in Turkey], Social Services and Child Protection Institute – UNICEF, April 2000, Ankara, http://www.die.gov.tr/CIN/CIN-TR/prereporttr/prereporttr.htm, (10.12.2008)

97 Statistical Data on Persons with Disabilities, Ministry of Family and Social Policies General Directorate of Services for Persons with Disabilities and the Elderly Department of Research, Development and Projects, March 2014, p.15.

is no precise numerical data, it is estimated that more than 20 thousand children within the age group of 5 in Turkey have one or more disabilities. According to the 2013–2014 school year data published by the Ministry of National Education, 1225 students received education in nursery classes within the special education schools in Turkey, while the number of students who attended inclusive education in nursery classes was only limited to 91. According to the 2013–2014 school year data, the total number of students who attended pre-school education (with or without disabilities) is 1 059 495. The rate of schooling in pre-school education within the 2013–14 school year is 28% in the 3–5 age group; 37,9% in the 4–5 age group. The rate of schooling in pre-school education in the 5-age group is 42,5%.[98] As is seen, the rate of participation in education in the pre-school period is quite low in terms of the general population in Turkey. However, although pre-school education is included in the compulsory education period of persons with disabilities, it is observed that persons with special needs encounter bigger problems compared to their peers in accessing pre-school education.[99]

It is observed that, the higher the education tier gets, the limited it becomes to access education for persons with disabilities. Among 280,014 persons registered in the National Database for the Impaired,[100] 22% finished elementary school, 10% finished primary education (i.e. 8 years) and only 7% finished high school and higher institutions. As of the 2013–14 school years, the number of students who attended special education services within the formal education system in Turkey has reached 242 716. Among these, 92 295 pursue education as primary education students (First Tier 4-year education period) in special education schools, special education classes and under inclusive education. The remaining 150 421 students study in secondary schools and general and vocational high schools under inclusive education or in special education classes, Third Tier Special Education Work

98 National Education Statistics Formal Education 2013/14, Official Statistics Programme Publication, p.1.

99 Türkiye Eğitim Sisteminde Eşitlik ve Akademik Başarı Araştırma Raporu ve Analiz [Research Report and Analysis of Equality and Academic Achievement in the Turkish Education System], Eğitim Reformu Girişimi (ERG) [Education Reform Initiative], May 2014, p.22.

100 The National Database on the Impaired (OZVERI) created within the General Directorate of Services for Persons with Disabilities and the Elderly was built by compiling the data on persons with disabilities who received a Report of Disability from the Medical Boards of authorised health institutions and filed an application for any reason to some public institutions and organisations from which data could be transferred to our database. Therefore, it does not include all persons with disabilities living in Turkey. See: Statistical Data on Persons with Disabilities, Ministry of Family and Social Policies General Directorate of Services for Persons with Disabilities and the Elderly Department of Research, Development and Projects, March 2014, p.13.

Practice Centres and Special Education Vocational Training Centres.[101] In Turkey, the number of students who attend inclusive education has increased regularly in the last ten years in primary and secondary education and during the last years, there has been a remarkable increase particularly in the number of students who attended inclusive education in primary education. The number of students who attend inclusive education in secondary education also increases, however this increase has a slower progress compared to primary education. Additionally, when the numbers of students who attend inclusive education in primary and secondary education are compared, it can be seen that the number regarding secondary education is dramatically lower. This level of loss during the process of transition to secondary education indicates that problems are encountered during the transition of persons with special needs to secondary education. The increase in this number compared to the previous years is a significant progress, however most of persons with disabilities still cannot access the special education services they need.[102]

As of 2012, the rate of children who are at the primary education age (6–13) but not enrolled in any schools in Turkey is 6%. Schooling tendencies only constitute the initial dimension of the discussion of equal access to quality education. The duration of attendance within the education period by the students who are provided with access to education, rates of graduation and whether they achieve academic success at school constitute the foundation of the discussion on quality and equality in education. An integrative analysis can be conducted in this regard by examining those who are not enrolled in schools as well as the rates of absence and drop-outs in primary and secondary education. Until the 2010–11 school year, Ministry of National Education have been sharing the data on the rate of absence and drop-outs in primary education with the public. For the last three years no data have been shared in this regard. According to the last year when data was shared, in the 2009–10 school year, the total rate of absence in primary education was 10,4%. Regarding the secondary education level, Ministry of National Education Strategy Development Department published data on the 2012–13 school year. According to this data which shows absence more than 10 days, the issue of absence in secondary education is at a prominent level across Turkey. While the rate of absence in general secondary education is 27,4%, it is 39,1% for vocational and technical secondary education. Another serious problem encountered in secondary education is the right rate of drop-outs. Similar to the data on absence, the last data published by the Ministry of National Education in 2011 was examined. In general, in all programme types except for the high schools admitting by academic selection, it indicates an

101 National Education Statistics Formal Education 2013/14, Official Statistics Programme Publication, p.36.

102 Türkiye Eğitim Sisteminde Eşitlik ve Akademik Başarı Araştırma Raporu ve Analiz [Research Report and Analysis of Equality and Academic Achievement in the Turkish Education System], Eğitim Reformu Girişimi (ERG) [Education Reform Initiative], May 2014, pp. 22–23.

important problem that the average rate of drop-outs is 10%. There is no data available in this regard for the students who pursue special education.

Regarding the actualisation of the compulsory education practice, it is equally as important to enrol children to educational institutions and to ensure their continued attendance and graduation. Convention on the Rights of the Child imposes and obligation on States in its provision on the right to education, to encourage regular attendance to education and prevention of drop-outs (Art. 28/1-e). Committee on Economic, Social and Cultural Rights, in its General Comment on the right to primary education, states that the compulsion refers to the "lack of choice of parents, guardians or the State on whether the child will begin education or not".[103] The obligation of families and the State is not only to prevent children from beginning school, but also an active obligation to ensure that they begin and continue their education. Regarding the achievement of such requirements of compulsory education, States should take legal measures to make compulsory education a right for children and an obligation for families and impose sanctions for actions against this compulsion. The discharge of the legal duty should be ensured via monitoring and oversight activities of the administrative units of the State.

In the legal regulations about special education, the school administration should be imposed the obligation to take all measures for ensuring the continued attendance to education within the compulsory education period, and in return, structural and administrative positions of schools should be reviewed, administrators and educators should be allowed to take initiative and implement them. Measures such as allowing to change the teacher or the class and if necessary the education programmes, letting the child to do only the activities he/she enjoys for a while and increasing extra-curricular social activities will be able to ensure that children willingly participate in education. School administrators, in addition to the measures they will take within schools, should also be enabled to create urgent solutions for parents who does not/cannot bring their child to school. About the access to education, which will be addressed in detail in the following sections, regarding eliminating the obstacles concerning the child and the family, the school administration should have powers such as urging central and local administrations to take action and cooperating with non-governmental organisations. Units should be established at Directorates of National Education comprising of experts who will develop urgent solutions and assist the school administration in their implementation, and whatever or whoever the cause of absence is about, it should be resolved in the shortest time and the child should be enabled to continue his/her education. Of course, it should also be kept in mind that all administrative, institutional, financial and personnel related needs should be met in order to put such legal measures in practice.

The main purpose of the minimum period obligation for education is to ensure that everyone obtains the basic knowledge and competences to carry out the

103 CESCR, Plans of action for primary education (Art. 14). 10/05/99. E/C.12/1999/4. (General Comments), para.6.

fundamental necessities of life and lives an independent and self-sufficient life within the society. To this end, States are obliged to take compulsory education seriously as a fundamental human right, recognise it as a minimum standard of the right to education and take effective measures to make sure that everyone enjoys this right. The lack of precise figures on all children in the age of compulsory education and the lack of knowledge about this age on the exact number of children who have disabilities/special educational needs hinder the healthy knowledge on how many of persons with disabilities are excluded from education. It is extremely important that public entities and private institutions offering public services meticulously keep records on persons with disabilities while offering services and that persons with disabilities who can be diagnosed during birth are referred to early intervention and special education services and therefore ensured to benefit from compulsory education. In addition to this, measures for increasing the frequency of local level baby and children health screenings and accelerating information and awareness raising activities on disabilities for families and the society[104] will increase the success rate in early diagnosis and intervention and serve for enabling persons with disabilities to begin their education at an early age.

Committee on the Rights of the Child laid emphasis in its Concluding Observation of May-June 2012 on Turkey's Combined Second and Third Periodic Report on the insufficiency of the data on children with disabilities and advised for a comprehensive data collection system to be established for analysing the data collected as a basis for evaluating the development achieved in actualising the rights of the child and policy and programme design for the implementation of the Convention. Regarding the access of persons with disabilities to education, in spite of the efforts of the State Party for ensuring the access of children to education, it is stated that there is a concern caused by the high percentage of children with disabilities in special education programmes and that many children with disabilities at the school age are not able to enjoy their right to education. Moreover the Committee pointed out that the State Party did not provide adequate information on whether the support provided to children with disabilities reached them everywhere or whether they are reintegrated in the society and recommended that efforts should be increased for ensuring full enjoyment of the rights by children with disabilities and in the following report, information should be provided on the scope, nature and results of the services and programmes offered to children with disabilities. Another recommendation of the Committee which makes a reference to the General Comment No. 9 on the rights of children with disabilities (2006) is to make the

104 For causes of post-natal disability, prevention and early response, see: *I. Özürlüler Şurası Çağdaş Toplum, Yaşam ve Özürlüler* 29 Kasım-2 Aralık 1999[*First Council on the Impaired, Modern Society, Life and Impaired* 29 November-2 December 1999], Başbakanlık Özürlüler İdaresi Başkanlığı Yayınları [Prime Ministry Administration for the Disabled People Publications], Ankara, pp. 292–310; for recommendations pp. 410–411.

schools in Turkey more accessible and inclusion of children with disabilities in the formal education system and the society and their integration via providing special trainings to teachers.[105]

2. Inclusive Education

Inclusive education,[106] or integrative education as known in the international human rights law, is a system which possesses the belief that education is a fundamental human right and aims to ensure that everyone has the opportunity to receive education according to their needs.[107] According to the integrative education perspective, it is the simple and easy way to lay the problems encountered by persons with disabilities during the education process completely on their disabilities. Instead, emphasis should be laid on the problems directly caused by the aspects of the education system. Education programmes, deficiencies of educators in terms of quality and quantity and difficulties in accessing buildings and structures each should be regarded as obstacles to learning for children with disabilities. As is known, regulations in the Convention on the Rights of Persons with Disabilities are also based on this philosophy. The emphasis on "integration" in the Convention is laid on the whole education system (Art. 24/1). Therefore, the education system should be structured in a manner to take into account the differences and special needs, without referring to categorisations such as persons with disabilities, highly talented or any other discriminating/excluding categorisations, in order to regulate and implement education as a "human right". The "integration" pointed out by the Convention is a key principle that should be considered in all measures to be taken for ensuring that persons with disabilities enjoy their human rights as other people in all areas of life (social, cultural, economic and political areas such as education, health and working). Convention not only defines integration as a principle, but also presents a framework which includes the objectives of education systems via integration and imposes certain obligations on States and international organisations for ensuring quality integration for all children and teenagers with special needs.

It is possible to say that the integrative (inclusive, as called in the Convention) education on which the Convention is based consists of two dimensions. First one

---

105 Committee on the Rights of the Children, 60th Session 29 May–15 June 2012, Review of Reports Submitted by States Parties pursuant to Article 44 of the Convention; Concluding Observations: Turkey, p.5, p.12.

106 Since the legislation in Turkey uses "integrative" or "integrated" education, we will continue to use the same term. S.Ç.

107 **Olof Sandkull,** "Strengthening Inclusive Education by Applying a Rights-based Approach to Education Programming", *ISEC 2005 Paper,* August 2005, UNESCO, Bangkok, p.6; For dissenting views on inclusive education system, see: **Edward L Meyen and Thomas M Skrtic (Editors)** *Special Education Student Disability An Introduction Traditional, Emerging and Alternative Perspectives,* Love Publishing Company Denver, Fourth Edition, Colorado, 1995, pp. 647–648.

is the spatial aspect which refers to persons with disabilities attending education in the same environments together with other individuals while the second is about the nature of the education which refers to implementing reasonable accommodation in these environments in order to ensure that persons with disabilities access quality and suitable education and provided with the support they need. Starting points and priorities may differ for each national system for establishing or developing an integrative education system. States have to review their status and determine the obstacles and challenges before education as well as the situations that will facilitate integration and come up with a national plan which also includes the development process suitable for their own systems. However, the course of the measures required to be taken are generally obvious; initiating change on the legal level, amending the administrative structures accordingly and mobilising the resources.

While evaluating the current legislation on education in force in the Turkish law system, the first point that needs to be examined is whether integrative education is based on these elements and whether it reflects a view of integration that is in parallel with the philosophy and concrete provisions of the Convention.

In Turkey, integration mostly refers to a process and structure which is structured based on the need for education, moreover the need for special education. As we are going to explain in detail below, this relationship is not one-to-one. In addition, it has a nature of causing negative results for children with disabilities. It should be highlighted that there is no "special education" term used in the Convention on the Rights of Persons with Disabilities and explanations should be made accordingly.

In the Turkish law system on the other hand, education of persons with disabilities are regulated based on the need for special education and the institutional structure is established in line with this approach. Decree-Law on Special Education and Regulation on Special Education Services, as obvious from their names, are the regulations structuring the special education system. In the scope article of the Decree-Law on Special Education, it is prescribed that the Decree-Law encompasses persons in need of special education and the education services to be provided to them directly or indirectly; schools, institutions and programmes which will provide these services (Art. 2). In this legislation which determines the principles for the structures and rules based on which the special educational needs will be fulfilled, integration ("inclusion" as called in the legislation) is only one of the methods for fulfilling special educational needs. In the Decree-Law, "inclusion" is defined as, *educational settings developed for ensuring that persons in need of special education have mutual interaction with other individuals and actualising their educational goals on the highest attainable level* (Art. 3/c).

There are similar regulations in the Regulation on Special Education Services as well (Scope: Article 2). In the Regulation, instead of "inclusion", the term "inclusive education" is preferred and although this education is enriched in terms of content to a certain extent, in essence, it is the same as the Decree-Law. Moreover, Regulation clearly refers to inclusive education as a special education implementation.[108] Pursuant to the Regulation, another way of special education practice is the education at special education institutions. Such a distinction creates the perception that there is only one education system (general education system) and that special education is a type of education within the general education system. But this is an illusion. When different educational needs are called as "special education", the system gets segmented on its own in terms of education. This segmentation can be observed in the whole structure from the organisational chart of the Ministry of National Education to the legislation on national education.

Education of persons with disabilities is addressed within the national education system in Turkey and is supported by provisions or regulations specific to persons with disabilities. As previously mentioned, pursuant to the Article 42/7 of the Constitution of 1982 which regulates the right to education and training, the obligation to "take necessary measures to rehabilitate those in need of special education so as to render such people useful to society" belongs to the State. In the Basic Law of National Education, which is regulated as a Constitutional imperative and recognised as the basic law on the right to education, there is no detailed provision regulating the education of persons with disabilities. Under the title "Equality of opportunity and facility", it is prescribed that special measures shall be taken for raising children in need of special education and protection (Art. 8/2). In the Law on Primary Education, in the provision which also encompasses the education of persons with disabilities, "schools and classes to be established for children in need of special education" are also included in the compulsory primary educational institutions (Art. 6/a-5).[109] When the provisions in the basic laws on education are considered, persons with disabilities have the right to attend general or vocational-technical educational institutions within both the formal and adult education system. However, when it is considered that the concept of "need for special education" becomes prominent in the assessment of persons with disabilities in terms of education and that this concept is mostly related to the education of persons with disabilities, the method of fulfilling special educational needs within the education system and the measures taken for this regard should be taken into account and the system should be evaluated together.

As mentioned before, LPD No. 5378 have been through a comprehensive amendment in 2014. The right to education was rewritten in line with the standards and principles of the Convention with a regulation different than the old provisions and turned into a qualified right. Pursuant to the new provision, persons with disabilities

108 Art. 23(1) – *Education by way of inclusion is the practice of special education based on that individuals with special educational needs receive pre-school, primary, secondary and non-formal education including supportive education services in public and private schools along with their counterparts without deficiencies.*

109 Law No. 222 on Primary Education, Date of Enactment: 05/01/1961, Official Gazette: 12.01.1961/10705, Publication Series: Edition 4, Volume 1, Page 1460, Article 6 – (Amended: 12/10/1983 – 2917/2 Art.)

will be provided with the opportunity for integrated education in the environment they live in for their whole lives. The provision which points out to taking into account the special conditions and differences of persons with disabilities in education and providing them education on the basis of equality without discrimination, also makes reference to the standards and principles on which this process will be dependent (Art. 15/1, Amended: 6/2/2014 – 6518/73 Art.). Relevant article of law lays down the main rule for the implementation of integrative education and draws attention to the necessity of integrating persons with disabilities in the general education system via planning to ensure that receive education at all levels (Art. 15/2). Here this refers to education being provided in a setting to meet all needs of persons with disabilities in terms of both spatial and service-related aspects via integrative planning to ensure that persons with disabilities receive education at all levels within the general education system on the equal basis with others (Art. 15), or more explicitly, the integration of the education system.

Education system, as known, refers to the whole bureaucratic structure relevant to education and training, institutions where education is provided, educators and other officers in these institutions, students and their families, the education and education-related services offered by the institution, in short, the legal and institutional structure in which the educational setting is regulated. Educational setting is not only a form-based or material concept which indicates only the educational settings or only the contents or methods of education. It refers to all measures to be taken for meeting the education related needs of each student without discrimination, based on the principle of equality and by considering special conditions and differences and therefore ensuring suitable and quality education and training. The provisions of the former Law No. 5378 were far from establishing the right to education of persons with disabilities to universal principles and standards. It only mentioned that integrative education will be regarded as the basis and then moved on to ways and methods for facilitating the education for persons with disabilities in their transition to higher education. However, unless measures are implemented for ensuring quality and suitable education in the primary and secondary education period starting from the pre-school period, it is not possible for persons with disabilities to reach the higher education period. Amending the old provision which ignored this well-known fact and defining education as an aggregate of principles and standards that will encompass the whole life of persons with disabilities, as well as expanding the area of obligation of the State is a positive step. As explained before, it should also be recognised as a significant progress that the Law No. 5378 has been recast by incorporating principles such as the prohibition of discrimination, equality, equality of opportunity, lifelong learning and respect for differences which constitute the foundation of the Convention on the Rights of Persons with Disabilities and mediate for protecting and actualising the right to education of persons with disabilities along with their all human rights.

The Decree-Law on Special Education which comprises principles and rules for fulfilling the special educational needs of persons with disabilities and constitutes the basis for the legal scheme of special education is far behind the Law No. 5378 and the Convention on the Rights of Persons with Disabilities in terms of the language used, principles and standards. Another factor that will support our previously mentioned recommendation on completely repealing the Decree-Law lays in the point of view and meaning given by the Decree-Law on the integration principle. For one thing, the Decree-Law still uses the term "inclusion". It should be repeated once more that in order to achieve unison in terminology of the education legislation this term should be replaced with "integration-integrative education".

Besides the form-related elements such as the terminology, there are also problems about the contents of integration. The most important part of legal regulations in the nature of laws is the provisions defining "fundamental principles". The reason for which the law is issued, its goal, subjects of rights and services as well as its subject-matter should be interpreted in the light of these principles. In the "fundamental principles" article of the Decree-Law, the concept of inclusion is not even directly referred and special education is mentioned as a matter of service. It is possible to say that the principles which explain that special education services will be carried out in a manner that will not separate persons in need of special education from their social and physical environments as much as possible; adaptations will be made in the goals, contents and teaching processes by taking into account the educational performances of persons in need of special education and priority will be given to ensuring that they are taught together with other individuals; and special education services will be planned in a manner to include the process of interaction and mutual adaptation of persons in need of special education and the society implicitly refer to integrative education. However, the articles regulating primary and secondary education contravene with this interpretation.

In the article of the Decree-Law which regulates the primary education period, it is clearly stated that persons in need of special education will pursue their primary education in special education schools and/or other primary schools, and for those who are in no condition to actualise the goals of compulsory primary education programmes, institutions will be opened with education programmes prepared by taking account their performance levels in developmental areas. Similarly, it is prescribed that they will pursue secondary education in special education schools and/or other general and vocational technical secondary schools (Art. 8, Art. 9). Regarding the higher education stage, it is only stated that necessary special measures will be taken for them to benefit from higher education opportunities and there is no phrase used for making reference to integration in adult education. The "and/or" used in the provisions regulating special education in primary and secondary education periods and the phrase "special education schools" used before that do not represent a strong will based on fulfilling special educational needs via integration.

In the *Educational Settings* section of the Decree-Law, the environments where special education will be provided are regulated in a dual structure by two separate articles as inclusion and special education schools and in the following article it is resolved that special education support will be provided in order to actualise the educational goals of the education programmes pursued in both environments (Art. 12, Art. 13, Art .14). Inclusion refers to education pursued by persons in need of special education together with their peers at all types and levels of schools and institutions by using suitable methods and techniques according to individualised education plans prepared (Art. 12). Education in special education schools on the other hand, refers to persons in need of special education who need to pursue their education in a separate school or institution together with their peers who have similar deficiencies receiving education in special education schools and institutions arranged with suitable inclusion models (Art .13). Inclusive education which is regulated as one of the educational settings, corresponds to the spatial togetherness (i.e. "co-location") element of integration since it refers to the education to be provided together with peers who do not need special education. Individualised education plan of the education provided in the scope of inclusion and the fact that it will be implemented by making reference to suitable methods and techniques indicate a unity also in terms of education programmes. From this aspect, the view of Decree-Law on inclusion matches integration. However, this view, based on the abovementioned reasons, is not reflected on the whole Decree-Law. In other words, there are discrepancies among the provisions of the Decree-Law pointing out inclusion/integration in education.

Similarly, the provision stipulating that regular school programmes will be implemented in special education schools and classes but arrangements will be made in these programmes by taking into account the characteristics and learning competences of students without disturbing the equivalency partly supports the equality of opportunity in education (Art. 15/2), however this statement does not comply with the goals of the programmes of special education schools and classes explained in the following sections. It is an accurate approach that the programmes to be implemented in special education schools and classes aim to ensure that students obtain competences to pursue their education in regular schools with their peers, however it does not seem realistic that special education will be provided in these programmes without disturbing equivalency (15/2) and it does not comply with the meaning of "special education" defined in the definitions provision of the Decree-Law. Because, the Decree-Law defines special education as *education pursued in settings suitable for the disability condition and properties of persons in need of special education in order to meet their educational needs by the personnel trained specially for this purpose, via specially developed education programmes and methods* (Art. 3/b). This definition is problematic in terms of both legislative technique and content. A definition developed based on the term "person in need of special education" needs to be defined on itself. While the intention is to define "special education", making a reference to the need by using the same term is a faulty method in terms of both linguistics and legislative technique.

When it is addressed in terms of content, the point which should be examined is whether *the special development of educational programmes* which is used as an obligatory element in the definition is the same as implementing a common programme by adapting it for a person with disability. In our opinion, these two have different meanings. To explain with an example, education programme developed for persons with autism is special and specific to the education of persons with autism. Certain adaptations can be made for a person with autism who is able to pursue the same education programme with his/her normal peers despite being in a special education school or class to attend this programme. However, this does not mean that the child receives special education, but means that special education methods are used, in other words he/she receives regular education with special education support. This is also the reason for the existence of resource rooms or as known today, the support education rooms which are mandatory to be allocated in schools for the use of students with disabilities who pursue their education in regular schools under integration. As emphasised in the definition made in the Regulation on Special Education Services, support education room is "*a setting arranged to provide support education services to students who pursue their education within inclusive practices or those who are highly talented in areas they need*" (Art. 4/1-ı). However, the students in special education schools and institutions or classes represent a group which has similar deficiencies and pursues special programmes developed specially for these deficiencies and the special education provided in such schools/institutions also comprises all kinds of support services.

This problem about the Decree-Law which we tried to explain briefly is caused by the fact that the issue of the education or persons with disabilities is defined with a reference to special education in the Turkish law system. All disability groups may not require special education. For the persons with disabilities who can follow regular educational programmes without any amendments required, only certain physical adaptations may be sufficient, and this may ensure that they take part in education as equals with others. For instance, this applies to many persons with orthopaedic disabilities. While it is not possible to explain the condition of these children with special education, they are not even required to be officially included in the scope of integration. It is absurd to open separate schools/institutions for persons with disabilities within this group under the name of special education. If close attention is paid, the Convention on the Rights of Persons with Disabilities regulates the right to education without creating a link between the education of persons with disabilities and special education, based on reasonable accommodation in accordance with the needs of persons with disabilities and providing them the support they need within the general education system in order to ensure that they effectively benefit from general education. Since it points out adaptations and amendments in terms of both physical and educational aspects (Art. 24/2-c, d, e), reasonable accommodation is usually adequate for persons with disabilities to receive education on the basis of equality. The phrase "support they need within the general education system" used in the Convention provision is usually a reference to individual support. While this support may be towards education, it may also be in the form of physical aid facilitating the utilisation of the educational setting as well as all types of guidance and counselling support. If the person with disability still cannot properly benefit from education in spite of all these support and adaptations, he/she will need to pursue education in completely in separate institutions via special programmes and methods.

Regulation on Special Education Services partially answers our criticism on the definition of special education by its definition of "person in need of special education" (Art. 4/1-z). However, the "special education" definition in the same article, while being slightly expanded in terms of scope, is still made based on the need for special education similarly to the Decree-Law. According to the definition, special education is the education pursued in suitable settings based on the characteristics of persons in need of special education in all development areas as well as their competences in academic disciplines by personnel trained specially to fulfil their educational and social needs, via specially developed education programmes and methods (Art. 4/1-y). Thus, special education has been transformed into a type of education which is provided by taking into account not only academic but also all development aspects of individuals, which aims to meet their educational needs as well as social needs and, in this regard, fulfils almost all needs of the individual in all areas of life. It should be repeated once more that naming the fulfilment of all educational and/or education related needs of persons with disabilities as special education exceeds the meaning and the objective of special education. If educational support and/or all types of support required for the continuance of education (for instance not toilet training, but the support or aid provided to the person with disability to satisfy his/her need to use the toilet at school) are called as special education, general education becomes completely meaningless. When the simple support provided to those who can pursue general education programmes under integration is also called special education, this distinction also becomes meaningless. The definition of special education schools and institutions made by the Regulation also supports our view. Because, special education schools and institutions are defined as, *all types and levels of boarding and day, public and private schools and institutions affiliated with the Ministry, which offer services to persons in need of special education, where specially trained personnel are employed, and specially developed education programmes and methods are applied* (Art. 4/1-ü).

As is seen in this definition, special education has three pillars; specially trained personnel, specially developed education programmes, education via special methods. Support, aid or adaptations which do not comprise all three of these elements within the education period should not be called as special education and those who do not need these should not be defined as persons in need of special education. Therefore, support education should not be defined based on the need for special education as well. Support education service which is defined in the Regulation as, *"providing expert personnel, materials and equipment and education and counselling services to persons in need of special education according to their educational needs determined as a result of medical and educational assessment and diagnosis as well as their families, teachers and school personnel"* has a content which also includes those who are not in need of special education. For instance, additional exercises conducted in company with a teacher by a student who does not have a right hand and cannot use his/her left hand quickly in order to write in a quicker manner can be regarded as support education but is not special education. Or printing out the course notes for this student and excusing him/her from taking written notes and attending written examinations or providing him/her additional time at examinations cannot be called as special education as well. If the education related problems of persons with disabilities can be resolved by reasonable accommodation and/or educational support, naming should also be done accordingly.

If the types of support which are provided individually to persons and do not include methods and education programmes specific to special education in terms of content are not named as special education, this will also prevent the labelling of these students as inclusion/integration students. Fulfilment of such needs should be left to the school administration and a board consisting of administrators, educators and counselling experts with the participation of the relevant student and the family should plan what kind of measures should be taken for the person with disability as well as who should provide this support and for how long. This plan can also be called an individual support plan. If education related special needs cannot be fulfilled via measures taken within the school and problems cannot be resolved, the person with disability can be referred to medical and/or educational assessment and counselling services may be obtained from competent experts and persons. In short, we try to explain that special education and special need for support do not mean the same thing. An abandonment of the wording in the legislation on education that persons with disabilities are indicated categorically as those needing special education, any reasonable accommodation and support which will be provided to any when required for education are named as special educational needs will not only alleviate the burden on bureaucratic processes, but also better protect the students' right to education and alleviate the burden on the families.

Regulation on Special Education Services defines inclusive education as, *special education applications which are based on the practice of persons in need of special education pursuing their education together with their peers without deficiencies while being provided with support education services in public and private; pre-school, primary education, secondary education and adult educational institutions* (Art. 23/1). This definition demonstrates that persons with disabilities who do not require special education in the sense we tried to explain above do not need to receive education under the name of integration. Another salient point of the definition is that it presents the need for special education and the support education service as two separate choices for fulfilling the education related needs. Therefore, it can be concluded that support education service, as we explained above, is not considered only as a service to be provided to those in need of special education.

In the same article of the Regulation, the principles to be considered during the inclusive education practices are also regulated. Accordingly, first it will be ensured that persons in need of special education pursue their education in the same institution as their peers who have no deficiency. It can be concluded from the explanation in the provision following the definition which states that inclusive education can be pursued full-time in the same classes as peers without deficiencies or part time in special education classes that, the practice of inclusion is predicated on the basis of institutional unity. The explanation stating that part time inclusion practices will be carried out via participation of students in certain courses or extra-curricular activities together with their peers who do not have any deficiencies indicates that part time inclusion can be carried out through two options in practice. Part time inclusion to be implemented under these conditions carries the risk of misuse of the right.

Complaints in practice indicate that one of the risks is caused by the places chosen for special education classes. Although being in the institutions where regular education is provided, special education classes opened in a far away corner, distant from other education classes or in separate corridors will cause the persons with disabilities to become excluded and isolated again. Due to the selection of the location, it is not even possible for persons attending courses in these classes to run into their peers without deficiencies during breaks. Breaks comprise most of extra-curricular activities. If there is a dining hall at the school, inclusion of the students in the special education class with others is not possible except for gathering during the lunch break. Unless standards are defined for the continuous and effective participation of these students in official holidays and flag raising ceremonies as well as excursions outside the school and other social events, the benefit expected from such an inclusion practice cannot be achieved and also the phenomenon of socialisation which is one of the goals of this education cannot be actualised. Practice may vary based on institutions according to the initiative of the school administration and teachers, it may be implemented to different extents or may be completely ignored. In this regard, the arrangement in the Regulation is not sufficient. In the Regulation, measures are incorporated stating that the location of these classrooms in schools shall be determined by taking into account the type of deficiency of students and arrangements shall be made for ensuring that students who attend special education classes in schools and institutions participate in certain courses and social activities together with their peers who do not have any deficiencies (Art. 27/2-1, h). However, there is no explanation on how these provisions will be implemented and audited. As far as we know, the Ministry has no circulars or directives in this regard.

Convention on the Rights of Persons with Disabilities is based on the access of persons with disabilities to integrative primary and secondary education within the environment in which they live, on the equal basis with others. According to the Convention, integration is one of the ways to socialise persons with disabilities through education and maximise their academic and individual development. Integration in education is a principle for ensuring that persons with disabilities receive the same education as others in terms of educational setting as well as education opportunities and services. The practice of special education classes does not comply with the integration philosophy of the Convention. Implementing the education programme used in the school for some of the persons in the special education classes while for others implementing the education programme of special education schools and institutions opened for persons with same deficiencies ultimately creates inequality between these two groups. Because, persons with disabilities who are in no condition to follow the programmes of primary or secondary educational institutions are given a completion certificate instead of a diploma which would enable them to continue to higher levels of education when they graduate.

Persons with disabilities who receive education in such classes during the primary education period will not be able to continue their education at the same status at the same institution, even if the institution has a secondary education section. Because, in the Regulation, it is prescribed that special education classes shall be opened within secondary education and adult educational institutions only for those in need of special education but able to follow the programmes of primary or secondary educational institutions. Special education class students other than these shall continue to special education institutions which offer education under the names such as work schools, education centres etc. after primary school. Statements and complaints of families also point out that special education classes of such nature do not actually serve for integration in practice and inclusion only seems to be effective in appearance. Regulation should either be recast in a manner to make education functional in these classes in accordance with the principles and goals of integration or this practice should be abandoned.

It is impossible to understand why persons with disabilities who are in special education classes but also able to follow education programmes of the institution pursue their education in separate classes. Since it is a legal obligation to open support education rooms, conduct Individualised Education Programmes (BEP in Turkish) and establish relevant units in these institutions, while it is possible for students with disabilities to pursue their education in the same classes with their peers when these measures are implemented effectively, it is against the Convention to opt for separation. Such practices should be ceased.

Regulation regulates in detail the principles regarding the inclusion practices and measures to be taken. The following will be put into practice on the basis of certain principles: the number of children in classrooms, equal distribution of students with disabilities to the classrooms, establishment of BEP units, educating students according to this plan, opening support education rooms, making arrangements in physical, social and psychological environments in accordance with the deficiency of the student, providing special materials and equipment and education materials in order to ensure that the education services provided to the student are carried out effectively, providing information to the personnel and other students in the institution and their families by relevant persons in the Counselling and Research Centre (RAM in Turkish) and BEP development unit in line with the planning conducted by the school administration on the characteristics of individuals in need of special education and the assessment of success. It is obvious that such measures will serve for the integration of person with disabilities via education and in education in practice.

However, all regulations on inclusive education in the Regulation target schools and institutions in which inclusive education practices are implemented. Many provisions are regulated by making reference to *schools and institutions where inclusive education practices are implemented.* However, public and private primary and secondary educational institutions are candidates for inclusion and obliged to implement this practice. A part of the obligation of educational institutions in this regard is the obligation which needs to be discharged based on the possibility of having students with inclusion status one day, even if the institution does not have any at the moment. Measures regarding the physical and institutional structure of the school/institution possess this nature. For instance, BEP units, support education rooms, and accessible buildings arranged in accordance with the universal design will serve for the solution of the problems of persons who have temporary disabilities, those who had disabilities afterwards for any reason and students who had psychological or psychiatric problems in their childhood or adolescence periods which were reflected on education regarding these conditions. It is possible to eliminate education related failures by preparing an individual working plan for the student, carrying out this plan effectively and providing support education. Reasonable accommodation will work in such periods. Therefore, a match will be achieved with the meaning associated by the Convention with inclusive education by building new school and institution buildings in compliance with the universal design, structuring BEP units and support education rooms as a standard in all schools and organising educational staff in a manner to put these units and rooms into practice in a functional way. Besides, when a student enrols for inclusive education in schools which do not have such a structure, it takes a certain time for schools to create such structures and the fulfilment of the educational needs of the students gets delayed. However, it is a well-known fact that the earlier the intervention to the education of persons with disabilities, the more positive and effective the result becomes.

For the fulfilment of special educational needs, of course the education in schools/institutions opened for this specific purpose (in separated settings) can also be preferred. However, when separated education is regarded as the fundamental method for the education of persons with disabilities, two major problems may appear in terms of the right to education. First, special education institutions are not in the condition to serve for all children with disabilities which are excluded from the general education system in terms of quantity and capacity.[110] According to the calculations of the World Health Organisation, only 5% of the children with disabilities in developing countries can benefit from all kinds of services and support, while the attendance to school is under 2%. One of the most important causes of this situation is the fact that children with disabilities are usually the children of poor families in poor countries.[111] Even if the family's economic power is adequate, unless they find a proper school to send their children, they still get excluded from education. Exclusion of the majority of these children from education due to not being accepted to regular schools, the low number of special education schools or the fact that they are not suitable for the disability types cause discrimination and

110 For examples of practices in the Latin American and Caribbean countries, see: **Porter L. Gordon** "Disability and Education: Towards an Inclusive Approach", *SDS Working Paper*, 2001, p.6.

111 **Porter L. Gordon** "Disability and Education: Towards an Inclusive Approach", *SDS Working Paper*, 2001, p.6.

inequality both between children with disabilities and their peers without disabilities as well as among persons with disabilities. Another negative effect of special education in separate schools on the right to education is that, some children with disabilities who can pursue their education in regular schools when proper support is provided, and their educational needs are met are forced to attend special education schools. This results in serious disadvantages for these children. First of all, particularly in developing countries, special education does not have the quality to ensure that children with disabilities pursue an independent and honourable life.[112] Moreover educating persons with disabilities in separate settings or in special classrooms inside regular schools is a practice which reinforces discrimination and exclusion. Another negative result is that, after graduating from these schools, persons cannot continue to educational institutions within the general system and there is no equivalency between special and general education systems in terms of graduation as well. With this practice, the essence of the right to education of children is damaged who has the capacity to pursue education in regular schools and get to the high levels of formal education regardless of the diagnosis or level of their deficiency and the right itself gets taken away.[113]

In order to prevent a misunderstanding about the integrative education system this addition should be made. In the integrative education approach, the need for special schools and centres and the special education classes within regular schools is not completely denied. In cases of disabilities with complex challenges and for those who cannot achieve success in education in spite of all the support provided in regular classes or those who will disturb the education programme of their peers may require education in special classes. When the framework for integrative education is drawn as "100% integration" it is already hard to achieve a universal success in practice and moreover, this system may not be beneficial for all children with disabilities to the same extent. Unless the need for assistive teachers or experts for implementing the education programme suitable for the children with disabilities within the crowded classes is met, and in certain cases, the necessary one-on-one support is not provided, students with disabilities cannot benefit from this education effectively. Regarding the placement of children with disabilities in the regular school programmes, attitudinal obstacles should also be considered in addition to the institutional arrangements. However, the practice of top priority should be to take necessary measures to ensure that students with disabilities pursue their

---

112 While it is not the comparative data showing the academic achievements, preparation for higher education, participation rates in work and other spheres of social life; some studies on students with disabilities in secondary education in 1985 found out that the academic performance of those who studied in regular schools was 80% whereas that of those educated in separated/special educational institutions was 50%. **R. Weiner,** *Impact on the Schools,* Capitol Publications, 1985 quoted by "Special Education Inclusion", 15 March 2007, http://www.weac.org/resource/june96/speced.htm, (18.03.2008)

113 CRC/C/SR.418, para.2.

education with their normal peers. Research also supports this realistic objective. Comprehensive research across the world shows that, the number of children and teenagers with severe disabilities is quite low. 80–90% of those in need of special education are in the condition to pursue their education in general education schools and regular schools when the necessary prerequisites are met.[114]

Transition to integrative education is not a process which can be ensured via simple technical or institutional changes. It is a current of thought with clear philosophical foundation based on certain principles. Efforts were made to popularise this philosophy and put it into a normative framework via international declarations, conventions and reports. In the Convention on the Rights of Persons with disabilities which is the most recent example in this regard, the integrated society and integrated education perspective and principles reflect a philosophy which penetrated the whole Convention. In that sense, the priority of States which adopted the Convention should be to transform their internal law order to be in harmony with the norms and standards in the Convention on integrative education. In other words, States are obliged to make new legal regulations to repeal practices which hinder persons with disabilities from receiving education on the equal basis with others, review existing regulations and amend provisions which prevent integration in accordance with universal acceptance.

a. Integration Process

Integrative education consists of two stages in terms of the process: the referral to integrative education and placement, and the integrative education period.

aa. Educational Assessment, Diagnosis and Referral

In Turkey, education of children with disabilities under inclusion or in special education classes and special education institutions depends on the referral after educational assessment and diagnosis. In Law No. 5378, it is prescribed that processes regarding the educational assessment, diagnosis and referral of persons will be carried out by the Special Education Assessment Board established under the counselling and research centre. However, during all stages of this process, families shall be informed, and their participation shall be ensured. Special Education Assessment Board refers persons in need of special education to formal and adult educational institutions in accordance with their interests, desires, development properties, competence in academic disciplines and educational needs [Article 16 – (Amended: 6/2/2014-6518/74 Art.)].

The regulation in the Decree-Law on Special Education is also of a similar nature. However, despite a couple of minor amendments, the original text from 1997

114 **Ture Jonsson & Ronald Wiman**, "Education, Poverty and Disability in Developing Countries", *A Technical Note Prepared for the Poverty Redaction Sourcebook*, 21 June 2001, pp. 6–7.

has been kept the same, so the term "placement" is used in the Decree-Law and the term "referral" is not incorporated. This situation, which can be accepted as normal in those years due to the lack of an organisation such as Special Education Assessment Boards, should be accepted as a deficiency at the moment. According to the Decree-Law, diagnosis is a process which can be carried out at any stage for determining the educational performance level of the individual, evaluate his/her properties in development areas and decide for placement of the individual to the most suitable educational setting by planning the educational goals and services in accordance with the results of this assessment (Art. 5).

Regulation on Special Education Services regulates the whole process in detail. Regulation also defines the term diagnosis in its "Definitions" article. This definition includes not only educational diagnosis but also the assessment of the individual in medical and psycho-social aspects. However, the subject of "diagnosis" which refers to the assessment process which is conducted regarding medical, psycho-social and educational aspects for determining characteristics of persons in all development areas as well as their competent and incompetent features, personal features and interests is those who need special education. The definition of "diagnosis" which is made with a reference to special education, is another example which demonstrates that the basis in Turkish law is the assumption that all persons with disabilities require special education. We previously explained with examples that this relationship is not absolute and all persons with disabilities do not necessarily need special education. Besides; the medical diagnosis mentioned in the definition is a process which is carried out by evaluating the competence or deficiency as well as development related properties of the person via medical materials and methods, without considering whether he/she is in need of special education. If a relationship is absolutely required, it can be established between medical diagnosis and the persons with disabilities and their disability status. The Regulation on the Impairment Criteria, Classification and Medical Board Reports to be Issued for the Impaired which entered into force on 30 March 2013[115] comprises the medical board reports for the impaired requested to enjoy the rights and services provided, authorised medical institutions which can issue medical board reports for the impaired as well as classifications and criteria on the impaired (Art. 2/1). One of the goals of the Regulation is to develop a common practice in areas where grading, classification and definitions are required for the impaired and popularise the use of international classifications and criteria (Art. 1/1).

Since the Regulation on Special Education Services is a special education themed Regulation, it is acceptable that definitions are made based on the "need for special education", however it is not possible to say that this is always consistent and accurate. Because, the process that will determine whether the person needs special education is the educational diagnosis itself. As in the example where the parents

115 While the Regulation is relatively new, its language is old. The terms impaired, impairment etc. in the Regulation should be replaced by disability etc.

notice the different developmental aspects, deficiency or competence beyond the measurement scale (for children with superior intelligence) of their children and go to Counselling and Research Centre and request an educational assessment, whether the child requires special education or not will be decided after the psycho-social and educational tests. Therefore, the phrase *need for special education* should be removed from the definition of "diagnosis".

In the article titled *Educational Assessment and diagnosis* of the Regulation, the educational assessment and diagnosis process is explained without making a reference to the "need for special education" (Art. 7/1). The sentence "Persons whose need for special education is determined after educational assessment and diagnosis" in the same article of the Regulation also lays down that the special educational needs are usually determined as a result of this process (Art. 7/4). According to the Regulation, educational assessment and diagnosis will be carried out *with an educational purpose in order to identify the characteristics of the persons in all development areas and competences in academic disciplines as well as educational needs and decide on the least restricted educational setting and special education service* (Art. 7/1) and *will be repeated upon the request from the parents or school/institution when necessary by taking into account the transition into all types and levels of education as well as the educational performance and needs of the individual* (Art. 7/3).

The decision made for persons about where and how they will receive education whose need for special education is identified after their educational assessment and diagnosis, or those who already started special education but was subject to educational assessment again is called as "referral". This process is regulated in the Regulation on Special Education Services with its principles. The main principle of the process is that the individual pursues education in *the least restricted environment* according to the *developed education plan.* When the environments where persons with special needs can pursue education are listed, *from the most restricting to the least restricting* it goes as; special education boarding school – special education day school – special education class – part time inclusion – resource room supported inclusion – full-time inclusion.[116] In Turkey, the special education provided in special education and rehabilitation centres should be added into this order.

While the least restricting educational setting for many students with special needs is full-time inclusion, for a smaller portion, it is the resource room supported inclusion. The fact that steps become narrower as one goes up means that the number of students required to be in those educational settings gradually decreases.

---

116 *Kaynaştırma / Bütünleştirmenin Etkililiğini Arttırmak İçin Politika ve Uygulama Önerileri Projesi Türkiye'de Kaynaştırma/Bütünleştirme Yoluyla Eğitimin Durumu* [*Project on Policy and Practice Recommendations to Increase Efficiency of Inclusion/Integration: State of Inclusion/Integration Education in Turkey*], Yayına Hazırlayanlar [Prepared for publication by: Ayşe Nal/Işık Tüzün], Eğitim Reformu Girişimi – Tohum Otizm Vakfı [Education Reform Initiative -Tohum Autism Foundation], 2011, p.11.

For instance, a very small portion of students with special needs require the most restricting environment, which is the special education boarding schools.

In Turkey, students with special needs can pursue their education in separate special education schools, in special classes within general education schools or as inclusion students in general education classes. The regulation on special education schools was made in the Article 18 of the Decree-Law No. 573 on Special Education as "Day or boarding special education schools shall be opened for persons whose conditions require special education in a separate school according to their impairments and characteristics". In these schools, the aim is to ensure that students obtain academic and occupational skills. In Article 20 of the Decree-Law, it is prescribed that students with special needs can pursue their education in special classes within general education schools.[117] We previously made our criticism on the practice of special education classes.

There are several recommendations in the international law as well on the kind of schools where children with disabilities should be educated. In this regard, United Nations Committee on the Rights of the Child (CRC) advocates for minding the "best interest of the child". The principle of "best interest of the child" which is one of the four fundamental principles of children's rights in the United Nations Convention on the Rights of the Child, refers to "best interests of the child being a primary consideration in all actions concerning children, whether undertaken by public or private social welfare institutions, courts of law, administrative authorities or legislative bodies". Children in need of special education should pursue their education in general schools and should only attend special schools with adequate equipment in cases when their best interest cannot be ensured.[118]

While adopting the principle of educating children with disabilities in the general education schools with their peers, the emphasis is laid on taking necessary measures for the integration of children with disabilities and providing adequate support. Measures and types of support stated by the CRC are training teachers in this regard, ensuring that the physical environment is accessible and preparing the school curriculum by considering the needs of children with disabilities. Another point stressed by the Committee is determining the number of children who cannot receive education and their educational needs in terms of general and Vocational education and thus ensure access of these children to education. In the General Comment published by CRC on children with disabilities, it is mentioned that prohibition of discrimination on the basis of disability should be incorporated explicitly in the legislation and that ultimate responsibility regarding the services provided to persons with disabilities belongs to the State. It is highlighted that resources allocated for children with disabilities should be used first for making all schools physically accessible for children with disabilities, and then for training teachers, carrying out education campaigns, providing income support to families

117 Ibid. pp. 11–12.
118 Ibid., pp. 17–18.

and providing assistive materials and equipment. The European Committee of Social Rights (ECSR) which is the oversight body of the European Social Charter of 1961 and the Revised European Social Charter emphasises that children with disabilities should be educated in general education schools and refers to it as "the right to be educated in general schools on an equal basis".[119]

International human rights legislation imposes an obligation on States to prohibit discrimination on the basis of disability regarding the access to education. Education of children with disabilities in general education schools is adopted as a principle. Only in cases when it is required for the best interest of the child it is deemed appropriate to attend special education institutions. It is emphasised that all individual needs of children with disabilities should be met in both private and general educational institutions otherwise it is also considered as discrimination. It is stipulated that, when necessary, adaptations should be made with regard to education methods, curriculum and assessment and the physical environment should be arranged by taking into account the children with disabilities. Moreover, the State is also obliged regarding the access of children with disabilities to education for training adequate number of teachers, building schools and providing special education support.[120]

In Finland, which is one of the good examples in this regard, all students including those with special needs participate in the same basic education system and almost all children (99,7%) complete their basic education. Only 2% of all children go to special education schools. Again, more than 96% of these children receive preschool education. Various steps were taken in the education system, school settings and pedagogic sense in Finland in order to ensure that every child receives education with adequate support in general education schools and achieves multifaceted development. In the regulations in force called Finnish Basic Law on Education (1998) and Basic National Curriculum for Basic Education (2004), it is emphasised that every child has the right to receive education in the general education school closest to him/her and receive individual support; instead of focusing on the problems of one student, the whole school and the learning environment should be improved.[121]

Children with special needs achieved significant gains regarding receiving quality education in the least restricting educational settings with the movement for the rights of persons with disabilities which was as a part of the human rights movement initiated in the 1950s and 1960s in the USA. Achieved rights were followed closely by families and they pressured states and schools to actualise the practices incorporated in the legislation. As a result of all these developments, students with special needs in the USA started receiving education in the least restricting

119 Ibid., pp. 17–18.

120 Ibid., pp. 17–18.

121 Project on Policy and Practice Recommendations to Increase Efficiency of Inclusion/Integration: Best Practices of Inclusion/Integration Education in Turkey and in the World, ERG, 2011, p.14.

environments where they could be together with their peers the most, while their educational needs are also met in the best way possible. With the Individuals with Disabilities Education Act (IDEA) adopted in the USA in 1990 and entered into force in 1997, rights of children with special needs regarding benefiting from free education in the least restricting environment were expanded. However, this did not happen on its own, families pressured schools to undertake legal obligations when their children did not receive adequate service and court decisions and human rights movements had impact on this change. Therefore, more and more students with special needs in the USA started going to closest general education schools instead of special education schools, various institutes and home schooling. A sound infrastructure was established for early diagnosis, assessment and providing required services for the education of persons with special needs, the number of special education teachers was significantly increased, and these teachers were provided with more comprehensive education and ensured to integrate better with schools. More students with special needs started attending general education schools in their neighbourhoods and developing their academic skills on a wide scale. According to the data, in 2008, 95% of the students with special needs in the USA started attending general education schools close to where they live. In addition, there was an increase in reading skills of students with special needs and this increase significantly reduced the academic gap between students with special needs and other students.[122]

Its impact on placement decisions makes educational assessment and diagnosis important for the right to education of persons with disabilities.[123] Problems stemming from the structure and operation of counselling and research centres which will carry out assessment and diagnosis result in discussions about the reliability of the reports issued by these institutions. Problems caused by the institutional structure become legal problems and result in discrimination allegations or appeals against assessment and diagnosis decisions as well as placement decisions. Appeals lodged against educational assessment and diagnosis and placement decisions are resolved by Special Education Services Boards (Art. 16/1-ğ). However, there are personnel from the counselling and research centre (RAM) in the Special Education Services Board and decisions are made with the majority of votes. When there is only one RAM in the province and the same RAM personnel participates in the Special Education Services Board, the principle of impartiality becomes compromised during the assessment of appeals. Same problems apply to the placement decisions

122 *Project on Policy and Practice Recommendations to Increase Efficiency of Inclusion/ Integration: Best Practices of Inclusion/Integration Education in Turkey and in the World*, ERG, 2011, pp. 19–20.

123 According to the Regulation on Special Education Services, the board of special education services decide along the board of special education assessment reports (Art.16/a).

as well. The appeal against the placement decision is lodged to the Board which issues the decision and there is not superior board to evaluate appeals.

In accordance with the objective of increasing the effectiveness of diagnosis mechanisms and strengthening the trust of different actors in this process, the roles of RAMs, schools and families in the diagnosis process in Turkey should be reviewed in favour of children and mechanisms should be developed for establishing mutual trust among these three actors. It is particularly important that a multifaceted and multi-step assessment system is developed for students with special needs and this assessment is repeated periodically. For instance, it is observed in England that a uniform assessment and education approach is not adequate for determining and fulfilling the needs of all children with special needs and therefore, a five-step special education assessment and teaching system was established. While informal assessment and inclusion is implemented in the first three of these steps, formal assessment and, when necessary, separation is carried out in the following two steps. These steps can be summarised as follows:

1. Step: Class or branch teacher informally assesses a student who he/she thinks that is not able to benefit fully from the education and prepares an individualised education programme for the student. In this regard, teachers consult the special education coordinator and the coordinator keeps records of these students.
2. Step: At this stage, first the special education coordinator becomes responsible for the student with special needs. Special education coordinator works together with the class teacher and conducts an informal assessment and prepares an individualised education programme.
3. Step: Special education coordinator receives support from experts outside the school and conducts an informal assessment and prepares an individualised education programme for the student with special needs. Support education personnel such as audiologists or language and speaking experts are provided by local education administrations or via special education institutions.
4. Step: At this stage, special education coordinator sends the student with special needs to the local education administration with a request for a formal assessment. At this institution, the services previously provided to the student at the school by his/her teacher and special education coordinator are examined, and a decision is made for whether he/she needs formal assessment. When it is deemed necessary, formal assessment is carried out by an inter-disciplinary team. As a result of the assessment, a decision is made on the educational setting where the student will pursue his/her education.
5. Step: A decision is made by the local education administration on whether the child will be identified as having special needs. Official identification may be required for certain special education services.

Such a multi-step assessment ensures that the needs of students are determined in the best way possible, while also establishing effective communication among the class teacher, special education coordinator and other experts.[124]

ab. Principles and Rules About the Placement and Education Processes

aba. Placement

Law No. 5378 has laid down several general principles regarding the services to be provided to persons with disabilities and some of these are: prohibition of discrimination and combat against discrimination, equality of opportunity in enjoyment of rights and services, accessibility for full and effective participation in independent living and the society, protection of family integrity, minding the best interest of the child, preventing multifaceted discrimination against women and girls with disabilities and participation in processes of decision making and service delivery (Art. 4-Amended: 6/2/2014-6518/64 Art.). These principles are quite important and meaningful for the right to education of persons with disabilities. Also, they are in compliance with the CRPD. These principles must be considered when making placement decisions on where and how persons with disabilities pursue will their education. In the provision on the right to education regulated in Article 15 of LPD, some of these articles were incorporated separately and it was indicated that the right to education of persons with disabilities cannot be actualised fully without these principles. However, in the Law, there is no special provision on the placement of persons with disabilities in educational institutions.

In the Decree-Law on Special Education, after the principles for special education are listed, the education and training process is regulated. Placement, which is one of the leading processes, was defined as placement to the most suitable educational setting and the nature of the process was taken into account. It is laid down that planning shall be conducted based on the goals of the education of the individual before the placement and opinions of the family shall be taken and their participation shall be ensured at every stage (Art. 5).

The Regulation on Special Education Services regulates the placement process with a detailed separate provision. Accordingly, the placement decision is a decision to be made by the Special Education Services Board in line with the special education assessment board report (Art. 12). While this article is based on the placement of the individual in the suitable public school or institution, if the special education assessment board report and the family request so, a decision can be made for the student to pursue education via inclusive education in the school in which he/she is already enrolled. In the second paragraph of the article, the points to be considered for the placement of individuals in suitable educational settings are listed: while

124 *Project on Policy and Practice Recommendations to Increase Efficiency of Inclusion/Integration: Best Practices of Inclusion/Integration Education in Turkey and in the World*, ERG, 2011, p.14.

making a placement in the school or institution closest to the place of residence, attention shall also be paid in order to ensure that the environment is as little restricting as possible. A provision among these principles which prescribes that placement shall be carried out according to the type and degree of the deficiency of persons, their performance in all development areas and academic disciplines, educational needs, interests and desires is attention-grabbing in these aspects: It will be possible to learn about the type and degree of deficiency of the individual from his/her medical board report, if available. However, the medical performance and educational performance of persons who has never received any education and will just start special education for the first time will be different.

Medical board reports issued via medical assessment of the individual and determination of the level of disability are unfortunately insufficient in Turkey for measuring the actual performance and functioning of the person. The reason behind this is that, although the Regulation on the Impairment Criteria, Classification and Medical Board Reports to be Issued for the Impaired (Effective date: 30 March 2013) states that disability classifications as well as diagnosis and criteria will be carried out by taking into account the international criteria (ICF classification of the World Health Organisation), these criteria are not properly used in diagnosis and assessment of persons with disabilities. In the International Classification of Functioning, Disability and Health (ICF) developed by the World Health Organisation and used for assessment and planning of the services about the treatment, rehabilitation, education and employment of persons with disabilities;

1. Focus is on the whole functioning system of a person; functions are assessed on a wide scale ranging from, 'no impairment in function and structure' to 'full impairment in function and structure'.
2. Classification mostly aims to reveal the impact of impairments on persons, rather than the causes of impairment. The existence and impact of environmental factors are addressed in a larger extent in the framework of both the person and the relationships with the society.
3. Health and health-related areas are defined in two lists as body functions and structures and the activities and participation.
4. Functioning is used as an umbrella term encompassing all body functions, activities and participation; while disability serves as an umbrella term for impairments, activity limitations or participation restrictions. In addition, environmental factors in interaction with these structures are also listed.[125]

---

125 *ICF, İşlevsellik, Yetiyitimi ve Sağlığın Uluslar arası Sınıflandırılması*, Çevirenler: **Elif Kabakçı / Ahmet Göğüş**, T.C. Başbakanlık Özürlüler İdaresi Başkanlığı-World Health Organization 2004 [*ICF, International Classification of Functioning, Disability and Health*, Translated by: **Elif Kabakçı / Ahmet Göğüş**, T.R. Prime Ministry Administration for the Disabled People – World Health Organisation 2004]; Children and Disability in Transition in CEE/CIS and Baltic States, Innocenti Insight, UNICEF 2005, p. 2.

The Schedule of Impairment Rates prepared as the annex to the Regulation on the Impairment Criteria, Classification and Medical Board Reports to be Issued for the Impaired and used for determining the disability rates in Turkey (Annex 2) is not in compliance with the coding of ICF classification system. Some of the determinants in the Schedule are not clearly and explicitly defined and unlike ICF, examples are not provided. According to the Schedule, functions and disabilities of the person are mostly assessed based on impairments in functions or diseases and the unplanned participation and performance limitations which persons may encounter within natural life as well as the impact of environmental factors on these areas are not considered sufficiently. It is impossible to say that such measurements and assessments always end in accurate results for what a person with disability can do under appropriate circumstances and with support, if necessary. In addition, this may result in different measurements by different healthcare institutions as well as different impairment rates for the competences and functions of the same person.

What we are trying to say is that, type and degree of disability of a person cannot be determined by focusing on a condition based on his/her disability or caused by his/her disability. It is hard to make a clear decision on what a person can and cannot do via medical examinations and couple of tests conducted at a hospital without considering the environment and other mechanisms we refer as external factors. Because, a person may show a much better performance in a proper setting with proper support, or in contrast, he/she may not show all of his/her competences and performance in an improper setting. Therefore, it is important to amend the Schedule of Impairment Rates prepared as an annex to the Regulation in a manner to correspond to the ICF system completely and carry out measurements and classifications, which affect the actualisation of many rights of persons with disabilities including education, in accordance with the international system.

Similarly, the fact that their "performance in all development areas and academic disciplines" will be taken into account in placement of persons in educational institutions according to the Regulation, as explained above, should be via assessments which have been controlled for effectiveness through several stages, to be conducted in proper settings, by competent experts, by using suitable tests and other methods. Placements made based on diagnosis and educational assessment conducted without a multi-step assessment method suitable for determining academic, social, psychological and other development areas of persons to an extent closest to accurate, and if the environment in the school/institution in which the child is placed (physical conditions, quality of educators and administrators, attitudes of other students and families etc.) is also not suitable, result in an education off to a bad start and will affect the whole education life of the child negatively, harm his/her right to education and deprive him/her of the chance to quality and proper education.

According to the Regulation, another point to be taken into consideration in placement is taking into account the personnel status, number of students and the education setting in the school or institution in which the persons will be placed. While this provision seems to be positive in terms of acting according to the principle of best interest of the child while fulfilling his/her special educational needs, on the other hand, it implies that it is accepted that not all schools or institutions in Turkey have a structure suitable for the requirements of integrative education. As we previously criticised, unless all institutions providing education at all types and levels within the compulsory education period are structured in a manner to potentially provide inclusive education, fundamental principles on the right to education of the Convention such as providing special education in the least restricting environment possible, best interest of the child, full and effective participation in society and equality of opportunity will not be put into practice. Schools/institutions should have a structure and functioning suitable for inclusive education from the start, not after an inclusion student is sent to them. In terms of full actualisation of these principles of the Convention and the right to education, it should be recognised that a child in need of special educational needs to be placed in the most suitable educational setting within *a structure of such quality.* Therefore, all provisions of this nature should be amended starting from the relevant laws and moving to the lowest level regulations, a law system should be established based on actual integrative education.

The provision which regulates appeals against placement decisions is also open to criticism. This provision stipulates that parents of the person can lodge an appeal within 70 work days following the decision date, and the executive commission on guidance and psychological counselling at the school or institution which is subject to the placement decision can lodge an appeal within 70 work days following the date of enrolment. This time period may not always be sufficient for making the right decision on the nature and the suitability of an education like special educational needs, which provides a result in the long term, for the child. In the following section of the provision, it is stated that *a new decision can be made for placement in a new school or institution at all stages of education according to the condition of the person based on his/her development and educational performance*, and an opportunity is provided to the child and the family. However, due to the fact that the child usually shows a development to the better, this opportunity is based on the perception which refers to, for instance, the transition of the child from a special education institution to an inclusion school or from a special education class to an inclusion class.

ac. Principles and Measures Regarding the Education Period

This period refers to the education provided under the rules and principles applicable during the time the child starts inclusive education and afterwards as well as the educational setting. The most indicative aspect of this period is the preparation of an education plan and programme specific to the child and carrying out the general education within integrative education as well as the special education based on these plans.

aca. Individualised Education Programme (BEP in Turkish)

This is prescribed in the Decree-Law on Special Education as; *It is essential that individualised education plans are developed for persons in need of special education and education programmes are implemented via individualisation* (Art. 4/f). Similar phrases are used in the Regulation on Special Education Services as; *Individualised education plans shall be developed by taking into account the individual competences of persons in need of special education as well as their characteristics in all development areas and competences in the academic disciplines and education programmes shall be applied via individualisation* (Art. 6/1-e). Principle of individualised education for persons in need of special education has been materialised in both legal regulations. Pursuant to the Decree-Law, education programmes in special education shall be implemented by considering the educational performance of persons and adapting the goals of the programme to the individual (Art. 15).

Decree-Law incorporates a different provision in terms of education programmes compared to the Regulation on Education Services. That is; regular school programmes shall be implemented also in the special education schools and classes; however, arrangements shall be made on these programmes by considering characteristics and learning competences of students in a manner to maintain the equivalency. Programmes of special education schools and classes shall be prepared with an approach which aims to ensure that students achieve the competence to pursue their education in regular schools together with their peers (Art. 15). However, according to the Decree-Law this is not an absolute situation and special education programmes can also be implemented in special education schools and classes with periods and contents prepared according to the characteristics of students.

In the provision titled *Education programmes* of the Regulation, a certain distinction was made by prescribing that general and Vocational education programmes prepared by the Ministry shall be implemented in schools and institutions to which the persons in need of special education attend while special education programmes with contents prepared according to the characteristics of students shall be implemented in special education schools, institutions and classes (Art. 68/1). This distinction also exists in the provision of the Regulation which regulates inclusive education. Accordingly, if persons who participate in inclusive education pursue their education in the same classes with their peers without any deficiencies, they shall follow the education programme implemented at the school in which they are enrolled; and those in special education classes shall follow the education programme prescribed in Articles 26 and 27 of the Regulation depending on the type of the classes. Based on the programmes followed by students, BEPs shall be prepared in accordance with the educational performances and needs of students. Without repeating what we previously said about the practice of special education classes, this can be said: Article 26 of the Regulation prescribes that in the special education classes opened for persons of the compulsory education age who are able to follow the primary or secondary education programmes, the same programme shall be followed as their normal peers, while Article 27 prescribes that in special education classes opened for those who cannot follow these programmes, the programmes of special education schools and institutions opened for persons with similar deficiencies in terms of education and training shall be followed and therefore the inclusive education has been hollowed (i.e. its contents have been impaired).

Individualised education programme is defined in the Regulation as, *a special education programme which is prepared in accordance with the goals targeted in line with the development characteristics, educational performances and needs of persons in need of special education which also include the support education services to be provided to these persons* (Art. 69/1). Inferences made from this definition are as follows;

1. Individualised education programmes are prepared only for persons in need of special education. If we go back to the point we previously addressed and criticised, Regulation regulates all matters based on the "need for special education" and excludes persons with disabilities who do not need such education but are still in need of certain types of support or special arrangements in education. Therefore, we would like to emphasise once more that rather than a legislation regulating the special education period, a legislation regulating the "education of persons with disabilities" in a more general sense is required.
2. Individualised education programme also comprises the support education services to be provided. As we previously explained, support education may be required for any child in any period of their education life regardless of being in need of special education. This also supports our comment above.
3. Individualised education programme is an umbrella concept in terms of individualisation of education. According to the Regulation, this concept includes (Art. 69/2);

   a) Annual goals in the education plan as well as the short-term goals determined based on the education programme(s) followed by the student,
   b) Type, duration, frequency of the support education to be received by the student as well as the persons who will provide this service,
   c) Methods and techniques, materials and equipment and education materials to be used in teaching and assessment,
   d) Arrangements regarding the educational setting,
   e) Methods and techniques to be implemented in order to prevent or reduce behavioural problems,
   f) Personal information of the student.

An individualised education programme with such a broad scope has a nature of being implemented for all students within the compulsory education period who has temporary disabilities, psychological-psychiatric problems as well as behavioural and social relationship related issues. In this regard, it will be beneficial to ensure that the BEP concept covers the whole education system including all students within the compulsory education period without being limited to students in need of special education and to recast the education legislation (general education-special education) in a manner to develop such a practice.

4. BEP is not a process which is completed once it is prepared, it can be renewed according to the changing needs of the person and the situations encountered during the implementation of the programme. The education plan within the BEP must be renewed every year (Art. 13/2).

As is seen, the BEP concept, which is regulated in detail in the Regulation in connection with the need for special education, is a key notion for the education of persons with disabilities besides those in the compulsory education period but not in need of special education. In other words, it seems to be a notion which encompasses all of the 4 elements we used in our explanations on the content of the right to education of persons with disabilities and the duties and obligations of the State; existence, accessibility, adaptability and admissibility. Due to the importance of this establishment in terms of ensuring that persons with disabilities receive equal, suitable and quality education; the composition, officers, duties and powers and the oversight of this establishment are quite important and indicative. According to the Regulation on Special Education Services, individualised education programmes shall be prepared under the cooperation of the Special Education Assessment Board and BEP development unit (Art. 69/3). Individualised education programme development units comprise of the following persons within the schools and institutions in which students in need of special education pursue special education: (Art. 72/2) Under the chairmanship the school/institution director or a deputy director to be delegated by him/her;

a) A teacher who provides special education on a mobile basis,
b) A guidance counsellor,
c) A teacher assigned to prepare education programmes,
d) Class teacher of the student,
e) Branch teachers which offer the courses of the student,
f) Parents of the student,
g) Student.

Participation of a member from the special education assessment board shall be ensured to the BEP development unit, in order to consult when necessary. Working principles and procedures of this unit shall be determined by the school/institution administration (Art. 72/3-4).

Special education assessment board shall be established under RAM upon the proposal from the RAM and approval from the directorate of national education (Art. 19/1). With the amendment made in 2009, the members of the board are as follows: (Art. 19/2 – Amended: OG-31/7/2009-27305)

Special education assessment board, under the chairmanship of the deputy director to be designated by the RAM director or the head of the department;

a) Special education services department head,
b) A guidance counsellor who can use psychological measurement instruments,
c) One of the class teachers for persons with visual, hearing or intellectual impairments,

d) If found, a teacher who provides special education on a mobile basis,
e) Parents of the person.

The main duty of special education assessment boards is to conduct educational assessment and diagnosis. However, according to the Regulation on Special Education Services, boards also have the duty of preparing the education plans of persons in need of special education and deciding on the type and duration of the support they will receive (Art. 21/1-c, d). Special education assessment boards cannot properly carry out the duties assigned to them with these staff. Because, every expert needs to work separately but in cooperation with each other to accurately solve the personal/developmental codes of persons with many types of disabilities as well as those who have multiple disabilities or atypical properties and also to conduct educational diagnosis and assessment to a proper accuracy in order to fulfil the actual needs of the child. Regulation states that certain external experts can be invited to participate in the board in order to resolve this problem: members of occupations such as education programmers, audiologists, psychologists, psychometrists, social workers, language and speech therapists, physical therapists and specialist physicians as well as representatives of institutions for apprenticeships and adult education and the representatives of the institution where the person in need of special education works can participate in the board as members. Similarly, in order to be consulted by the special education assessment board; class and branch teacher of the person who is in need of special education, class guidance counsellor, director of the school or institution in which he/she is enrolled, representative from the applicant institution, special education services board member, faculty members from relevant departments of universities and representatives from non-governmental organisations can also be invited (Art. 19/3,4).

However, it does not seem realistic that the invitation and participation of such external experts in the board is ensured in practice. First of all, in practice, an appointment is made with the RAM beforehand for the educational assessment and diagnosis and the assessments of children are carried out accordingly. Particularly in initial assessments, the RAM personnel see the child for the first time. If it is believed that the assessment and diagnosis would be difficult to carry out with the existing staff or that it will lead to more proper results with the participation of certain experts in the board, a decision can be made to invite those experts and gather the board again on a future date. However, in cases when there is no mechanism to force or supervise the participation of these experts in the meeting held on that date or when they cannot be sent due to the heavy work load at the institutions they work at, diagnosis, assessment and educational planning will be carried out by the existing board members. When it is also considered that the number of special education teachers and guidance counsellors in Turkey is quite low,[126] it will

126 For data and assessments on the matter, see: Project on Policy and Practice Recommendations to Increase Efficiency of Inclusion/Integration: State of Inclusion/Integration Education in Turkey, pp. 15–16. It is expected that some improvements

not even be possible for such boards to gather with all members at all times. The Regulation specifies that the quorum for decisions is the majority of votes but does not mention the quorum for meeting.

On the other hand, counselling and research centres also have the duty of providing support education as well as guidance and psychological counselling services to the persons in need of special education and their families (Art. 49). However, CRSs are not institutions with certain powers and duties in terms of special education services. Pursuant to the Regulation on Guidance and Psychological Counselling Services of the Ministry of National Education[127] RAMs also have the duty of carrying out all works necessary for providing guidance and psychological counselling services at education and training institutions in an effective and efficient manner (Art. 21). It is not possible for RAMs to successfully carry out such a comprehensive range of duties with its existing institutional structure and personnel.

In practice, there are many complaints lodged regarding the functioning of RAMs in terms of special education. The fact that RAMs are assigned with the duty of serving to all institutions offering general and special education is one of the factors which negatively affect the process of providing efficient and fast service. RAMs need to be improved in terms of quantity, opened in provinces where required and in central locations where persons in need can easily access and their buildings and surroundings should have appropriate physical aspects as well as adequate number of guidance counsellors and special educators. Regarding the improvement of RAMs in terms of quality, it is important to change the institutional structure, duties and functioning and ensure that the education and counselling services to be provided by these institutions to persons with disabilities are offered in a structure and functioning to protect and actualise the right to education of persons with disabilities at international standards. Legal and administrative measures should be taken for their rearrangement as institutions equipped with physical conditions, suitable and competent personnel, assessment methods which follow scientific developments and consist of multiple steps which test and complement each other, as well as proper instruments, equipment and materials, with reduced duties and

will be made through a recent Regulation on the matter. That is, the Regulation on Standard Job Positions of Administrators and Teachers for Educational Institutions of the Ministry of National Education was published in the Official Gazette of 18 June 2014 and entered into force. This Regulation increased by 100% the standard job positions for counselling teachers and special education teachers in Counselling and Research Centres (RAMs). The Regulation added approximately 550 positions for counselling teachers and 1,500 positions for special education teachers in 224 RAMs as determined on the basis of population within the area of responsibility of each RAM. http://www.mebpersonnelleri.com/meb-personneli/mebde-norm-patlamasi-h3810.html (26.08.2014). The new and old numbers of standard job positions and increased numbers for RAMs by population can be accessed at the same source.

127 O.G. 17.4.2001/24376.

powers or an organisational structure able to carry the existing work load. While the Regulation on Special Education and Counselling Services, which is currently a draft, cannot produce a complete solution to this problem, it seems to regulate that positive changes are made in the organisational structure of RAMs and to distribute the work load. According to the draft Regulation, counselling and research centres *shall be opened by the Ministry at the province and/or district level in order to regulate guidance and psychological counselling services as well as special education services, to ensure that they are carried out in coordination and to monitor and assess them. RAMs consist of a) Guidance and psychological counselling services unit, b) Special education services unit, c) Education programmes and materials unit, ç) Research, monitoring and assessment unit. (3) A unit coordinator shall be assigned for every unit in RAMs (Art. 32).* Duties of the special education unit are as follows (Art. 34):

a) *Carry out works and processes regarding the persons who applied or were referred to educational assessment and diagnosis.*
b) *Provide support on special education services to schools where inclusion practices are implemented.*
c) *Organise activities for informing individuals, families, teachers and administrators about special education.*
d) *Carry out necessary works and processes in the RAM Module for taking examination measures for students in need of special education at the central system examinations conducted by the Ministry as well as examinations conducted under protocol.*
e) *Cooperate with relevant institutions and entities regarding services when necessary.*
f) *Carry out other duties relevant to the area as assigned by the Director.*

While the draft Regulation comprises regulations, which will take the right to education of persons with disabilities backwards on other issues, such a structure for RAMs seems to be a positive and temporary measure. More radical structure changes are needed. In this regard, a structure model can be recommended which consists of institutions that will only provide services for diagnosis, assessment, referral and placement regarding special education services as well as monitoring and oversight on the education process and the planning of education within this process and services for counselling and support to the individual, his/her family and the educational institution, in a quantity which provides easy access to individuals and families, with mild bureaucracy and appropriate and effective functioning.

Duties and responsibilities of the individualised education programme development unit are listed in Article 74 of the Regulation on Special Education Services. One-by-one definitions of duties are also provided for each of the members of this unit in various provisions of the Regulation. As is seen in the aggregate of these provisions, preparation of BEPs is primarily the duty of the Special Education Assessment Board. BEP development units at schools or institutions are partners of cooperation and responsible for coordination of practices within the school/institution. However, these units play an active role in preparation, implementation, monitoring of these individualised education plans as well as the resolution of problems and are indicative in the course of the process.

The preparation and implementation of a BEP is an inseparable step for ensuring that the child with special needs benefit from the suitable educational settings and support education services to the largest extent possible which aim to fulfil the developmental and educational needs of him/her. However, according to a recent study, 23,1% of teachers state that BEPs are not prepared, 44,3% of parents state that BEPs are implemented partially, and again, 21,9% of parents state that BEPs are not implemented. These findings have the nature which supports the literature. Surveys conducted on directors, class teachers and parents in primary education first tier schools where inclusion practices are implemented, in the scope of the study from the Ministry of National Education, Department of Research and Development of Education (EARGED) titled *Assessment of Inclusion Practices in Primary Schools* also provide important up-to-date data in this regard. Research indicate that, the regulations in the Regulation on Special Education Services for inclusive education regarding the number of students in classes, fulfilment of the needs of students with special needs, implementation of individualised education plans and ensuring cooperation between teachers and families are not adequately put into action in practice. For instance, according to the study published by EARGED in 2010, approximately one third of school administrators do not act in accordance with the legislation on the number of students in classes and the number of inclusion students per class. It is observed that in approximately one-third of schools which provide inclusive education, the number of students in classes in which inclusion practices are implemented are more than 35. It is highlighted that this situation may result in teachers having negative attitudes about inclusion and makes it more difficult for all students in the class to achieve effective teaching. In the same study, the crowdedness of classes becomes prominent as an answer frequently referred by school administrators, teachers and parents among the problems encountered during the inclusion practices. In summary, it is not yet possible to say that the comprehensive regulations in the legislation regarding inclusive/integrative education are completely put into practice. While ensuring that more students benefit from inclusive/integrative education, on the other hand, perpetual, integrative and intense efforts should be made to eliminate the gaps between the legislation and the practice.[128]

According to the relevant legislation, BEP is also an indicative factor that should be regarded as the basis for evaluating the success of the student. Relevant articles

---

128 *Kaynaştırma / Bütünleştirmenin Etkililiğini Arttırmak İçin Politika ve Uygulama Önerileri Projesi Türkiye'de Kaynaştırma/Bütünleştirme Yoluyla Eğitimin Durumu* [*Project on Policy and Practice Recommendations to Increase Efficiency of Inclusion/Integration: State of Inclusion/Integration Education in Turkey*], Yayına Hazırlayanlar [Prepared for publication by: Ayşe Nal/Işık Tüzün], Eğitim Reformu Girişimi – Tohum Otizm Vakfı [Education Reform Initiative -Tohum Autism Foundation], pp. 12–13.

of the Regulation on Special Education Services explain some of the systems for success assessment via examination methods according to the type of deficiency of persons and the education programme of the school/institution in which they pursue their education. Apart from that, technique, measurement instruments and assessment duration, assessment time, assessment intervals, persons responsible for assessment and the setting in which the assessment will be conducted shall be determined in line with the opinions and recommendations of the BEP development unit (Art. 24). Regardless of being and inclusion student, the common point for all persons in need of special education is that the goals of BEPs will be taken into account when their educational success is assessed. However, as indicated by the data provided above, BEP applications in Turkey are quite weak and far from providing the desired benefit. Therefore, major problems are also encountered in the assessment of success. Practices against students are encountered in many areas ranging from the settings where examinations are held, durations given, person-specific supports, to types of examinations and measurement techniques, an actual assessment cannot be achieved.

ad. Supportive Education Services

A fundamental principle of inclusive education is to provide special education support to students with special needs and their teachers in the general education classrooms. It is possible to distinguish between intra-classroom and extra-classroom supportive education services.

ada. Intra-classroom supportive education services

Counsellor-assisted general education classroom: The student with special needs receives special education in an all-day general education classroom through the class teacher. A special education counsellor provides the class teacher with advisory services in the fields of adapting the teaching process and materials to the needs of the student, coping with problematic behaviours and increasing the social inclusion of students with special needs.

Special education teacher-assisted general education classroom: The student with special needs receives special education in a general education classroom from a special education teacher in addition to the class teacher. The special education teacher works to solve the adaptation problems of the student, facilitate the class teacher's working with the student, and create positive interaction among students.

Collaborative teaching-assisted general education classroom: In this practice, the class teacher and the special education teacher work together continuously in the general education classroom and share the responsibilities for students.

adb. Extra-classroom supportive education services

Resource room: In the resource room, the student with special needs receives, either individually or in small groups, education from the special education teacher in addition to the education received in the classroom. The student spends at least 21% to at most 60% of a school day here. For the successful implementation of this mode, the resource room teacher and the class teacher should be in good communication and cooperation.

Mobile special education teacher: Under this practice, the special education teacher goes from one school to another to provide supportive education services to students with special needs. Students with special needs spend most of their school day in their classrooms and leave the classroom for certain periods to receive education from the mobile teacher.[129]

Such services related to special education as language, speech therapy and physiotherapy that play a major role in successful inclusive education are provided by supplementary service personnel to students with special needs in the inclusive schools.[130]

Studies on inclusive practices in Turkey point out to the inadequacy of supportive education services as an integral part of inclusive education in respect of the problems experienced in the inclusive education by class teachers, school principals, parents and students with special needs. In a study on schools with inclusion is practised at primary education first tier; school administrators, teachers and parents were asked whether educators and parents received support/assistance, and students received supportive education. As shown in the following table, only a part of administrators and teachers indicated that they received support/assistance on inclusive education. Parents believed at higher rates that they received support/assistance, however about half stated that the students were not provided supportive education. While drawing a more positive picture when compared to the responses by parents, the responses by school administrators and teachers signalled that not many children received supportive education. The same study found that four fifths of the schools did not have any special education teacher, and about one fourth of the schools lacked a counselling department.

Administrators, teachers and parents who stated that supportive education was provided to students under inclusion responded rather variously to the question which mode such education was provided through. EARGED interpreted the results as follows: *"About half of the school administrators and parents who stated that supportive education was provided to students under inclusion indicated that students received supportive education through intra-classroom assistance; while teachers who similarly responded to the same question stated that students received supportive*

129 *Kaynaştırma / Bütünleştirmenin Etkililiğini Arttırmak İçin Politika ve Uygulama Önerileri Projesi Türkiye'de Kaynaştırma/Bütünleştirme Yoluyla Eğitimin Durumu [Project on Policy and Practice Recommendations to Increase Efficiency of Inclusion/Integration: State of Inclusion/Integration Education in Turkey]*, Yayına Hazırlayanlar [Prepared for publication by: Ayşe Nal/Işık Tüzün], Eğitim Reformu Girişimi – Tohum Otizm Vakfı [Education Reform Initiative -Tohum Autism Foundation], pp. 13–14.

130 Ibid. pp. 13–14.

education from a special education institution. When these rates are assessed taking into account the rates of respondents who stated the student received supportive education, very few students received supportive education through the supportive education room and the intra-classroom assistance. Based on these results, it may be concluded that the supportive education at school is inadequate".[131]

	School administrators	Teachers	Parents
Receiving support/assistance for inclusive education	**34.6%**	**36.4%**	**78.2%**
School providing supportive education to inclusion students	**68.0%**	**64.3%**	**52.4%**
School having a special education teacher	**18.3%**	**18.8%**	**21.1%**
School having a counselling department	**75.9%**	**80.4%**	**78.0%**

Source: Compiled from EARGED (2010) findings.

The Regulation on Special Education Services defines supportive education services as *"services of expert personnel, equipment and materials, education and counselling to a student, family, teachers and school staff in accordance with the educational needs identified as a result of medical and educational assessment and diagnosis on the individual with special educational needs"* (Art. 4/1-h). As would be seen in the definition, supportive education involves not only the student but also families, teachers and expert personnel considering that teachers, school staff and families as part of such education should be given support so that supportive education can succeed, thus establishing a triangle of mutual support, cooperation and communications. However, "supportive education" is not regulated in the Regulation in such scope and content that can fulfil the requirements of this definition. To give a concrete example, the provision of the Regulation which enumerates the fundamental principles of special education lacks any provision on supportive education, which is an important shortcoming. While it is enumerated, in the context of special education, as fundamental principles that cooperation should be ensured with institutions and organisations that will provide rehabilitation services, BEPs be developed and implemented; no fundamental principle is laid down which points out to enabling elements that achieve the objectives of special education such as information, education on theory and practice, assistance, support etc. all parameters, i.e. students in need, families, normally developing students and families, administrators, teachers, educators and other personnel in the institution.

131 Ibid. pp. 14–15.

The subsequent provisions of the Regulation explain supportive education over BEP and in relation to the functions and powers of the boards, teachers and educators involved in this process in connection with BEP, and the family's participation. This approach however is based on that individuals receive education on the basis of individualisation peculiar to their special needs. In other words, it describes the individualisation of supportive education. However, the notion of support/supportive education requires that the process in general be planned before the need arises, and certain fundamental principles and standards be laid down as to how the institutional arrangements and practice be established. Supportive education should be conceived, in the process of educational assessment and diagnosis of the individual, not only as a procedure for the person, but also a process that requires structuring the institutional system accompanied by preparatory works for informing and educating the educator, administrator, teacher and personnel of the school/institution, and the student and parents before the need arises. This process should be directed to all students, parents and personnel of the school/institution; designed to identify, prevent in advance the need for support/supportive education; and if required, include a roadmap showing how the process could be operated better and more efficiently. To give a concrete proposal; the entire text including particularly the chapter "fundamental principles" in the Regulation on Special Education Services should address support and supportive education as two distinct processes; all actors of the process should be holistically described including their interests; the process should be clearly regulated in terms of the subjects, qualities, principles and standards of the support both to be provided and to be received, guiding the objectives and outcomes.

Considering that the provision in the Regulation that "Information shall be provided the personnel in the schools and institutions which practice inclusion, other students and their families by relevant persons in RAM and BEP development unit in line with the planning conducted by the school administration on the characteristics of individuals in need of special education" (Art. 23/2-f) is indeed an act supporting the inclusion, this provision should be readdressed. It is mandatory to rewrite the provision that "Necessary arrangements shall be made to ensure that students under inclusive education receive supportive education services. To that end, supportive education services may be in the form of intra-classroom assistance as well as be given in the supportive education rooms" (Art. 23/2-h) in a more inclusive and explanatory manner. In summary, support and supportive education refer to all types of support including educational measures that will help exercise the right to education in the best manner by responding to concrete and special needs relating to or affecting education for each student in the education process. In this context, everybody (students, parents, teacher, educator and other personnel) in the education process must be supported by education and/or other methods. "Supportive education" should be adopted, in the Regulation, as one of the measures included in the "support to be given/taken" and be arranged separately but as a part of the whole in respect of all legs of the process, relevant people and institutions, and the basic concept should be "educational support". In other words, if the support to be given internally and/or externally aims to meet the educational needs of the student, it should be named educational support whatever its nature is; and the supportive education to be given to students, teachers, personnel and families should be conceived as part of this process. Because the listed persons will not be able to exercise the right to education at equal footing with others without such support.

The draft Regulation on Special Education and Counselling Services has not mentioned either what type of support will be given to teachers in the context of inclusion. While the first paragraph of Article 74 the draft governing the duties and responsibilities of teachers lay down the duties and obligations of teachers assigned to special education schools, and the second paragraph lays down the duties and obligations of teachers working in all types of schools, the draft is primarily designed to regulate the special education schools. Educational support to be provided to the teachers instructing the classes that include inclusion students should be explicitly regulated. The draft, while including the matters of cooperation between the teachers on one side and the BEP unit, counselling units or the units in RAMs, appears to have overlooked the fact that teachers need assistance and support beyond cooperation.

The literature including studies with teachers, administrators and inspectors notes that frequent problems include that teachers have difficulty in controlling the class due to the presence of inclusion students, no preparations are made for inclusive education at schools and classes, students are not selected through appropriate methods, and teaches fail to adapt the inclusion programme. Teachers also have difficulty in assessing the achievement, passing to a higher grade and graduation of students with special needs; they need supportive services in this field. According to a study on the opinion of teachers, administrators and parents on the inclusion practices:

- 86.4% of the responding 907 class teachers indicate that they are not adequately knowledgeable on inclusive education;
- 89.7% of the teachers do not request more information on the matter;
- 77.1% of the teachers indicate that individualised education programmes cannot be prepared for the students with disabilities, whereas 70.9% state that they implement the present curriculum.

Administrators and teachers are not provided adequate information on inclusive education; training is limited, and more information is needed for all including those who receive MoNE's in-service programmes. According to a study published in 2010, about two thirds of administrators and more than half of the teachers in primary schools with inclusive education state that they are not informed prior to the implementation of inclusive education. 59.4% of the responding school administrators and 55.1% of the responding teachers state that they have been trained on inclusion, and 86% of school administrators and 73.9% of teachers indicate that they want to be informed on inclusive education. Further, the preparatory process for inclusion at schools also needs development. Important factors to the success of inclusion practice are listed as receiving information on the student, making physical arrangements for inclusion, sharing information with teachers who have inclusion students, preparing other students and parents for inclusion; and it is indicated that the ratio of administrators who engage in such efforts in schools is not adequate.[132]

Human is the most important factor for education. Teachers, educators, administrators, parents and persons to receive education are the basic components for efficient and successful education. While the physical structure of schools/institutions, technological novelties and supports, equipment and materials are the material components of education, these are too elements created, developed and used by human hand and mind. Therefore, prospective legislative arrangements should prioritise the human factor which must always be considered when planning for the institutional setup of education and deciding on the equipment and materials to be used, and the curricular programmes and techniques. Prospective legislative arrangements should take care that educators to serve both in inclusive and separated institutions must be provided with support and assistance commensurate with their duties and obligations. Similarly, explicit arrangements are needed to inform the families of other children receiving education at the same premises with the children with special needs, raise their awareness, foster their confidence to overcome difficulties and develop positive attitude.

The Centre for Studies on Inclusive Education (CSIE) in the United Kingdom has developed an Integration Index to promote the transition of schools in Australia into inclusive education. The index provides a framework to assess schools, and develop the integration of school culture, policy and practices, and includes various indicators and events for various dimensions. It emphasises that such dimensions do interact, and a transformation of school culture depends on formulating and implementing a policy in schools. The indicators in the index aim to:

- Identify the existing knowledge and understanding in the school on school culture, policies and practices,
- Identify priorities to develop the school and teachers,
- Manage and document the transformation process.

Building on the idea that teachers are key to the reform in schools, personal development model was implemented in a primary school in Queensland. This model aimed that teachers would learn from colleagues, an academician working on integration and another researcher who assumed the role of a supportive education teacher by providing feedback in dialogue, and at the same time transform the school culture towards integration. In the primary school selected under the project, researchers

132 *Kaynaştırma / Bütünleştirmenin Etkililiğini Arttırmak İçin Politika ve Uygulama Önerileri Projesi Türkiye'de Kaynaştırma/Bütünleştirme Yoluyla Eğitimin Durumu [Project on Policy and Practice Recommendations to Increase Efficiency of Inclusion/Integration: State of Inclusion/Integration Education in Turkey]*, Yayına Hazırlayanlar [Prepared for publication by: Ayşe Nal/Işık Tüzün], Eğitim Reformu Girişimi – Tohum Otizm Vakfı [Education Reform Initiative -Tohum Autism Foundation], pp. 16–17.

studied how the use of Integration Index impacted the personal development of teachers, and what changes it entailed in the school's culture, education policy and teaching practices. As reported on this model implemented in a primary school in Queensland, Australia, the Integration Index offered a useful framework to develop the school staff personally in the direction of integration. The project resulted in improvement in two core areas. The first involved the analysis of existing beliefs and values on school policy and practices across the school, and a reassessment of such beliefs and values in terms of integration. The second result was that the knowledge and skills of teachers individually were improved. During the project, school stakeholders were particularly encouraged to address problems through communication and cooperation. The use of indicators in the index contributed to the enrichment of teacher-student relations, focusing on pedagogy and curriculum, making assessment to respond to training, learning and personal needs of teachers. In addition, the study aimed to strengthen and maintain the culture of change, as well as boosting the motivation of teachers.[133]

The Committee on the Rights of the Children to emphasises this factor in the General Comment on the Rights of Persons with Disabilities. The Committee holds that the substance of the matter is the support and assistance to be provided to institutions, educators and the children with disabilities for them to receive education with their peers by inclusion in regular educational institutions.[134] The most important barrier to effective and quality education for children with disabilities in regular schools arises from the non-recognition of education as a fundamental human right, not from problems of finance or budget.

The Committee on Economic, Social and Cultural Rights interpreted the education support far broadly in its General Comment on Persons with Disabilities. The Committee emphasises the obligation to provide and secure the necessary support to elevate the educational level of students with disabilities to that of those without.[135] The said support refers to any and all support necessary to ensure that persons with disabilities access to any type and level of education offered at formal and non-formal educational institutions, maximally benefit from educational services, and acquire an occupation following the education, thereby live independently in all spheres of social life.

---

133 For further information on the study, see: *Project on Policy and Practice Recommendations to Increase Efficiency of Inclusion/Integration: Best Practices of Inclusion/Integration Education in Turkey and in the World*, pp. 20–23.

134 General Comment No. 9: The Rights of Children with Disabilities, CRC, 17/10/2006, CRC/C/GC/9, 27 February 2007, para.62–63; Hodgkin Rachel/ Newel Peter; Convention on the Rights of the Child Practical Handbook, UNICEF, 1998 (translation), pp. 306–308.

135 The right to education (Art. 13): 08/12/99. E/C.12/1999/10. (General Comment No. 13), CESCR Committee on Economic, Social and Cultural Rights, Twenty-first session 15 November – 3 December 1999, para.35.

The Convention on the Rights of Persons with Disabilities refers, in similar language, the support to be provided to the education for persons with disabilities. The Convention obliges, in the article governing education, the States Parties ensure that "Persons with disabilities receive the support required, within the general education system, to facilitate their effective education" and "Effective individualised support measures are provided in environments that maximise academic and social development, consistent with the goal of full inclusion" [Art. 24/2(d, e)]. Unlike other Conventions, the Convention on the Rights of Persons with Disabilities prioritises that the support be provided to the students with disabilities themselves. The priority matter in enabling the exercise of the right to education of persons with disabilities is not the support to be provided to schools, educational institutions or educators, but the provision of support to the student both within and without the general education system to meet the student's personal educational needs and enable him/her to effectively enjoy education. Effective education that cannot be provided through universal design and reasonable accommodation must be provided through the provision of required support. For instance, to successfully deliver an education programme to a student with speech disorder, it is necessary that a specialist on the matter within or without the institution give the student speech education; or a translator of sign language must be allocated to a student with hearing disability who receives education in a regular school. An educational environment and administration based on solidary will be created to ensure that classmates and educators assist the student on all matters. In short, the relevant student must be provided with any and all support and assistance to eliminate barriers to enjoyment of education and respond to personal educational needs, provided that such relate to education.

3. *Quality and Appropriate Education*

While it is difficult to define what quality education is, the definitions so far emphasise to core aspects. The first is cognitive (relating to cognition, i.e. understanding) development, as a priority matter of education. The achievement in cognitive development is measured by the effectiveness of education. The other relates to creative and emotional development aspect of education. This aspect involves development of an understanding and sensitivity for peace, equality, security, respect for global and cultural values, human rights and environment.[136] In other words, the quality of education is assessed on the basis of achievement of educational objectives.

The goals and objectives of education are laid down by the international human rights instruments and updated through the decisions and general comments of

136 A Human Rights-Based Approach to Education for All, UNESCO/UNICEF, 2007, p.32; for views of rights-based approach to education quality, see: **Katarina Tomasevski**, "Manual on Rights-Based Education, Global Human Rights Made Simple", *Asia and Pacific Regional Bureau for Education*, UNESCO-Bangkok, 2004, pp. 30–38.

the convention supervisory bodies.[137] The Convention on the Rights of Persons with Disabilities requires the States Parties to pursue the following three objectives (Art. 24/1):

"a. The full development of human potential and sense of dignity and self-worth, and the strengthening of respect for human rights, fundamental freedoms and human diversity;
b. The development by persons with disabilities of their personality, talents and creativity, as well as their intellectual and physical abilities, to their fullest potential;
c. Enabling persons with disabilities to participate effectively in a free society".[138]

The best way to achieve these objectives is to include the persons with disabilities in the integrative education system. While the development of human potential and sense of dignity and self-worth of the persons with disabilities is influenced by the family and environment, it is contemplated that the best outcomes can be obtained through starting education as early as possible. The children, youth and adults with disabilities who receive education along with those without at all stages including career and vocational education and life-long learning will believe their dignity is preserved and develop self-confidence and personally when they feel the recognition and worth in such environments. They will develop creativity using various ways and methods of communicating with different others; and develop mentally and physically by observing, listening and mutual assistance, and strengthen their personality. Education is the most effective way to integrate persons with disabilities in all spheres of life. In that sense, the education provided to persons with disabilities is of good quality and appropriate as long as it achieves the said objectives.

The goals of education and underlying principles as prescribed by the Decree-Law on Special Education and the Regulation on Special Education Services can, while having some deficiencies as mentioned earlier, be interpreted to prevent discrimination against persons in need of special education in the sphere of right to education, and to ensure that they have equal educational opportunities as others. The problem however with the legislation on special education is that it treats the raison d'etre of special education differently than the approach in the Convention on the Rights of Persons with Disabilities, overlooks the nature of education as a "right", and attempts to regulate education in a service delivery approach. Special education is based on the fact that not everyone can enjoy education under the ordinary methods and rules that some persons need to have education through special educational methods and rules of varying types and degrees. Thus, it is necessary to treat special education

137 Article 29 of the Convention on the Rights of the Child, Article 1371 of the Covenant on Economic, Social and Cultural Rights and Article 2471 of the Convention on the Rights of Persons with Disabilities lay down the purposes of education.

138 Convention on the Rights of Persons with Disabilities, Art. 24/1, www.un.org/disabilities/documents/convention, (19.08.2008)

not as an alternative to general education, but complementary to the latter; take the delivery of special education in separated schools and institutions as an exceptional method and enact the legislation through such approach.

While the Turkish education legislation addresses special education as an integral part of general education, special education does not yet occupy its deserved place in the legislation governing general education. The Basic Law on National Education, Law on Primary Education and Law on Higher Education are not laws focusing on general education and training, but laws merely governing general education, and overlooking the education of persons with disabilities. The principle that special educational needs will be addressed in general educational institutions is prescribed only in the legislation on special education. Special education can become a part of the general education only if that same principle is laid down in the legislative texts governing the general education, and the functions and powers of the provincial organisation of the national education and of the general educational institutions are regulated accordingly. The fundamental requirement must of course be to take into account the rules and principles specific to special education within the general education system and implement appropriate and necessary measures to respond to special educational needs.[139]

There are certain parameters and conditions to achieving the goals of education specific to persons with disabilities. The quality and appropriateness of education; how, where and by whom the persons with disabilities will be educated; or in other words, how the curricula and programmes are structured; how educational material and supportive methods are employed; the qualification of educators, specialists and other personnel are closely related to the appropriateness of educational environment. This framework will be the basis of the following assessments relating to how parameters that affect appropriate and quality education should be managed.

a. Use of Appropriate Curriculum and Effective Materials

Educational programmes and curriculum and educational materials accordingly structured are the elements that mediate and set the direction of education. Where persons with disabilities are concerned, the programming and contenting of education and use of materials tend to be a more sensitive issue. The programme

139 As emphasised in the annex to the Circular of the General Directorate of Counselling and Guidance for Special Education Services of the Ministry of National Education on "Inclusive Education Practice", while general and special education resemble in respect of teaching methods and techniques, special arrangements are necessary to meet the special educational needs within the framework of inclusive education. Special arrangements must include such areas and topics as educational equipment and materials, instructional methods and techniques and assessment. See: "Recommendations to Teachers on Inclusive Education Practice", Annex to the Circular No. 2008/60 of 02.09.2008 on Inclusive Education Practice No. 3601, p.1.

and curriculum applied to students with disabilities in the special education institutions are tailored to the types and degrees of disabilities, and supported with special materials, thus leading to fewer problems. Since persons with similar deficiencies are educated in the special education institutions, the same educational programme and curriculum is applied. However, since it is not possible that every person with disabilities cannot benefit from such education at the same level, the content and objectives of the education in special education programmes must also be formulated specific to individuals. Individual educational plans programmes should be developed in accordance with the goal of maximising individual development and capacities considering the characteristics, interests, skills and learning needs of each child or youth receiving special education.

The Regulation on Special Education Services provides that children with special educational needs receive education under the same programme and curriculum in the inclusion classroom as with their peers, however the programme and curriculum is adapted through BEP to their educational needs. Educational methods and techniques, educational equipment and materials, and the type of supportive education based on an assessment of achievement are planned so that the child can continue with the inclusive education.

According to the Regulation, another method of meeting special educational need is to provide education in special education classes set up in the regular education schools. As mentioned earlier, the educational programme of the school is applied partly in such classes and the educational programme applicable to deficiencies in special education schools and institutions is applied partly. We have criticised such separation of classes in various aspects. We may add here specifically for the topic: the application of unified education in special education classes is a practice that disregards the personal nature of special education and violates the right to education. The Regulation provides that unified education will be practised in classes that are set up for the students with visual and hearing deficiency who are capable of attending the educational programme in the school and for the students with intellectual deficiency or autism (Art. 26/1-c, d). The unified class practice will continue in classes set up for students with visual and hearing deficiency until Grade 5; from thereon, these students will have education along with their peers in the same class (Art. 26/1-c). For this category of persons with disabilities, joint education is provided in the same classroom with their normally developing peers. Students with intellectual deficiency or autism will have the entire duration of compulsory education (Grades 1 to 4, and 5 to 8) in the unified classes (Art. 26/1-ç).

Whatever the duration is, it is simply impossible to overlook the adverse impact of the unified education practice on the students with disabilities for certain categories of disability. Education in unified classes is a practice of education by one teacher for a group of students brought together by the unification of more than one class. Accordingly, the ages, academic and cognitive developmental levels of students in unified classes are different. The only common aspect of such a heterogeneous group is that they have the same type of deficiency. When individuals of the same type of deficiency are classified merely according to such criterion, no homogenous group will come into being due to the differences in their personal characteristics, the duration and nature of individual education each has had so far, family structure and other external factors. Individual BEP application for each will not alleviate the problem either because, according to the Regulation, the lessons in such classes will be addressed mostly by the class teacher, and some other classes by the branch teacher. Setting aside the difficulty for the class teacher alone to give education to such a group that is heterogeneous in all respects except for the type of deficiency, it is almost impossible for such education to fulfil the best interests of the child, equality, individuality etc. principles, or be called quality and appropriate education. It is merely a dream that such a teacher will provide each child with BEP-adapted education. Such classes can at best follow a common route, focusing on whether the duration of education under inclusion is completed, not how far each child has benefited from the education.

The Ministry of National Education itself has criticised this method applied to normally developing children in some villages, and called such practice as "difficult and complex teaching by its circumstances".[140] In the light of the fact that MoNE admits that the efficiency desired of such practice depends on the teacher who knows and practices well the instruction in unified classes, it is simply incomprehensible that MoNE implements such self-criticised method for the children with disabilities through an amendment on 21.07.2012 to the Regulation on Special Education Services. The provisions of the Regulation which allow such practice must be amended in the shortest time possible. It is also observed that the same practice is maintained in the draft Regulation on Special Education and Counselling Services (Art. 24–25).

The Regulation on Special Education Services provides that special education classes may be opened in secondary education and formal educational institutions for individuals in need of special education and capable of following the educational programme of the school. For this group of students, the unified class practice is not explicitly stated, but instead it is provided that "in such classes, necessary arrangements will be made considering the *educational programme of the school or institution, physical conditions and personnel of the school, deficiencies and developmental characteristics of individuals in need of special education and individual competences*" (Art. 26/1-j). This provision is wide open to the practice of unified class practice. It is explicitly stated that for individuals incapable of following the educational programme, unified class practice shall be implemented (Art. 27/1-c).

As known, the Regulation on Special Education Services includes arrangements that allow opening of many special education schools and institutions of various types in the compulsory education process. It is provided that in some of these schools and institutions, the programmes of schools where individuals without deficiency receive education will apply; and in some, special education programmes

140 http://mebk12.meb.gov.tr/meb_iys_dosyalar/63/01/718146/dosyalar/2012_12/18071249_birletirilmisnflardaretim.pdf (5.4.2012)

specific to types of deficiency will apply [(Art. 38–46) 39. and 41. Have been repealed; and Article 43 should be disregarded because it relates to the education of highly talented individuals]. Those relevant provisions do not include unified education practice for places other than the schools and institutions opened for individuals institutionalised in health institutions; the number of students per class is limited to certain figures. As is known of the practice, individuals of similar type of deficiency receive education in the same class in such schools and institutions despite their differences in age and developmental level.

The fact that educational programmes are designed on the basis of type of deficiency, and the curricula are developed along such programmes in the Turkish special education system results in an education system that disregards the child's social, cultural and economic competences, interests and desires. We cannot say that persons with disabilities receive quality and appropriate education that enables a dignified, independent life in the sense of the convention unless and until practical education is provided which takes into account the child's present and future needs, considers developing abilities,[141] teaches basic cognitive skills and life skills as well as academic knowledge designed to empower the person to overcome problems in all spheres of real life, and meet his/her needs. It is only through education that persons with disabilities can acquire skills of healthy and safe lifestyle, establishing proper relations, learn the means of overcoming difficulties of life, develop ability of judgment to make consistent decisions to enable them to live independently to the extent possible within the society, as compared to other person who learn such skills by themselves in the course of life.[142] For children and youth with disabilities incapable of living independently, the objective and content of educational programmes will of course be different. Education for this category should be provided in limited academic content considering the personal needs of each, mostly designed to strengthen knowledge, skills and social communications to meet self-care and basic personal needs and develop self-expression and anger control. However, it should be kept in mind that the purpose of education for this group too is to ensure independence in as many as spheres possible.

For integrative education system, the issue is more complicated. The curriculum and educational materials are all the more important in overcoming the challenges in providing the theoretical and practical programme and courses, classes and other educational activity jointly to students with and without disabilities. The issue of what content and how education programmes will be presented to students, and how educational outcomes will be assessed should be considered in a context that takes into account the students with disabilities as well as those without who will receive education in the same class or school.

141 General Comment No. 1, The Aims of Education, CRC/GC/2001/1, para.9.

142 A Human Rights-Based Approach to Education for All, UNESCO/UNICEF, 2007, pp. 68–69.

The first step to develop a curriculum that covers all students in the full-time inclusive education classes is to expand the definition of learning in an inclusive manner. The habitual method of learning based on transfer of knowledge from teacher locks schools in the strictly organised curriculum and teaching practices. The development of programmes that allow active involvement of students in the learning experience and assessment of knowledge and findings, and the encouragement of project-based team work will also provide students with disabilities with opportunities to achieve collectively with others, develop and exhibit the abilities both groups in social communications, cooperation and research and development.[143] Relaxing the content and method of delivery of education programmes to ensure access by all students, formulating work plans and programmes, and according the same flexibility to teach on the methods of delivery will lead to intensive, planned interaction between the teacher and the class.[144]

Learning by touching, trying, seeing and mutual communication should be viewed as a method that will increase the opportunities for students with disabilities to receive education. For persons with disabilities who have learning difficulty and difficulty in reading-writing-comprehending, and persons with intellectual disabilities; it is difficult to listen to and understand theoretical lessons. It may be necessary that theoretical education that can be given to other students in conventional means should be given by different methods with support of different materials. For instance, using such methods as the narration of history or geography lesson supported by pictures and illustrations, presentation of language lessons in storytelling with the use of appropriate audio-visual materials; solution and illustration of mathematical problems on the practical applications in life; providing the education through the channels for each student where his/her learning capacity has developed will likely to achieve successful results in education.

However, it should not be preferred to apply a curriculum to students with special educational needs wholly different than that applied to other students in the same programme or class. Same topics should be taught in simplified, abridged manner but with no change in substance or nature; necessary additional support be provided to the children so that they can get education of same quality.[145]

---

143 For countries which have obtained positive results from such practices, see: *Open File on Inclusive Education Support Materials for Managers and Administrators,* UNESCO, 2001, pp. 96–98; Guidelines for Inclusion: Ensuring Access to Education for All, UNESCO 2005, pp. 25–26.

144 Guidelines for Inclusion: Ensuring Access to Education for All, UNESCO 2005, pp. 16–17.

145 "The Salamanca Statement and Framework for Education on Special Needs Education", *Adopted by the World Conference on Special Needs Education: Access and Quality,* Salamanca, Spain, 7–10 June 1994, UNESCO, 1994, para.28–34 ; for standards of developing appropriate curriculum in Australia, see: **Philip Maxwell Ruddock**, *Disability Standards for Education 2005,* 17 Marc 2005, Australia, pp. 17–18; for

The inclusion of knowledge and practices designed to provide a recognition of occupations and vocational skills in the educational programmes starting from the primary school, and adding controlled workplace apprenticeship training to the education provided intensively in vocational education branches selected according to abilities well identified in the secondary education age may create vital opportunities to students with disabilities as well as to other students who are not apt to academic education. Making vocational education compulsory beyond the compulsory education time[146] will help achieve the goal of an inclusive society for the majority persons with disabilities if such compulsion is accompanied with availability, accessibility, acceptability and adaptability.

It is very important that the curricula, from the early education age onwards, include alternative communication forms for children with disabilities and use appropriate materials accordingly. In addition, course books and other printed educational materials should be worded in clear and simple language for all students and supported by illustrations. Further, all topics of theoretical courses must be printed in Braille and reviewed and updated every year. Care must be taken that the curriculum for students with hearing disabilities include words amenable to communicate in sign language, and the assistance of an expert in sign language must be enrolled.

It is the State's obligation to develop educational programmes which will provide basic education to persons with disabilities of all ages who have received no education or dropped out of education or whose basic educational needs have not been met though having received education. Basic education, as a normative right, should not be conceived only as courses and programmes directed at literacy courses and basic life skills, but treated in a larger scope because the needs for basic education evolves depending on changing economic, social, cultural and environmental conditions. For instance, computer has become an important source of knowledge and communications for everyone and an integral part of education. In that sense, it should be addressed in the context of the basic right to education to give other knowledge and abilities that have become vital to the requirements of socio-economic life in addition to the mandatory skills and knowledge to live such as literacy and calculation. It is possible to teach an individual who lacks the ability to speak how to use computer and give drawing and arts education to an individual who lacks the ability to speak but has the ability to draw, thereby enable them to express themselves and establish communications. Therefore, when filling in the content of basic needs variable by person, the deprivations and abilities of each person, and the basic educational programmes be built on a rich framework. Turkey, as a State Party to the Convention on the Rights of Persons with Disabilities which establishes "life-long education" as a right for persons with disabilities should diversify both

---

other country experiences, see: "Diversity, Inclusion and Equity: Insights from Special Needs Provision", *Education Policy Analysis*, OECD 2003, 28.

146 General Comment No. 9: The Rights of Children with Disabilities, CRC, 17/10/2006, CRC/C/GC/9, 27 February 2007, para.68–69.

formal and non-formal education educational programmes, create educational and developmental programmes that do not exclude sports and art education from the development of persons with disabilities, open sports and arts centres to disseminate such practice to enable persons with disabilities to express themselves through various methods, become independent and integrate into the society.

In addition, it is possible to facilitate the education of students with disabilities within the integrative education system through making curricula more attractive to all students using appropriate technologies and reasonable accommodation. Educational materials of appropriate or simple category must be in place which will facilitate or enhance the education of each student with disabilities in the context of his/her personal learning needs; in addition, assessment should be made whether accommodation is reasonable in terms of assistance and supportive materials.[147]

The traditional practice in the regular education setup in the Turkish education system is based on acquisition of knowledge in passive methods, not designed to develop the ability of inquiry and reasoning. The educational programmes and curriculum have been built on such approach. It is not easy to introduce through theoretical training the realities of life out of school/institution in education based on school/institution. Education for children with normal developmental level does not include a system based on the principles and standards outlined above. It cannot be expected that persons with disabilities which receive inclusive education in such an education system can indeed receive education at the principles and standards recognised by international law and in the model and quality observed in best practice countries. Therefore, it is necessary to change the approach in the general structure of education in addition to the peculiar problems of inclusive education, restructure the education system and support the practice by an enabling legislation.

b. Appropriate and Qualified Educators

The presence of educators is of equal value both to special education and integrative education who know how to use educational materials properly to meet learning needs through appropriate and quality, can plan and individualise educational programmes according to particular needs of each student, have pedagogical knowledge and education to communicate with and understand any type of student. The priority action to ensure this is to make mandatory that educators to serve in special education institutions have higher education in special education. To teach the sign language in a school for students with hearing disabilities, it is extremely important to employ educators of an adequate number who know the means and methods of communicating with such children and have qualifications to assess their development and peculiar characteristics. It is incomprehensible to provide sound education in an institution that provides education to students with hearing disabilities through educators who have none or little of such qualifications. For

147 For standards relating to supportive services, see: **Philip Maxwell Ruddock**, *Disability Standards for Education 2005*, 17 Marc 2005, Australia, pp. 19–20.

instance, assigning an educator who does not know Braille as a class teach in a school for students with visual disabilities should be seen as the violation of the right to education of students in such a school. It is not difficult to imagine the difficulties for the teacher and children where a teacher of regular school who has received no education in the field of special education, has no idea on persons with disabilities starts to serve in a school or class where children with disabilities are numerous.

It is acceptable under certain circumstances that a class teacher who has finished an educational programme including courses on special education, not a higher education programme specifically designed for special education will serve in the integrative education class with students with disabilities. In such case however, teachers should at least be provided with expert assistance in designing, implementing and assessing the outcomes of the educational programmes for students with special needs.

It is required that educators who play a key role in supporting the system at all phases in the integrative education process have the following qualifications:

- Ability to understand the strengths and weaknesses of children in terms of personal and educational aspects, and assess their needs;
- Have the flexibility to adapt the education curriculum to the interests and abilities of the children;
- Ability to work with external professional educators to reinforce the children's education obtained within school and from other learning media;
- Ability to work with families;
- Ability to use existing technologies to support learning, monitor and assess the outcomes of the practice;
- Ability to employ positive norms on discipline and class administration;
- Ability to engage in teaching and group working in participative and interactive manner.[148]

Special education teachers who work in the integrative education system and have students with special needs in their class should be provided with an expert or competent assistant even if they have the qualifications above.[149] While the class teacher is in charge of general administration of the class and flow of lessons, the assistant teacher will help prevent a disruption of order in the class, observe and support the students with disabilities and endeavour to keep them learning at the learning rate of the class. Further, the assistant teacher will transfer his/her special education

148 "Promoting the Rights of Children with Disabilities", *Innocenti Digest No. 13*, Innocenti Research Centre, UNICEF, 2007, p.30; A Human Rights-Based Approach to Education for All, UNESCO/UNICEF, 2007, pp. 71–72; *Pathways to the Future: A Report of the Review of educational Services for Students with Disabilities in Government Schools*, Government of Western Australia Department of Education and Training, 2004, pp. 42–43.

149 **Gordon L. Porter,** Disability and Education: Towards an Inclusive Approach, *SDS Working Paper*, 2001,p.14.

experience to the class teacher such as providing supportive education to students in need, preparing and assessing the individualised educational programmes. The legislation on special education does not provide for such a system for full-time inclusive education. The Regulation on Special Education Services provides, in order to remedy such deficiency, to some extent, in special education classes under part-time inclusion practice, that the lessons will be provided by a class teacher who has received education per the prevalent disability; and for the branch lessons, the branch teacher will be accompanied by the class teacher. Pursuant to the relevant provisions of the Regulation, class teachers for students with hearing, visual and intellectual disabilities will be assigned in the special education classes opened for the students with deficiencies arising from visual, hearing, orthopaedic intellectual and autism conditions considering the types of deficiency (Art. 38/2-c, Art. 40).

These arrangements however show that the class teachers are burdened with all sorts of work relating to education including providing education to students with disabilities in inclusion schools and special education schools, solving problems in the class relating to education and students, taking up assignments in the preparation and implementation of BEPs, recommending necessary changes, and assessing achievements. The fulfilment of special educational needs indeed is so comprehensive a work that cannot be placed on one single individual; it is a process that requires specialist knowledge, support and assistance, and working in coordination and cooperation. The Regulation on Special Education Services introduces some provisions to alleviate the burden and responsibilities of teachers. In-school support and cooperation mechanisms such as BEP units, counselling and guidance services units are complemented by such out-of-school mechanisms as RAMs. None of such boards, institutions and units however is closely mingled with the students as the class teacher is. In an inclusion class, the teachers are required to supervise the children with disabilities along with other students, ensure that they participate in class, generate immediate solutions to emergent cases, and at the same time keep order and discipline in the class. The same is also true for class teachers serving in special education classes or special education schools and institutions. While the number of students in special education classes or special education schools and institutions is low, teachers alone educate students of varying developmental levels, different characteristics and habits. It is extremely important that class teachers and other educators receive intra-classroom support and assistance to ensure that students with disabilities receive quality and appropriate education on equal bass with others. Legal measures must be taken on this matter.

Another measure to ensure quality and appropriate education is to provide pre-service and in-service vocational training to all employees in the integrative educational institutions including teachers, educators and assistants, school administrators and assistant personnel. It must be legally mandatory that employees in the educational institutions receive vocational education to equip them with technical knowledge for pedagogical and special education such as types and degrees of disability, characteristics of students, interpersonal relations and communication, response to emergency behavioural problems. In-service training should be provided frequently where everyone will have a chance to express the challenges and experience and get responses to pending problems.[150] In addition, teachers should be given the opportunity to participate in courses and programmes where they can develop themselves, be encouraged to participate in scientific meetings, experimental work, meetings where knowledge and experience are shared, new methods and developments are discussed on meeting the needs in integrative education.[151]

The Article "Vocational Works" of the Regulation on Special Education Services provides that "Administrator and teachers in special education schools and institutions shall participate in vocational works from the end of classes to the first working day of July, and from the first working day of September to the start of the academic year, and for the designated times during the annual work plan [59/A – (Supplement: OG-14/3/2009-27169)]. While the provision appears theoretically to introduce an opportunity for professional development for all educators and administrators, it should be kept in mind that the feedback and assessments are important on the content of such processes in practice, or in other works, how it contributes to the development of education and development of administrators in respect of special education, what solutions are formulated to prevent the recurrence of problems identified and discussed in the upcoming academic year and whether they are implemented. Therefore, a system should be established and secured by the relevant legislation to generate a specific content, monitor, supervise and assess both the content and results of the professional development programmes in a manner to cover all educators and administrators working in special education school/institutions and inclusive education.

The State is responsible, to a large extent, for the professional qualifications of special educators and other educators to work in integrative education. It is not possible for the States to overlook special education needs in a world where the rights-based approach to education is fostering, and the practices of transition to integrative education system are prevalent. It is necessary that existing and

---

150 For detailed arrangement, see: "The Salamanca Statement and Framework for Education on Special Needs Education", *Adopted by the World Conference on Special Needs Education: Access and Quality,* Salamanca, Spain, 7–10 June 1994, UNESCO, 40–48; **Gordon L. Porter**, "Disability and Education: Towards an Inclusive Approach", *SDS Working Paper,* 2001, pp. 14–15; **Hildegunn Olsen**, *Inclusive Education: A Process of School Improvement,* UNESCO, Bangkok, p. 9 www.adb.org/Documents/Events/2002/Disability_Development/olsen_paper.pdf, (23.05.2008)

151 For example, such encouraging measures may be taken that score points may be assigned to each participation in scientific or experimental work and meetings, performance-based wages and bonuses etc. For experiences of some countries, see: *Thematic Studies Inclusion in Education: The Participation of Disabled Learners,* World Education Forum Dakar, Senegal 26–28 April 2000, Education for All 2000 Assessment, UNESCO, Graphoprint, France 2001, pp. 41–43; "Diversity, Inclusion and Equity: Insights from Special Needs Provision", *Education Policy Analysis,* OECD 2003, pp. 25–26.

prospective higher education institutions should include programmes compliant with the general principles of integrative education to provide quality education to educators as one of the pillars of education in accordance with such developments. The education provided by institutions that raise educators must include intensive internship programmes, prospective educators must come into contact and work with children with disabilities. Education must be given in such content and nature that such courses as psychology, pedagogy cover all new knowledge and experience on persons with disabilities; and experience be acquired in class administration, interactive education methods, project-based group works. It will be useful to include provisions on this matter in the higher education legislation.

In addition to such measures, there must be certain conditions and criteria to start the profession following the graduation. Such criteria as passing certain topical tests as psychology, psychiatry; achievement in compulsory internship and pre-service training will help carefully select those who will work in such sensitive areas. Working in special education and with persons in need of special education can be challenging and draining. Therefore, the field of special education may be made an attractive choice to encourage entry to the profession through such measures as establishing a special status similar to the employees of police and armed forces and providing various advantages in wages, career promotions and retirement. Satisfying the educators by social and economic benefits during their career, the presence of an administrative system that support and encourage them in the working environment will be effective in the success of integrative education. It will not be realistic to expect educators whose rights are violated to respect the rights of children.[152] Such advantages as relatively better wages, labour union rights will provide motivation for the selection of and staying in the profession.[153] The presence of an adequate number of committed educators in integrative education will bring about institutional success. It will be appropriate that the special education legislation or other relevant legislation include such incentives and facilitations.

152 A Human Rights-Based Approach to Education for All, UNESCO/UNICEF, 2007, p. 72; **Susan J Peters**, "Inclusive education: Achieving Education for All By Including Those With Disabilities and Special educational needs", *Prepared for The Disability Group The World Bank*, April 30, 2003, p. 32; for public and private law rights of educators, see: **Katarina Tomasevski**, "Removing obstacles in the way of the right to education", *Primers No. 1,* International Development Cooperation Agency, Sida, 2001, pp. 39–41.

153 For professional rights of educators, see: **Katarina Tomasevski**, "Human rights obligation: making education available, accessible, acceptable and adaptable", *Right to Education Primers No. 3,* International Development Cooperation Agency, Sida, 2001, pp. 23–25.

c. *Appropriate Educational Environment*

The practice of special education school poses two core questions in respect of the right to education of persons with disabilities. The first is that special education institutions are not capable, by number and capacity, of serving children with disabilities who are not admitted to the general education system.[154] The World Health Organisation estimates that only 5% of the children with disabilities in developing countries can benefit from all support and assistance; and the school enrolment rates remain as low as 2%. The most important reason is that children with disabilities are mostly the children of poor families in poor countries.[155] The children remain out of education as long as there is no appropriate school to attend, even if the families have the economic power.

The non-admission of a large majority of such children to regular schools, the few numbers of special education schools or lack of schools appropriate for the type of disability, children with disabilities are excluded from education where it creates discrimination and inequality vis-à-vis peers without disabilities. The right to education of persons with disabilities is thus violated. The most important impact of the provision of special education in separate schools on the right to education is that some children with disabilities who can receive education in regular schools if provided with appropriate support and educational needs met appropriately are forced to receive education in special education school. This leads to serious disadvantages on the part of such children. The first is that special education particularly in developing countries is not of adequate quality to enable children with disabilities to live independently in dignity.[156] Further, providing education to children with disabilities in separate premises or special classes in regular schools indeed reinforces discrimination and exclusion. Another negative outcome is that following graduation from such school, they cannot attend educational institutions in the general system; there is no equivalency in respect of graduation from special and general education systems. By such practice, the right to education of children is substantially degraded and the right itself is effectively dispossessed of the children

---

154 For examples of practices in the Latin American and Caribbean countries, see: **Gordon L. Porter,** "Disability and Education: Towards an Inclusive Approach", *SDS Working Paper*, 2001, p.6.

155 **Gordon** L. **Porter,** "Disability and Education: Towards an Inclusive Approach", *SDS Working Paper*, 2001, p.6.

156 While it is not the comparative data showing the academic achievements, preparation for higher education, participation rates in work and other spheres of social life; some studies on students with disabilities in secondary education in 1985 found out that the academic performance of those who studied in regular schools was 80% whereas that of those educated in separated/special educational institutions was 50%. R. Weiner, *Impact on the Schools*, Capitol Publications, 1985 quoted by "Special Education Inclusion", 15 March 2007, http://www.weac.org/resource/june96/speced.htm, (18.03.2008)

who, whatever the diagnosis or the level of deficiency, have the capacity to receive education in regular schools and move to the top levels of formal education.[157]

The provision of education to children with disabilities in separate institutions is a residue of the medical model of disability. The examples of this model are the practices of the States in the Central and East Europe and Baltic in the late 1990s. At that time, 317 000 children out of an approximately 1 million children living in institutions were children with disabilities in 27 countries in the said geography. Some were kept unnecessarily as inpatients for long time in such institutions for having epilepsy, cleft palate, scoliosis.[158] Education was provided to these institutionalised persons with disabilities by either the institution or another institution specific to persons with disabilities. Such tradition of separation results in a domino effect for all phases of life. Persons with disabilities are imprisoned in a rather narrow sphere of life through separate residence, separate education, separate work, separate lifestyle. The provision of education to children and youth with disabilities wholly or substantially by separate special education institutions and organisations outside the general system results in an isolation and exclusion of persons with disabilities from the society at large. Where the model that includes persons with disabilities in the general system of education starting from pre-school is preferred, they can fully and effectively participate in society, whereas the discriminatory and exclusion model of education separates persons with disabilities from all other spheres of life.

It is true that the transition from separated special education school system to integrative education is not easy. Following a serious analysis considering the best interests and needs of the children, it takes time and serious effort to enact legislative arrangements, formulate strategies and plans in cooperation with various sectors involved, set aside human and financial resources, and restructure the institutional system. When making such plans, care must be taken that a system be developed to avoid conflicts of interests considering the right to education and learning needs of other children who will have education with children with disabilities.

While the legislative measures and policies are various in those States which adopt the integration model for the education of children with disabilities and seek to minimise education in separated premises and classes, the common practice in developed countries is to transform the special education schools into resource centres for schools and educational institutions in the general education system. For instance, in such system that is becoming more pervasive in the North and Central European countries, the role of special education schools is defined as follows:[159]

---

157 CRC/C/SR.418, para.2.

158 "Promoting the Rights of Children with Disabilities", *Innocenti Digest No. 13*, Innocenti Research Centre, UNICEF, 2007, p.18.

159 **Susan J Peters,** *Inclusive education: Achieving Education for All by Including Those with Disabilities and Special educational needs*, Prepared for The Disability Group The World Bank, April 30, 2003, p.22.

- provide training and courses for teachers and other professionals in regular educational institutions,
- develop and disseminate materials and methods,
- support mainstream schools and parents,
- provide short-term or part-time help for individual students,
- support students in entering the labour market.

This practice is also taken up in countries in addition to European countries; educators and other experts in special education schools have started to transfer their knowledge and experience to the administrative and academic staff of the regular schools engaging in inclusive education in their area, provide pre- and in-service training, provide guidance, and deliver family support programmes.[160] In Jamaica and Brazil for instance, the integrative educational programmes piloted in the second half of 1990s started to provide support to educators and assistant personnel who gave education children who received education in regular schools but failed because their special educational needs were not adequately met. Educators were informed and trained on the teaching methods that must be adapted to the interest and development of every child, and methods of coping with in-class behavioural problems children with disabilities were taught. It was found out in the conclusion of the application that the feelings of fear and anxiety of educators in regular schools about the students with disabilities in their classes were alleviated or eliminated; and their self-confidence boosted through the skills of coping with such children, successful communication and teaching methods. The work was a useful start for special educators because they saw that they would always be needed and how they could be effective for the success of the integrative education system while indeed they thought that they would lose their jobs with transition into the integrative education system.[161]

As seen in the examples, special education schools and institutions can serve as valuable resources for the development of integrative education.[162] For integrative education to succeed, it needs professional guidance. They may play a significant role in transferring the knowledge and experience to teachers and teaching

160 **Seamus Hegary,** *Educating Children and Young People with Disabilities Principals and the review of practice,* UNESCO, 1992, p.41; "Promoting the Rights of Children with Disabilities", *Innocenti Digest No. 13,* Innocenti Research Centre, UNICEF, 2007, p. 30; for the new roles assumed by special educators and practices in the United Kingdom, see: *Open File on Inclusive Education Support Materials for Managers and Administrators,* UNESCO, 2001, p.50–51 and pp. 75–77.

161 **Gordon L. Porter,** Disability and Education: Towards an Inclusive Approach, SDS Working Paper, 2001, pp. 16–18.

162 See: "The Salamanca Statement and Framework for Action on Special Needs Education", *Adopted by the World Conference on Special Needs Education: Access and Quality, Salamanca, Spain, 7–10 June* 1994, UNESCO & Ministry of Education and Science Spain, pp. 11–12, Inclusive Schooling Children with Special Educational Needs, Department for Education and Skills, 2001, p. 21.

personnel in regular educational institutions and adapting the content and methods of educational programmes to the general system in responding to special educational needs. The trend of establishing close relations between special education schools and general schools is spreading in North America and Europe.[163]

The Decree-Law on Special Education that entered into force in 1997 without adequate prior research, review, analysis and assessments introduced an inclusion-based special education approach abruptly to the Turkish education system. Prior to any legislative effort, some preparations must be made. A piece of legislation which would radically change the education system should not have been adopted without knowing the number of persons with disabilities, number of persons in need of special education, types of disability, geographic distribution, level of educational needs, number of special educators and other special education professionals, qualifications, physical and service capacity of schools and institutions, and the cost likely to be incurred for inclusion. Consequently, too many problems were experience in the implementation of the -Law; then, the same mistake of attempting to set something right by legislative action was made again to issue the Regulation on Special Education Services in 2006. In the meantime, the Law on Amending the Law on Impaired Persons and Certain Laws and Decree-Laws (now called the Law No. 5378 on Persons with Disabilities) was enacted in 2005; and the principles and standards for the right to education of persons with disabilities were treated in a modern interpretation. However, the practice in Turkey relied on the Regulation on Special Education Services because it was a comprehensive regulation both for service provides and recipients in respect of special education.

The said Regulation structures, as noted earlier, special education services according to types of deficiency of individuals. Once this is adopted as the starting point, the entire Regulation is dominated by the institutional viewpoint on schools and institutions to be opened by types of disability/deficiency, and the functions, powers and standards relating to the education to be provided in such places. The Regulation set its tone right from the start by defining the types of deficiency in respect of individuals. The subsequent provisions of the Regulation, in an approach disregarding the goals and basic principles of special education in its very own text, put special education schools/institutions and classes to the forefront, and direct a large part of the persons with disabilities towards education in separated settings where unified class practice also exists. Inclusive education is regulated by only two specific provisions. While it is frequently emphasised that special education needs will be met under inclusion within the formal education starting from pre-school through higher education as well as non-formal education, the Regulation exposes itself as a legislative piece as a whole not serving such philosophy by allowing the establishment of a special education class, school or institution for almost each type of disability. As explained above, the Regulation on Special Education Services

163 "Promoting the Rights of Children with Disabilities", *Innocenti Digest No. 13,* Innocenti Research Centre, UNICEF, 2007, p.17.

cannot be called as an outcome of a will that requires the inclusion of persons with disabilities at the highest rates possible in inclusive education without highlighting the types of deficiency and does not allow the practice of such model education in the so-called part-time inclusion frame, i.e. special education classes or other schools and institutions.

It is not realistic to propose to shut down the existing special education schools in Turkey and have everybody receive inclusive education, nor is it feasible or appropriate for every child. Our proposal is to terminate the practice of special education class as arranged by the Regulation, amend the functions of special education schools and institutions to become resource centres.[164] It is obvious that such structuring of education will effectively fulfil the right to education of persons with disabilities or in need of special education in compliance with the Convention. First of all, educational institutions that may be called regular schools will, due to their high number and wide geographic dispersion, facilitate physical access by persons with disabilities. On the other hand, special education institutions pose access problems due to their low number and pattern of distribution across the country; thus, it is recognised that the latter result in inequality and discrimination among the persons with disabilities because few have access to it. Thereby, the problems relating to the availability and accessibility of education, as explained in the elements of right to education, will be resolved to a large extent. There remain the adaptability and acceptability of education for which we presented our proposals in our assessment of the inclusion system.

The concern that such a system will leave special educators unemployed or unusable is groundless either. On the contrary, special educators who are few in Turkey[165] like in many other countries have little time and opportunity to develop themselves, learn new techniques and system while trying to provide day-long education to many children with disabilities in isolated schools; they can then have time and the structural and other problems in special education schools, and low efficiency due to excessive workload will be resolved. Once special education schools

---

164 While it varies by country that resource centres are structured and assume roles, the purpose is to provide expert knowledge, suggestions and courses to educators on the types and forms of educational materials, how to treat students with disabilities and others having education together, and how to ensure order in the class, thereby ensure that students different than others can effectively benefit from education. See: *Open File on Inclusive Education Support Materials for Managers and Administrators*, UNESCO, 2001, pp. 76–77.

165 This problem is expressed even in relatively developed countries such as New Zealand. See: Human Rights in New Zealand Today: Chapter 15 The Right to Education, http://www.hrc.co.nz/report/chapters/chapter15/education01.html, (05.08.2008); for the view that the low number of teachers who have received appropriate education for all levels is a barrier to inclusive education, see: "Promoting the Rights of Children With Disabilities", *Innocenti Digest No. 13,* Innocenti Research Centre, UNICEF, 2007, p. 17.

are transformed into resource centres, special educators and experts will provide education to educators, and counselling to families and school administration in the regular school scheme in their time remaining after the limited time for providing education to children with disabilities. Thereby, they can engage in research and development activities to meet special education needs in an education setup of better quality and benefit more frequently from "training of educators" programmes to develop themselves.

To transform the Turkish education system accordingly, it is necessary to adopt a series of amendments in the Turkish education legislation including the operation and institutional structure of education, monitoring and inspection of practice, providing effective means of complaints and other application.

4. Monitoring and Supervision of Education

It is known that the States' adoption of legislation to prevent the violation of the right to education and other rights of persons with disabilities by third parties and institutions and ensure that persons and organisations providing public service are kept under supervision and oversight is of unique value in respect of prevention of actual discrimination, protection and fulfilment of rights. The most effective way to conduct education in accordance with the laws is to continuously monitor and supervise the practice. The State may generally discharge such function through administrative and judicial protection as well as through national human rights institutions.

The administration refers to the public administration and involves a "power" that includes all public organisations and affairs other than legislature, judiciary and governing to a certain extent.[166] Due to its functions of enforcing the laws and the decisions of the judiciary, establishing general regulatory acts concerning fundamental rights and freedoms and individual acts and actions, the administration is in closer relation with the society and individuals compared to other State organs. Therefore, it is highly likely that the administration commits violations of human rights. Looking the other way around, the function of the administration to protect fundamental rights and freedoms is equally valuable. It has an effective role in protecting the rights by such powers as preventing possible violations by itself due to acts and actions concerning rights and freedoms or by third parties, stopping any ongoing violations, operating the mechanisms to repair the damages to those whose rights have been violated, and imposing administrative penalties.

166 **A. Şeref Gözübüyük,** *Yönetim Hukuku [Administrative Law],* Turhan Kitapevi [Turhan Publisher], Onaltıncı Basım [Sixteenth Edition], Ankara, 2002, pp. 2–3, Gözübüyük states that the expression "... other than governing to a certain extent..." means that the government does not only have administrative duties but also political duties; therefore, the government can only be included in the concept of administration in respect of discharging administrative duties and powers.

The administration has two basic duties relating to the protection of rights freedoms: prevent violations and remedy violations. The administration's function of prevention of violations should be viewed in the context of a wider set of obligations. One is to inform the society on rights and freedoms through the State actors and non-State actors providing public services and prevent violations through increased awareness of rights through education. In addition, the obligation to facilitate and provide access to information and documents relating to the administration's acts and actions is important for the protection of rights. Another protection obligation of the administration is the obligation to remain compliant with laws in all acts and actions including regulatory acts and prevent violations. To that end, it must strike a balance between the public good and the protection of individual's rights, not promoting one over the other. It should be kept in mind that the obligation to act in accordance with laws and ensure that all others do so covers the supervision and oversight of public institutions and organisations and private persons and organisations providing public service (preventive administrative oversight).

The Constitution, administrative legislation and various laws govern the prohibition and sanctions that prevent the violation of human rights and freedoms and interests by the administration itself, and the obligation of the administration to prevent commission of such violations by third parties. From the viewpoint of the right to education of persons with disabilities, there are some monitoring and supervision mechanisms both in the general education and special education legislation to prevent violations of the right to education and ensure that individuals properly benefit from special education services. However, the complexity of legislation on special education services, and associated difficulties in understanding the institutional system and operation prevents beneficiaries and recipients of service from participating in the monitoring and supervision. The provisions in the legislation relating to right to education of persons with disabilities and special education services change so frequently that persons with disabilities and families as well as the practitioners have difficulty to keep abreast. Such changes also affect institutional structuring; the confidence is eroded in the continuity of powers and functions of the units operating the system. It is basic characteristics of the modern rule of law that laws must be clear, predictable, intelligible and not be changed unless necessary; Turkey, as a country that adopts the principle of rule of law in her Constitution, must in priority preserve and implement this principle. Therefore, it is of utmost importance that the entire legislation on education and special education be simplified in language and meaning; measures be taken for conflicting provisions; the provisions on rights, freedoms and services have fewer rules relating to the institutional and prevent frequent amendments.

The Ministry of National Education is the central administration within the education system. The organisation and operation of education as a right and service (from the centre to provincial and local administration units) is under the supervision and oversight of this Ministry. The Ministry is authorised to inspect both public and private educational institutions. However, it is not easy to smoothly operate the formal and non-formal education structure in the context of compulsory education process by all its components and rules at national level. It is too burdensome a job for a single central unit to plan and execute education as a multi-pillar system and as a right to be fulfilled on the basis of equality for all. In order to solve the problem, it will be effective to increase the number of units within MoNE, establish a special unit for the education of persons with disabilities, ensure that special education services and counselling and guidance services be delivered by separate units, and build a comprehensive organisational structure for inclusive education.

The administration's functions and powers to remedy violations include the obligation to establish objective institutions through which complaints of violations will be lodged and effectively operate such structures, enforce the decisions of judicial bodies and repair the damages.

a. *Remedying Violations and Consequences*

Upon becoming parties to international human rights covenants, States assume the obligation to protect and fulfil the rights arising from such covenants of everyone under their jurisdiction through all bodies and institutions within the State system. The importance has been emphasised of the part of the administrative body of the State which acts mostly as the service unit on the State's obligation to protect and fulfil. The administration must have taken all measures to prevent violations; identify, stop and remedy the consequences of any violations despite all measures so that the administration can be considered to have fulfilled its obligation to protect under the domestic law the rights governed by the Convention on the Rights of Persons with Disabilities. In view of the fact that preventive measures and methods are not always successful, and some violations do occur; it is necessary to admit that remedying of violations too protect the rights. The administration must take action to ensure such protection. The administrative bodies of States Parties to the international human rights covenants are under obligation to take positive action to remedy violations of rights. Such measures particularly include, among others, establishing independent institutions that will hear and resolve allegations and complaints of violations relating to the acts and actions of the administration under in the context of powers and responsibilities. It is equally important that where the problems not resolved by the administration or independent human right institutions are taken to court, the court decisions be enforced, damages be repaired, and the grievance of complainants be ended. The latter obligation refers to the opportunity of access by individuals, who claim that they are adversely affected, and their rights are violated by the administration's acts and actions, to an objective institution within the administrative structure but independent of the administration, and expedient and easy solution to such claims. The other refers to the impact of the enforcement by the administration of judicial decisions relating to the administration's acts and actions on the protection of rights.

b. Establishing an Impartial and Effective Complaints Mechanism

The United Nations General Assembly recommended, by a resolution in 1989, that all States to establish national institutions for the protection and promotion of human rights within their country and territory, emphasised that it was essential to enact appropriate national legislation to effectively guarantee international human rights standards. It was also noted that by establishing national human rights institutions and strengthening the existing ones, significant distance could be covered in protecting and promoting human rights and fundamental freedoms at national level, and the United Nations could play a catalytic role.[167]

The Vienna Declaration and Programme of Action as the conclusion document of the World Conference on Human Rights of 1993 highlighted the important and constructive role played by national institutions for the promotion and protection of human rights.[168] The resolution of the United Nation General Assembly, referred to as "Paris Principles", laid down the principles on the status of national human rights institutions, and their mandate should be set forth in a constitutional or legislative text.[169] The Committee on the Rights of the Children recommended, among the general measures of implementation to be taken by States Parties, that an institution of coordination, monitoring and supervision with a legal status within the administration but independent of the administration to ensure the fulfilment of all the rights recognised by the Convention. Among the child-focused and child-sensitive bodies and structures were mentioned children's rights units at the heart of Government, ministers for children, inter-ministerial committees on children, children's ombudspersons and children's rights commissioners and so on.[170]

Among such institutions, national human rights institutions stand out particularly because they are independent of the administration and used effectively and commonly in the practice.

ba. Establishing National Human Rights Institutions

While there is no consensus or unity of practice at international level on the definition of national human rights institutions, it is generally recognised that such institutions be structured and operate under the Paris Principles. The names and functions of national human rights institutions vary by States. The most frequent names in practice include ombudsman (or ombudsmen or ombudsperson), human

167 United Nation General Assembly, A/RES/44/64 78th plenary meeting, 8 December 1989.

168 World Conference on Human Rights Vienna, 14–25 June 1993, Vienna Declaration and Programme of Action, UN General Assembly A/CONF.157/23, 12 July 1993.

169 United Nation General Assembly, A/RES/48/134 85th plenary meeting, 20 December 1993.

170 General Comment No. 5 (2003) General measures of implementation of the Convention on the Rights of the Child (Art. 4, 42 and 44, para.6), CRC/GC/2003/5 27 November 2003, para.9.

rights commission (or committee), equality institution or commission. The bodies that exist fall into three main categories, but their titles and functions are often interchangeable. Ombudsman is usually an institution that deals with complaints relating to a particularly public administration's acts and actions, and is equipped with powers to monitor, inquire, research and assess in protecting person's rights and upholding justice and legality in the society. Equalities institutions are human right institutions established with a specific mandate to protect the rights of particularly vulnerable groups from discrimination in the exercise of those rights, lead in taking the administrative and legislative measures to ensure that they have and exercise equal rights with the rest of the society and prevent discrimination. These bodies use a variety of designations including ombudsmen or commissioners. Human rights commissions have a broad remit to address a wide range of human rights issues.[171]

Whatever their title is, pursuant to UN Paris Principles, every human rights institution should be established and operate on certain principles. The following are the principles that relate to the status of national human rights institutions:

- These institutions should have as broad a mandate as possible, set down in a constitutional or legislative text that specifies the institution's composition and sphere of competence.
- They should have responsibilities to provide its opinions, recommendations, proposals and reports on any matter concerning the promotion and protection of human rights to parliament, government and other competent bodies – either on request or through its power to consider such matters without higher referral.
- They should have the right to publish opinions and reports independently, including those on the current state of the law, on developments affecting human rights and on violations.
- They should have general duties and necessary powers to promote and ensure harmonisation of national legislation, regulations and practice with international human rights instruments to which the state is a party, and their effective implementation; to encourage ratification or accession to these instruments.
- They should have the right to contribute to the reports that states must submit to UN bodies and committees and to regional institutions, and, where necessary, to express an opinion on the subject, "with due respect for their independence"
    - to cooperate with UN and UN-related organisations and regional and national human rights institutions;

171 For a background and types of national human rights institutions, see: "Independent Institutions Protecting Children's Rights", *Innocenti Digest No. 8*, UNICEF, June 2001, pp. 2–3; Ombudsman for Children, Innocenti Digest No. 2, UNICEF 1997, pp. 2–3; **John Hucker,** "Bringing Rights Home: The Role of National Human Rights Institutions", in *Butler, Frances. (Ed.); Human Rights Protection: Methods and Effectiveness*, Kluwer Law International and British Institute for Human Rights, 2002, Chapter 2, pp. 29–36.

- o to help formulate and take part in programmes for teaching and researching human rights in schools, universities and among professionals;
  - o to publicise human rights and efforts to combat discrimination by increasing public awareness – particularly through information and education and use of the media.
- The composition of the national institution and the appointment of its members shall be established in accordance with a procedure which affords all necessary guarantees to ensure the pluralist representation of the social forces. Non-governmental organisations, Parliament, Government departments (only in an advisory capacity), universities and qualified experts, trends in philosophical or religious thought, trade unions, concerned social and professional organisations should be included.
- The national institution shall have an infrastructure which is suited to the smooth conduct of its activities, in particular adequate funding. The purpose of this funding should be to enable it to have its own staff and premises, in order to be independent of the Government and not be subject to financial control which might affect its independence. It must have, as a necessary characteristic of independence, the power to hear any person and obtain any information and any documents necessary for assessing situations on public acts and actions, Maintain consultation with the other bodies, whether jurisdictional or otherwise.[172]

Relating to their quasi-jurisdictional competence:

- A national institution may be authorised to hear and consider complaints and petitions concerning individual situations. They may be authorised to make recommendations to the competent authorities within the limits prescribed by the law, or seek an amicable settlement through conciliation or, within the limits prescribed by the law, through binding decisions or, where necessary, on the basis of confidentiality.
- It is also important and necessary to ensure access of individuals, groups and civil society to such institution to inform the party who filed the petition, operate the necessary resolution mechanisms.[173]

The Committee on the Rights of the Children refers to similar principles and rules in its General Comment No. 2 on the role and functions of national human rights

---

172 For guarantees of independence for ombudsman, see: "Ombudsman for Children", *Innocenti Digest No. 2,* UNICEF 1997, p.10, "Independent Institutions Protecting Children's Rights", *Innocenti Digest No. 8,* UNICEF, June 2001, pp. 7–8; **Dympna Glendenning**, "The Ombudsman for Children: an analysis of the Irish model as it relates to recognized schools", *Education and the Law,* Vol.16, Nos. 2–3, June/September 2004, Carfax Publishing Taylor & Francis Group, p. 139.

173 United Nation General Assembly, A/RES/48/134 85th plenary meeting, 20 December 1993, Annex.

institutions, and General Comment No. 2 on the rights of children with disabilities.[174] The Committee on Economic, Social and Cultural Rights also issued a General Comment in this line. The Committee pointed out the importance of national human rights institutions in protecting economic, social and cultural rights, and takes Article 2(1) of CESCR as the basis of the obligation to establish such institutions. Treating the matter in the framework of the article that requires the States Parties to take all appropriate measures to progressively achieve the realisation of the rights recognised by the Covenant, the Committee considers the establishment of national human rights institutions as one of the "appropriate measures".[175]

baa. Function of the National Human Rights Institutions to Protect the Rights of Persons with Disabilities

National independent human right institutions may be established to protect and ensure human rights in general as well as to protect and realise the rights of vulnerable and marginalised groups in the society as exemplified in many countries.[176]

In recent years, there is an increase in the number of national institutions on the rights of persons with disabilities which play an important role in preventing the violation of the rights and freedoms of persons with disabilities by public acts and actions, assisting in remedying such violations, and protecting and realising the rights of persons with disabilities in other activities. It is of utmost importance that the rights of persons with disabilities be protected by non-judicial mechanism because persons with disabilities are a group with the highest likelihood of being adversely affected by an act or omission of any government or administration. Generally, not taken into consideration in administrative measures, plans and programs, persons with disabilities therefore face many difficulties in all spheres of social life. Persons with hearing, visual or physical disabilities are not able to effectively benefit from the services provided on account of the difficulties they experience in accessing the public service areas, in communication and other areas. Such difficulties are also experienced in accessing judicial bodies, and the slow-moving judiciary

---

174 General Comment No. 2. The role of independent national human rights institutions in the promotion and protection of the rights of the child, CRC/GC/2002/2, para.1–28, General Comment No. 9 (2006), 27/02/2007. The Rights of Children with Disabilities, CRC/C/GC/9., para. 24; for general information on children's ombudsman, see: **Thomas Hammarberg**, "Children", in *Economic, Social and Cultural Rights, A Textbook,* Revised Edition, Edited by: Asbjørn Eide/ Caterina Krause/ Alan Roses, Marchinus Nijhoff Publishers, Durdrocth/Boston /London 2001, p.364.

175 The role of national human rights institutions in the protection of economic, social and cultural rights, 14/12/98. E/C.12/1998/25, CESCR General comment 10. (General Comments), para.1.

176 For examples of countries which have established national institutions to protect the rights of the child, see: "Independent Institutions Protecting Children's Rights", *Innocenti Digest No. 8,* UNICEF, June 2001, pp. 15–25.

weakens the acquisition and protection of rights. In addition, most persons with disabilities including particularly those with intellectual disabilities and children with disabilities are exposed to exploitation and abuse, and incapable of protecting themselves against violations. All this makes clear that legal remedies and venues should be expanded to protect the legal rights of persons with disabilities. National human rights institutions, by their formal and legal status, discharge a significant function using such power lacked by civil society organisations.

While the rights of persons with disabilities are protected, in some countries, by the national human rights institutions established to protect human rights in general, some other countries have specific institutions to protect the rights of persons with disabilities. For instance, the Australian Commission on Human Rights and Equal Opportunity is mandated by its organisational act to prevent and remedy all discrimination. Another function of the Commission is to protect the persons with disabilities and their rights protected under the Disability Discrimination act and other laws against practices and violations that create discrimination and inequality, and assist in solving problems.[177] While the Canadian Human Rights Commission, French Mediator, Dutch Equality Commission are mandated to protect and supervise human rights in general; the United Kingdom Commission on the Rights of Persons with Disabilities, Israeli Commission on Equal Rights for Persons with Disabilities are specifically mandated on the rights of persons with disabilities.[178] Establishing a national human rights institution specifically mandated to protect the rights of persons with disabilities will strengthen the protection of the rights of persons with disabilities. However, it is not necessary for such institutions to operate in subjective areas. The point is to build them to have certain powers and responsibilities. The success in protecting the rights of persons with disabilities through a new or existing national human rights institution depends on the responses to the following questions:

- Is the institution structured in accordance with Paris Principles?
- Does the institution have the powers to fulfil the requirements of the provision on "national implementation and monitoring" of the Convention on the Rights of Persons with Disabilities?
- Does the institution have staff and members who are with disabilities?
- Does the institution have adequate time and human resources to fulfil its obligation to protect, realise and implement national monitoring as required by the Convention on the Rights of Persons with Disabilities and other conventions and provisions relating to the rights of persons with disabilities?

177 International Disability Rights Compendium 2003, Center for International Rehabilitation/ Landmine Survivors Network/ Rehabilitation International, Second Impression, U.S.A. 2003, pp. 128–129,

178 International Disability Rights Compendium 2003, Center for International Rehabilitation/ Landmine Survivors Network/ Rehabilitation International, Second Impression, U.S.A. 2003, by order of countries p.137, 175, 277, 198,188.

- Does the institution have a policy to reach out persons with disabilities and are the institution's means of outreach adequate?

If the questions above can be answered affirmatively, it may be stated that such a human rights institution would positively contribute to the rights of persons with disabilities.

Article 33 "National Implementation and Monitoring" of the Convention on the Rights of Persons with Disabilities provides that "States Parties shall, in accordance with their legal and administrative systems, maintain, strengthen, designate or establish within the State Party, a framework, including one or more independent mechanisms, as appropriate, to promote, protect and monitor implementation of the present Convention. When designating or establishing such a mechanism, States Parties shall take into account the principles relating to the status and functioning of national institutions for protection and promotion of human rights (Art. 33/2).[179] This provision aims to implement the Convention effectively in domestic law and protect the rights of persons with disabilities in the maximum extent possible. States Parties are under obligation to accord the widest possible mandate to the national human rights institutions that they will establish or designate in their national law and administrative system to protect the rights recognised by the Convention.

Such institutions should be considered a separate and complementary venue to strengthen protection, not as an alternative to the judiciary in respect of protection of rights in the domestic law. In other words, such institutions cannot effectively discharge the function of protection unless they have the powers to receive individual and/or collective petitions, issue opinion, mediate and reconcile parties, present case files to the judiciary and participate in court action. Further, the mandate of such institutions should include both first tier and second tier rights and be regulated so as to ensure protection against both State apparatus and private actors providing public service.

In a world where public services are privatised or transferred to the private sector as a result of all-encompassing globalisation, it has become mandatory to protect the social, economic and cultural rights of persons with disabilities as a whole in the system. For instance, such acts which would be violation of the right to education as preventing a student with disabilities from receiving education provided by the State or private sector, being discriminated, being denied requisite opportunities, excluding from education must be stopped no matter where such acts come from, and the right be restituted and damages be repaired. Such violations of rights are first complained against the institution itself or the administrative units to which the institution is affiliated with or supervised by. However, leaving the powers and responsibilities to remedy the violations only to the administration and viewing the violations as an intra-administration problem will not provide adequate protection. Once the power to supervise is left only to the relevant institution or administration,

179 Convention on the Rights of Persons with Disabilities, UN General Assembly A/61/611, 6 December 2006.

it is always likely that the violation will not be remedied, and the case be covered up, and this is a serious danger for the subjects of rights. In addition, it will not become public unless taken to court. However, the information that a national human rights institution equipped with the said powers will disclose the case to the public will have a deterring effect on the educational institution where the right is violated, and the problem between the student with disabilities or his/her representative and the institution may be resolved by settlement. If the problem cannot be settled by the national human rights institution, the claim of violation will be taken to court; then the participation of the national human rights institution in the case and submission of the problem objectively with evidence and statement of its opinion will facilitate the work of the judiciary.

Consequently, national human rights institutions that are constructed in accordance with the said principles and rules will function as a brake and balance for the legislative, executive and even the judiciary power of the State. In addition, considering such institution as a venue that enables utmost protection of the rights of persons with disabilities, it may be effective in reducing the frequency of violations in time.

The executive organ and administration of a State Party to the international human rights covenants are under obligation to remedy violations of rights regardless of origin in vertical or horizontal relations. They are, as a requirement of the obligation to protect, to stop explicit violations, punish the perpetrators and repair the damages. Where a violation of domestic law or international covenant relating to the right is not explicit or clear, they are under obligation to inquire and investigate the allegations of violation and take all action to protect the right where any violation is identified. For instance, in a State Party to the Convention on the Rights of the Child, Covenant on Economic, Social and Cultural Rights or Convention on the Rights of Persons with Disabilities; such violations as where a student with disabilities who wishes to receive education in the State's educational institutions is denied education for no valid reason, or fails to receive appropriate education due to non-provision of the required support and assistance while means and conditions are adequate in the present educational institution, or excluded from educational possibilities through passive acts will be inquired immediately by the State administration, remedy the adverse consequences if violation is found to exist, repair the damages to the student in question, and punish the culpable persons, all of which make it possible to protect and ensure the exercise of the right.

In the Turkish Law, such acts as negligence in office, abuse of office are generally sanctioned by the Turkish Criminal Code, Law on Civil Servants and relevant legislation. The administrative legislation enumerates the responsibilities of the administration in terms of fault in service, the rights of service recipients, and legal remedies for the violations of rights and interests. Since teachers, educators and administrators in the public sector are civil servants, they are held liable under the civil servants' legislation. In addition, the legislation on general and special education describes duties, powers and responsibilities. However, it is necessary to establish an effective supervisory mechanism specific to special education as a field which is by its very nature sensitive where many violations of right to education may occur due to the structuring of service and/or acts of employees of schools/institutions or excessive workload.

Units whose mandate is solely to monitor and supervise should frequently inspect the structuring of the service for special education or education for the persons with disabilities; how duties, powers and responsibilities are discharged in reasonable conditions; the physical and service related structuring of schools/institutions; whether reasonable accommodation is provided; whether BEP units exist; how they are operated, whether supportive education rooms exist; whether they are used efficiently; whether the education provided at home or in hospital is adequate, effective and appropriate; and the problems and difficulties identified must be reported and solutions be generated. Units with such powers of monitoring, supervising and solving certain problems should be established within local governments or as semi-independent institutions in all provinces and districts, their powers and duties not be limited to public educational institutions and include special education institutions. Provided that such units operate with an adequate number of personnel and at a reasonable workload, they should be authorised to hear the complaints from families and employees of schools/institutions relating to special education or education for the persons with disabilities, examine and inquire on site, obtain documents and information, hear the relevant people, solve certain problems by reconciliation, trigger ministries and other relevant units to expedite solution, which will help prevent violations of special education as well as speedily remedy some of the violations. In addition, the power to remedy the adversities in the slow-moving bureaucracy between the central and provincial organisations of MoNE, solve the problems speedily on site without referring to the Ministry, refer to the centre those unsolved problems along with recommendations, and monitor whether problems are resolved will facilitate the relations between the centre and the local.

If the problem is not resolved by the administration, then taken to court and the court decision is finalised that the right of a student with disabilities has been violated, it is extremely important that the public or special education that committed the violation implement the decision of the judiciary without delay to protect the right. If the relevant right cannot be exercised or the damages arising from the violation is not repaired and left on the victim because the requirements of a judicial decision are not implemented in respect of the institutions owned by the administrative units of the State or under the supervision and oversight of the State, it must be possible to lodge a complaint on this case again. The possibility of communicating the complaints that the violation is going on or the damage is not repaired due to the failure of implementation of the relevant judicial decision to the relevant administrative units or higher authorities should be thought of as a legal remedy and serve to protect the right.

Conclusions and Recommendations

The right to education is explained in this Report in the meaning and content as recognised generally in international law and the normative elements of the right to education of persons with disabilities are described. The rights of persons with disabilities and right to education among them are explained in the specific context in international law. Such explanations devoted the most comprehensive section to the Convention on the Rights of Persons with Disabilities, and the Conventions is evaluated as a whole with the right to education of persons with disabilities and fundamental principles and other provisions relating to such right.

The second part of the Report examines the right to education in general in the Turkish legal system and right to education of persons with disabilities in particular; comparing the Turkish legislation to the Convention on the Rights of Persons with Disabilities and other international human rights covenants to which Turkey is a State Party.

The report further examines the structuring of the Turkish education system, how the education of persons with disabilities is treated in the context of what basic principles and goals, and institutions and rules relating to the structure and functioning. The relevant parts of the Report do not only provide explanations, but also evaluate specific provisions of the legislation, and provide criticism and recommendations. Therefore, we will not need to make another assessment in this conclusion section; we will suffice by stating some recommendations not expressed earlier.

Education is both a human right in and of itself and an inalienable instrument for the realisation of all other human rights. As an empowering right, education is the basic instrument for adults and children who are excluded from the society in economic, social and other areas to find the way to save themselves from poverty and participate fully in the society in which they live. Education has a vital role in empowerment of women as well as persons with disabilities, protecting children from exploitation and dangerous labour and sexual abuse, development and emplacement of human rights, democracy and the notion of active citizenship and protection of the environment. Based on this basic philosophy, we recommend that the following be considered in regulating the right to education in the Constitution:

- Education should be regulated with a content based on an individual oriented and rights-based approach as adopted in the international human rights covenants, not as a service mentality which puts forward the interests of the State and aims at raising good citizens. The goal, content and method of education should be laid down in accordance with the approach that considers individual differences, prioritises individual education needs and addresses the child's development in a holistic framework.
- Education should be physically and economically accessible by all, particularly by persons with disabilities and vulnerable groups, legally and actually in

accordance with non-discrimination. The new Constitution should appropriately regulate the accessibility of education which means that nobody is subject to discrimination in respect of the exercise of the right to education, that it is possible for all to physically access educational institutions, that nobody is excluded from education due to economic deprivation and all benefit fully from education given in educational institutions.

- The form and substance of education including curriculum and teaching methods should be acceptable to all students and parents as necessary considering the "best interests of the child", adaptable to the changing needs of communities, and flexible to respond to the educational needs of students from different social and cultural backgrounds and different characteristics.
- Measures to be taken to eliminate structural barriers to exercising the right to education by persons with disabilities other vulnerable (exposed to risk) and disadvantaged groups should be explicitly emphasised that they will aim to ensure full participation and equality of all in the society, and to that end, all persons with disabilities and other disadvantaged persons will have priority appropriately.
- It should also be emphasised that the special measures to be taken to ensure actual equality in education for girls, persons with disabilities and culturally, socially and culturally disadvantaged persons cannot be considered as discrimination.
- Education should be treated as a right that is child-centred, for the child and empowering the child; and it should be emphasised that the structure and processes of education be built on the "best interest" centred around the child.
- The individual and social goals of education should be laid down clearly. The individual goals of education should be based on a method that is centred on the child and individual and aims to meet different needs on the basis of differences, conducive to maximise individual and social development, and the best interest and participation of the child.
- The individual goals of education in the Constitution should be clearly stated, in a language consistent with the Convention on the Rights of the Child, the Covenant on Economic, Social and Cultural Rights and the Convention on the Rights of Persons with Disabilities to which Turkey is a State Party, that *education should aim to empower the child and ensure his full and active participation in all spheres of life through developing the child's abilities, learning and other competences, human dignity, self-esteem and confidence.*
- To that end, the necessity should also be emphasised that the education curriculum directly relates to the child's present and future needs, and teaching methods be formulated to suit differing needs of the child.
- While the individual goals to be pursued for the education of children with disabilities are based on the same basis, it should be clearly stated that *integrative*

education (inclusive education)[180] is adopted as the purpose which, in line with the Convention on the Rights of Persons with Disabilities, provides more opportunities of peer support to foster the self-esteem of persons with disabilities and facilitate their participation in all spheres of social life.

- There should be no Constitutional provision such as 42/7 that obliges the State to take measures to make those in need of special education useful to the society, because the priority objective of special education is not render the child to the society, but to achieve the child's individual and social development in all aspects to the maximum level, strengthen and make the child independent so as to enable him/her to fully participate in independent life.
- Further, it should be indicated as an obligation of the State to meet the needs of persons with disabilities in the general education system so that they can effectively benefit from the system; make reasonable accommodation and thereby ensure their attendance in education continuously.
- Similarly, the social purposes of education should be built on a philosophy that respects human beings and values human dignity; and include a list of objectives designed to build a way of thinking that fosters respect for democracy, human rights, own culture as well as other cultures, society and environment; respect for all nations, differences in race, religion, language, sex and any other differences on the basis of friendship.
- The compulsory education in the Constitution should be defined as a process to achieve the best interest and development of the child, prepare him/her in the best manner for future to attain the goal of educating all children on a strong basis in line with the scope and content in international law.
- The fundamental right to education should be considered as a right that applies to everybody whose "basic learning needs" have not been met as an integral part of adult education and life-long learning; the curricula and teaching methods

180 The Committee on the Rights of the Children, in its General Comment in 2006, defined inclusive education as a set of values, principles and practices that seeks meaningful, effective, and quality education for all students, that does justice to the diversity of learning conditions and requirements not only of children with disabilities, but for all students. The Committee emphasises that this goal can be achieved by different organisational means which respect the diversity of children. It is further noted that inclusion may range from full-time placement of all students with disabilities into one regular classroom or placement into the regular class room with varying degree of inclusion, including a certain portion of special education. The emphasis by the Committee on the practice is that close cooperation among special educators and regular educators is essential; schools' curricula must be re-evaluated and developed to meet the needs of children with and without disabilities; modification in training programmes for teachers and other personnel involved in the educational system must be achieved in order to fully implement the philosophy of inclusive education. General Comment No. 9 (2006): The Rights of Children with Disabilities, CRC/C/GC/9, 27 February 2007.

should be formulated to fit the needs of all age groups and basic educational needs of the persons with disabilities.

- The limits of the State's obligation to realise the right to education in the Constitution should be arranged to cover the following basic areas of obligations:
  - ✓ Guarantee the right to access to public/special education institutions and programmes without discrimination;
  - ✓ Guarantee that education conforms to social and individual goals; ensure that all benefit from free and compulsory primary and secondary education;
  - ✓ Prepare and implement the national education strategy for pre-school, basic education and higher education;
  - ✓ Guarantee that education can be freely selected without the intervention of the State or third parties within the "minimum educational standards".
- The general obligations of the State relating to right to education should be arranged in a scope that expresses the necessity to eliminate the practices that prohibit or prevent the enjoyment of right to education, take measures to prevent interference with the enjoyment of right to education, provide means and opportunities for individuals and communities to enjoy right to education, and take positive measures to facilitate the foregoing.
- To that end, the scope of the State's obligations should be enlarged, and obligations be expressed in explicit language. It should particularly be stated as the State's obligation to take all necessary measures to realise the right to education in a manner free of discrimination and in actual equality with others in the framework of the principles, standards, methods and goals as defined above for the disadvantaged segments of the society including particularly persons with disabilities.

The basic elements of a legislative text relating to the right to education of persons with disabilities should include the following:[181]

- The law should conform to the approach to disability in the Convention on the Rights of Persons with Disabilities, include all the notions of discrimination and areas where discrimination is prohibited on the basis of disability. It should include such important concepts as reasonable accommodation and universal design as defined in the Convention. It should have a content to lead in eliminating physical, financial or attitudinal barriers of access and exercising the inclusive right to education in all aspects. It should pursue the goal of ensuring that

181 For detailed information, see: *Disabilities from Exclusion to Equality Realising the Rights of Persons with Disabilities, Handbook for Parliamentarians on the Convention on the Rights of Persons with Disabilities and its Optional Protocol,* UN, UN OHCHR, Inter-Parliamentary Union, No. 14, 2007, pp. 51–76, "Economic, Social and Cultural Rights Handbook for National Human Rights Institutions", *Professional Training Series No. 12,* United Nations, 2005, pp. 17–18.

persons with disabilities enjoy the right to education in equal opportunity with others including equal and effective use of resources.

- The law should explicitly state the purposes and principles of education in general, and the education of persons with disabilities in particular; and outline the framework for the content and quality of education.
- The law should explicitly lay down the powers, duties, qualifications of the State and non-State actors engaged in the field of education, and the standards that the institutions must meet.
- The law should enable the relevant persons or groups to make claims of discrimination in the right to education, request inquiry and obtain appropriate solutions.
- The law should allow applications to be lodged to independent units other than the administration and judiciary bodies.
- The law should have provisions on the establishment of cooperation and coordination with other fields and sectors associated with the right to education of persons with disabilities.

Bibliography

- 6529 Sayılı Temel Hak ve Hürriyetlerin Geliştirilmesi Amacıyla Çeşitli Kanunlarda Değişiklik Yapılmasına Dair Kanun, Kabul Tarihi: 2/3/2014, RG Tarihi:13 Mart 2014, Sayı:28940 [Law No. 6529 on Amending Various Laws to Improve Fundamental Rights and Freedoms, Date of Enactment: 2/3/2014, OG Date: 13 March 2014, Issue: 28940]
- Ad Hoc Committee A/58/118 & Corr.1, 3 July 2003.
- Ad Hoc Committee, Report of the third session, A/AC/265/2004/5, 9 June 2004.
- Ad Hoc Committee, A/AC/265/2005/2, 23 February 2005.
- A Human Rights-Based Approach to Education for All, UNESCO/UNICEF, 2007.
- Basic Law No. 1739 on National Education, Date of Enactment: 14.06.1973, Official Gazette: 24.06.1973/14574
- "Bringing Rights Home: The Role of national Human Rights Institutions", in Butler, Frances(Ed.); *Human Rights Protection: Methods and Effectiveness*, Chapter 2, Kluwer Law International and British Institute for Human Rights, 2002.
- CESCR, Plans of action for primary education (Art. 14). 10/05/99. E/C.12/1999/4. (General Comments).
- **Colin, Barnes / Mercer, Geof,** *Disability*, Polity Press, 2003, London.
- Committee on the Rights of the Children, 60th Session 29 May – 15 June 2012, Review of Reports Submitted by States Parties pursuant to Article 44 of the Convention; Concluding Observations: Turkey.
- Committee on the Rights of the Child, General Comment No. 9 (2006) The rights of children with disabilities, CRC/C/GC/9, 27 February 2007.
- Committee on the Rights of Persons with Disabilities, "Guidelines on treaty-specific document to be submitted by States Parties under Article 35, paragraph 1, of the Convention on the Rights of Persons with Disabilities", CRPD/2/3. 18 November 2009.
- Committee on Economic, Social and Cultural Rights, General Comment No. 16 (2005), General Comment No. 16(2005), 11/08/2005. E/C:12/2005/4. (General Comments).
- Committee on Human Rights, General Comment No. 28: Equality of rights between men and women (Article 3) 29/03/2000, CCPR/C/21/Rev.1/Add. 10, General Comment No. 28. (General Comments).
- Committee on Economic, Social and Cultural Rights, General Comment No. 5, Persons with disabilities, Eleventh session, 1994 (Contained in Document E/1995/22)

- Committee on the Rights of Persons with Disabilities, CRPD/C/9/D/1/2010, Distr.: General 21 June 2013.
- Committee on the Rights of Persons with Disabilities, General comment No. 2 -Article 9: Accessibility, Distr.: General 11 April 2014 Advance Unedited Version Original: English
- Committee on the Rights of Persons with Disabilities, CRPD/C/7/D/3/2011, Distr.: General 21 May 2012.
- Committee on the Rights of Persons with Disabilities, CRPD/C/11/D/2/2010, Distr.: General 4 April 2014.
- Convention against Discrimination in Education Paris, 14 December 1960 http://portal.unesco.org/en/ev.php-URL_ID=12949&URL_DO=DO_TOPIC&URL_SECTION=201.html (24.06.2014)
- "Convention on the Rights of Persons with Disabilities", UN General Assembly A/61/611, 6 December 2006.
- Çağlar, Selda, *Uluslararası Hukuk ve Türk Hukuk Sisteminde Engellilerin Eğitim Hakkı ve Devlet Yükümlülükleri [Right to Education of Persons with Disabilities and State's Obligations in International Law and Turkish Law],* Beta, Istanbul, 2009.
- Çağlar, Selda, "Engelli Hakları Sözleşmesi'nde Ayrımcılık Yasağı ve Türkiye'nin Uyum Sorunu", *Türkiye Barolar Birliği Dergisi,* Eylül-Ekim 2011, Yıl:24, Sayı:96, ss.149–178 ["Non-discrimination in the Convention on the Rights of Persons with Disabilities and Turkey's Problem of Harmonisation", *Journal of Turkish Union of Bar Associations,* September-October 2011, Year: 24, Issue: 96, pp. 149–178].
- Çıraklık Eğitimi Merkezlerinde Parasız Yatılı Çırak Öğrenci Okutma ve Bunlara Yapılacak Sosyal Yardımlar İle Pansiyonların Yönetimi Yönetmeliği, RG. 30.04.1995/22273 [Regulation on Providing Free Boarding Education at Apprentice Training Centres and Social Aid, and Administration of Boarding Houses, OG.30.04.1995/22273]
- Decree-Law on Special Education, Decree date: 30.05.1997, No:573, Date of the Authorising Law: 03.12.1996, No: 4216, Official Gazette: 06.06.1997/ 23011(bis)
- "Disabilities from Exclusion to Equality Realising the rights of persons with disabilities", *Handbook for Parliamentarians on the Convention on the Rights of Persons with Disabilities and its Optional Protocol,* UN, UN OHCHR, Inter-Parliamentary Union, No. 14, 2007.
- "Diversity, Inclusion and Equity: Insights from Special Needs Provision", Chapter 1, *Education Policy Analysis,* OECD 2003, http://www.oecd.org/education/school/26527517.pdf (30.3.2018)
- "Economic, Social and Cultural Rights Handbook for National Human Rights Institutions", *Professional Training Series No. 12,* United Nations, 2005.
- Engelli Bireylere İlişkin İstatistiki Bilgiler, Aile ve Sosyal Politikalar Bakanlığı Engelli ve Yaşlı Hizmetleri Genel Müdürlüğü Araştırma Geliştirme ve Proje

Dairesi Başkanlığı, Mart 2014. [Statistical Data on Persons with Disabilities, Ministry of Family and Social Policies General Directorate of Services for Persons with Disabilities and the Elderly Department of Research, Development and Projects, March 2014] http://eski.bingol.edu.tr/media/225854/5engelliler-istatistik.pdf (14.08.2018)

- Engelli Hakları Sözleşmesi'ne ilişkin Türkiye Ulusal Rapor Taslağı [The draft Turkish National Report on the Convention on the Rights of Persons with Disabilities (designed as the inception report)] http://engelli.oyhgm.gov.tr/sozlesme/dosyalar/sozlesme/national_rapor/ (29.06.2014)
- **Espiell, Hector Gros**, *Significance of the Convention against Discrimination in Education* (1960), UNESCO 2005.
- *Eurybase The Information Database on Education Systems in Europe 2007–2008 Türk Eğitim Örgütlenmesi,* Eurybase – Turkey (2007–2008), http://eacea.ec.europa.eu/ressources/eurydice/eurybase, (16.12.2008)
- **Evadné, Grant** "Dignity and Equality", *Human Rights Law Review,* Volume 7, Issue 2, 1 January 2007, pp. 299–329, https://doi.org/10.1093/hrlr/ngm002
- **Gemalmaz, Mehmet Semih,** *Ulusal Üstü İnsan Hakları Hukukunun Genel Teorisine Giriş,* Güncelleştirilmiş ve Geliştirilmiş 5. Baskı, Legal Yayınevi İstanbul, 2005 [*Introduction to the General Theory of Supranational Human Rights Law,* Legal Publication, Updated and enlarged Fifth Edition, Istanbul, 2005]
- General Comment No. 1: **The Aims of Education** (Article 29/1), CRC/GC/2001/1, April 2001.
- General Comment No. 2. The role of independent national human rights institutions in the promotion and protection of the rights of the child, CRC/GC/2002/2.
- General Comment No. 9 (2006), 27/02/2007. The Rights of Children with Disabilities, CRC/C/GC/9.
- General Comment No. 5 (2003) General measures of implementation of the Convention on the Rights of the Child (Art. 4, 42 and 44, para.6), CRC/GC/2003/5 27 November 2003.
- **Glendenning, Dympna,** "The Ombudsman for Children: an analysis of the Irish model as it relates to recognized schools", *Education and the Law,* Vol.16, Nos. 2–3, June/September 2004, Carfax Publishing Taylor & Francis Group.
- **Gordon, Porter L.,** "Disability and Education: Towards an Inclusive Approach", *SDS Working Paper,* 2001.
- **Gözübüyük, A. Şeref,** *Yönetim Hukuku,* Turhan Kitapevi, Onaltıncı Baskı, Sixteenth Edition [*Administrative Law,* Turhan Publisher, Sixteenth Edition], Ankara, 2002.
- Guidelines for Inclusion: Ensuring Access to Education for All, UNESCO 2005.

- **Hammarberg, Thomas** "Children", in *Economic, Social and Cultural Rights, a Textbook,* Revised Edition, Edited by: Asbjørn Eide/ Caterina Krause/ Alan Roses, Marchinus Nijhoff Publishers, Durdrocth/Boston /London 2001.
- **Harris, Alison / Enfield, Sue,** *Disability, Equality and Human Rights A Training Manual for Development and Humanitarian Organisations,* Oxfam GB, 2003, ISBN 9780855984854, https://policy-practice.oxfam.org.uk/publications/disability-equality-and-human-rights-a-training-manual-for-development-and-huma-115363 (20.03.2018)
- **Hegary, Seamus,** *Educating Children and Young People with Disabilities Principals and the review of practice,* UNESCO, 1992.
- **Hodgkin Rachel/ Newel Peter;** *Convention on the Rights of the Child Practical Handbook,* UNICEF, 1998 (translation).
- http://www.un.org/esa/socdev/enable/rights/ahc4da7.htm (16.3.2018)
- http://yeniyasa.yok.gov.tr/?page=yazi&c=90&i=120. (10.07.2014)
- Human Rights in New Zealand Today: Chapter 15 The Right to Education, http://www.hrc.co.nz/report/chapters/chapter15/education01.html (05.08.2008)
- *ICF, İşlevsellik, Yetiyitimi ve Sağlığın Uluslar arası Sınıflandırılması,* Çevirenler: **Elif Kabakçı / Ahmet Göğüş**, T.C. Başbakanlık Özürlüler İdaresi Başkanlığı-World Health Organization 2004 [*ICF, International Classification of Functioning, Disability and Health,* Translated by: **Elif Kabakçı / Ahmet Göğüş**, T.R. Prime Ministry Administration for the Disabled People – World Health Organisation 2004], Children and Disability in Transition in CEE/CIS and Baltic States, Innocenti Insight, UNICEF 2005.
- "Inclusive Schools & Community Support Programmes", *Report 1996 – First Phase 1997,* UNESCO.
- "Independent Institutions Protecting Children's Rights", *Innocenti Digest No. 8,* UNICEF, June 2001.
- *International Disability Rights Compendium 2003,* Center for International Rehabilitation/ Landmine Survivors Network/ Rehabilitation International, Second Impression, U.S.A. 2003.
- İlköğretim ve Eğitim Kanunu, Kanun No.222, Kabul Tarihi: 05/01/1961, RG. 12.01.1961/10705 [Law No. 222 Primary Education Law, Date of Enactment: 05/01/1961, OG. 12.01.1961/10705]
- **Jonsson, Ture & Wiman, Ronald,** "Education, Poverty and Disability ın Developing Countries", *A Technical Note Prepared for the Poverty Redaction Sourcebook,* 21 June 2001.
- **Karan, Ulaş,** "Türk Hukukunda Ayrımcılık Yasağı ve Türk Ceza Kanunu'nun 122. Maddesinin Uygulanabilirliği", *Türkiye Barolar Birliği Dergisi,* Sayı 73 [Non-discrimination in Turkish Law and Applicability of Article 122 of the Turkish

Criminal Code, *Journal of Turkish Union of Bar Associations*, Issue 73], 2007, pp. 146–173.

- *Kaynaştırma / Bütünleştirmenin Etkililiğini Arttırmak İçin Politika ve Uygulama Önerileri Projesi Kaynaştırma/Bütünleştirme Yoluyla Eğitimde Dünyadan ve Türkiye'den İyi Örnekler*[Project on Policy and Practice Recommendations to Increase Efficiency of Inclusion/Integration: Best Practices of Inclusion/Integration Education in Turkey and in the World], ERG, 2011.
- *Kaynaştırma / Bütünleştirmenin Etkililiğini Arttırmak İçin Politika ve Uygulama Önerileri Projesi Türkiye'de Kaynaştırma/Bütünleştirme Yoluyla Eğitimin Durumu* [*Project on Policy and Practice Recommendations to Increase Efficiency of Inclusion/Integration: State of Inclusion/Integration Education in Turkey*], Yayına Hazırlayanlar [Prepared for publication by: Ayşe Nal/Işık Tüzün], Eğitim Reformu Girişimi – Tohum Otizm Vakfı [Education Reform Initiative -Tohum Autism Foundation], 2011
- **Makkonen, Timo,** "Measuring Discrimination Data Collection and EU Equality Law", *Anti-Discrimination Law Review,* Issue No. 4, November 2006, European Commission, pp. 7–87.
- **Marks, Susan / Clapham, Andrew,** *International Human Rights Lexicon,* Oxford University Press, 2005, ISBN: 9780198764137.
- **McGoldrick, Dominic,** "The United Nations Convention on the Rights of the Child", in *Children's Rights* Volume II, Edited by Michael D.A. Freeman, Ashgate/ Dartmouth, 2004, ISBN: 075462336X (alk. paper) 9780754623366 (alk. paper).
- **Meyen, Edward L and Skrtic, Thomas M (Editors),** *Special Education Student Disability An Introduction Traditional, Emerging and Alternative Perspectives,* Love Publishing Company Denver, Fourth Edition, Colorado, 1995.
- Millî Eğitim Bakanlığına Bağlı İlkokul, Ortaokul, Lise ve Dengi Okullarda Burs, Parasız Yatılılık ve Sosyal Yardımlar Yönetmeliği, Bakanlar Kurulu Kararı: 05.10.1983-83/7166, RG. 8.12.1983/18245 [Regulation on Scholarships, Free Boarding and Social Aid in Primary and Secondary Education Institutions of the Ministry of National Education, Decree of the Council of Ministers: 05.10.1983-83/7166, OG. 8.12.1983/18245.
- Milli Eğitim Bakanlığı Özel Eğitim Okulları Çerçeve Yönetmeliği, RG: 22.7.2005/25883, Tebliğler Dergisi: Ağustos 2003/2551 [Framework Regulation on Special Education Schools of the Ministry of National Education, OG: 22.7.2005/25883, Journal of Communiques: August 2003/2551].
- Milli Eğitim Bakanlığı İlköğretim Kurumları Yönetmeliği, RG: 27.08.2003/25212, Tebliğler Dergisi: Eylül 2003/2552, Düzeltme: Ekim 2003/2554, Madde 6/f **(Değişiklik: 2.05.2006/26156 RG.)** [Regulation on Primary Education Institutions of the Ministry of National Education, OG. 27.08.2003/25212, Journal of Communiques: September 2003/2552 Correction November 2003/2554, Art. 6/f **(Amended: 2.05.2006/26156 OG.)].**

- Milli Eğitim Bakanlığının Teşkilat ve Görevleri Hakkında Kanun, Kanun No.3797, Kabul Tarihi: 30.04.1992, RG. 12.05.1992/21226 [Law No. 3797 on Organisation and Functions of the Ministry of National Education, Date of Enactment: 30.04.1992, OG. 12.05.1992/21226]
- Milli Eğitim İstatistikleri Örgün Eğitim 2013/14, Resmi İstatistik Programı Yayını, [National Education Statistics Formal Education 2013/14, Official Statistics Programme Publication]. ISBN 978-975-11-3808-8, https://sgb.meb.gov.tr/istatistik/meb_istatistikleri_orgun_egitim_2013_2014.pdf (14.08.2018)
- **Morris, Jenny,** "Impairment and Disability: Constructing an Ethics of Care that Promotes Human Rights", *Hypatia,* Vol.16, No. 4, 2001, pp. 1–16.
- Okul Öncesi Eğitim Kurumları Yönetmeliği, RG: 08.06.2004/25486, Tebliğler Dergisi: Temmuz 2004/2562, m.10/c (Değişik: 21.07.2012/28360 RG) [Regulation on Pre-school Educational Institutions, OG. 08.06.2004/25486, Journal of Communiques: July 2004/2562, Art. 10/c (Amended: 21.07.2012/28360 OG)].
- **Oliver, Michael & Sapey, Bob,** *Social Work with Disabled People, Practical Social Work,* Series Editor: Jo Campling, BASW, Second Edition, 1998.
- **Oliver, MJ.,** "The Disability Movement and the Professions", *International Journal of Therapy and Rehabilitation,* Vol.6, Iss.8, 1 August 1999, pp. 377–379.
- Özel Eğitim Hakkında Kanun Hükmünde Kararname, Kararname Tarihi: 30.05.1997, No:573, Yetki Kanununun Tarihi: 03.12.1996, No: 4216, RG. 06.06.1997/23011(Mükerrer) [Decree-Law on Special Education, Decree Date: 30.05.1997, No: 573, Date of the Authorising Law: 03.12.1996, No: 4216, OG. 06.06.1997/23011(bis)]
- Özel Eğitim Hizmetleri Yönetmeliği, RG. 31.05.2006/26184, **(Değişiklik 21.7.2012/28360 RG.)** Regulation on Special Education Services, OG.31.05.2006/26184, **(Amended 21.7.2012/28360 OG.)**
- *Özürlüler Şurası Çağdaş Toplum, Yaşam ve Özürlüler* 29 Kasım-2 Aralık 1999, Başbakanlık Özürlüler İdaresi Başkanlığı Yayını [*First Council on the Impaired, Modern Society, Life and Impaired* 29 November-2 December 1999, Prime Ministry Administration for the Disabled People Publications], Ankara.
- *Pathways to the Future: A Report of the Review of educational Services for Students with Disabilities in Government Schools,* Government of Western Australia Department of Education and Training, 2004.
- **Peters, Susan J.,** "Inclusive education: Achieving Education for All by Including Those with Disabilities and Special educational needs", *Prepared for the Disability Group the World Bank,* April 30, 2003.
- **Porter L., Gordon;** Disability and Education: Towards an Inclusive Approach, SDS Working Paper, 2001
- "Promoting the Rights of Children with Disabilities", *Innocenti Digest No. 13,* Innocenti Research Centre, UNICEF, 2007.

- "Recommendations to Teachers on Inclusive Education Practice", Annex to the Circular No. 2008/60 of 02.09.2008 on Inclusive Education Practice No. 3601.
- **Rehman, Javaid,** *International Human Rights Law: A Practical Approach,* London, Longman, 2003.
- **Ruddock, Philip Maxwell,** *Disability Standards for Education 2005,* 17 Marc 2005, Australia.
- **Sandkull, Olof,** "Strengthening Inclusive Education by Applying a Rights-based Approach to Education Programming", *ISEC 2005 Paper,* August 2005, UNESCO, Bangkok.
- **Shakespeare, Tom & Watson, Nicholas,** "Defending the Social Model", Chapter 18, in *Disability Studies: Past Present and Future,* edited by Len Barton and Mike Oliver, Leeds: The Disability Press, 1997, pp. 263–273.
- "Standard Rules on the Equalization of Opportunities for Persons with Disabilities", UN General Assembly resolution 48/96 of 20 December 1993, A/RES/48/96, 4 March 1994.
- "Tallinn Guidelines for Action on Human Resource Development in the Field of Disability", UN General Assembly, A/RES/44/70, 8 December 1989.
- The challenge of universal primary education, Strategies for achieving the international development targets, Department for International Development (DFID), January 2001. http://www.albacharia.ma/xmlui/bitstream/handle/123456789/31760/1604Target_Strategy_Paper__The_challenge_of_universal_primary_education%5B2001%5Dn.pdf?sequence=1 (04.3.2018).
- *Thematic Studies Inclusion in Education: The Participation of Disabled Learners, World Education Forum Dakar,* Senegal 26–28 April 2000, Education for All 2000 Assessment, UNESCO, Graphoprint, France 2001.
- "The Right to Education for Persons with Disabilities: Towards Inclusion, an EFA Flagship", *Conceptual Paper December 2004.*
- The Right to Education, Commission on Human Rights Resolution 2002/23, 49th meeting, 22 April 2002 [Adopted without vote. E/2002/23-E/CN.4/2002/200].
- The Right to Education, Commission on Human Rights Resolution 2005/21, 51st meeting, 15 April 2005 [Adopted without vote. E/CN.4/2005/L.10/Add.10] General Comment No. 1: **The Aims of Education** (Article 29/1), CRC/GC/2001/1, April 2001.
- The right to education (Art. 13): 08/12/99. E/C.12/1999/10. (General Comments), CESCR Committee on Economic, Social and Cultural Rights, Twenty-first session 15 November–3 December 1999.
- The role of national human rights institutions in the protection of economic, social and cultural rights, 14/12/98. E/C.12/1998/25, CESCR General comment 10. (General Comments).

- "The Salamanca Statement and Framework for Action on Special Needs Education", Adopted by the World Conference on Special Needs Education: Access and Quality, Salamanca, Spain, 7–10 June 1994, UNESCO & Ministry of Education and Science Spain.
- **Tomasevski, Katarina**, Human rights obligation: making education available, accessible, acceptable and adaptable, *Right to Education Primers No. 3*, International Development Cooperation Agency, Sida, 2001.
- **Tomasevski, Katarina,** "Manual on Rights-Based Education, Global Human Rights Made Simple", *Asia and Pacific Regional Bureau for Education*, UNESCO-Bangkok, 2004.
- **Tomasevski, Katarina,** "Removing obstacles in the way of the right to education", *Primers No. 1,* International Development Cooperation Agency, Sida, 2001.
- Türkiye Büyük Millet Meclisi İnsan Haklarını İnceleme Komisyonu Engelli haklarını İnceleme Raporu, 24. Dönem 3. Yasama Yılı 2013 [Turkish Grand National Assembly Commission on Human Rights Inquiry Rights of Persons with Disabilities Inquiry Report, 24th Assembly 3. Legislative Year 2013] https://www.tbmm.gov.tr/komisyon/insanhaklari/docs/2013/raporlar/engelli_haklari_inceleme_raporu.pdf (14.08.2018)
- Türkiye'de Çocukların Durumu Ön Rapor, Sosyal Hizmetler Ve Çocuk Esirgeme Kurumu- UNICEF, Nisan 2000 [Preliminary Report on the State of Children in Turkey], Social Services and Child Protection Institute – UNICEF, April 2000], Ankara, http://www.die.gov.tr/CIN/CIN-TR/prereporttr/prereporttr.htm (10.12.2008).
- Türkiye Eğitim Sisteminde Eşitlik ve Akademik Başarı Araştırma Raporu ve Analiz [Research Report and Analysis of Equality and Academic Achievement in the Turkish Education System], Eğitim Reformu Girişimi (ERG), May 2014.
- Türkiye'de Engellilik Temelinde Ayrımcılığın İzlenmesi Raporu Raporu 1 Ocak – 30 Haziran 2010, Hazırlayanlar: Arzu Şenyurt Akdağ ve diğerleri, İstanbul Bilgi Üniversitesi İnsan Hakları Uygulama ve Araştırma Merkezi, Şubat 2011, İstanbul [Report on Monitoring Discrimination on the Basis of Disability in Turkey 1 January – 30 June 2010, By Arzu Şenyurt Akdağ et al, Istanbul Bilgi University, Human Rights Application and Research Centre, February 2011, Istanbul].
- United Nation General Assembly, A/RES/48/134 85th plenary meeting, 20 December 1993, Annex
- United Nation General Assembly, A/RES/44/64 78th plenary meeting, 8 December 1989.
- United Nations Committee on the Rights of the Child, Day of General Discussion, CRC/C/66, Annex V, 16th Session, 6 October 1997. http://www.ohchr.org/EN/HRBodies/CRC/Documents/Recommandations/disabled.pdf (20.03.2018)

- UN Enable Daily Summary related to Draft Article 18 – Participation in political and public life, Volume 3, # 5, January 9, 2004
- UN Enable Daily Summary related to Draft Article 24 – Participation in cultural life, recreation and leisure, Volume 3, #7, January 13, 2004.
- UN Enable – Towards a Convention Comments on the Draft Text, Draft Article 15: Living independently and being included in the community, UN General Assembly, A/60/266, 17 August 2005.
- UN General Assembly sixty-first session, A/61/611, 6 December 2006 Ad Hoc Committee on a Comprehensive and Integral International Convention on the Protection and Promotion of the Rights and Dignity of Persons with Disabilities, Eighth session, New York, 14–25 August 2006.
- **Uyar, Leyla (Derleyen),** Birleşmiş Milletler'de İnsan Hakları Yorumları İnsan Hakları Komitesi ve Ekonomik, Sosyal ve Kültürel Haklar Komitesi, 1981–2006, İstanbul Bilgi Üniversitesi Yayınları, 1. Baskı, Eylül 2006 **[(compiled by)** *Human Rights Comments in the United Nations, Human Rights Committee and Committee on Economic, Social and Cultural Rights,* 1981–2006, Istanbul Bilgi University Publications, First Edition, September 2006]
- **Weiner, R.,** *Impact on the Schools,* Capitol Publications, 1985. Transmitting "Special Education Inclusion", 15 March 2007, http://www.weac.org/resource/june96/speced.htm, (18.03.2008)
- Yükseköğretim Kurumları Özürlüler Danışma ve Koordinasyon Yönetmeliği, RG. 20.06.2006/26204 [Regulation on Higher Education Institutions Disability Advisory and Coordination OG. 20.06.2006/ 26204]
- Yükseköğretim Kurumları Özürlüler Danışma ve Koordinasyon Yönetmeliği, RG. 14.08.2010/27672 [Regulation on Higher Education Institutions Disability Advisory and Coordination OG. 14.08.2010/27672]

www.ingramcontent.com/pod-product-compliance
Ingram Content Group UK Ltd.
Pitfield, Milton Keynes, MK11 3LW, UK
UKHW021014120926
8556IPUK00040B/1141

9 783631 766521